"Only once in my 30 years in Nashville have we been blessed with what I would consider 'true talent' on the airwaves. I, like most everyone in town, would look forward to waking up and tuning in to the humor, quick wit, and reflective wisdom of Gerry House—he was always far more than a jock—his timing was impeccable, but the cards that he brought to the table were Will Rogers good! He bailed on us and left a void on the radio that may never be filled."

—Kix Brooks,
singer/songwriter and nationally syndicated radio host

"Gerry House, radio personality, a songwriter of note in the Nashville recording community. So now my friend Gerry writes a book... (insert cricket sounds here)... No doubt the closest thing to a death blow the literary world will have suffered to date."

—Michael McDonald,
Grammy Award–winning singer and artist

"There's nothing more uncomfortable than being around someone that tries to be funny and isn't. Gerry House IS f***ing funny!"

—Ronnie Dunn

"Gerry is the funniest, most knowledgeable, creative, and interesting person I know. From the day we met, he has made me think, laugh, and stare in amazement at the way he can make the simplest things in life interesting and compelling. He's traveled the world, sat with sinners and saints, cheated death when no one thought he could, and made a name for himself like no other. He became an icon to an industry that often forgets fast about the great people that built Country music and radio. He is in the Hall of Fame for a lot of reasons (an even bigger honor because he's still alive), but even if he weren't, he would definitely be at the top of my ballot every time!"

—Clay Hunnicutt,
Executive VP of Programming, Clear Channel Media & Entertainment

"Gerry is simply the very best at what he does. The radio sounds lonely without him on it."

—**Jay DeMarcus, Rascal Flatts**

"I've spent more than 20 years building a reputation as a trusted, responsible leader. And now I've thrown that away overnight by admitting that I know Gerry House."

—**Dave Ramsey,**
New York Times **bestselling author**
and nationally syndicated radio host

"Gerry House is a personal friend of mine. I cannot think of another single person with as much talent and imagination as he possesses. We have been friends for many years. He has written things for me to use on television and in my road shows. When we get the chance to go out and have dinner together, I can verify that his table manners are impeccable. He married pretty well, too."

—**Barbara Mandrell, recording and television star**

COUNTRY MUSIC Broke My Brain

*A Behind-the-Microphone Peek
at Nashville's Famous and Fabulous Stars*

COUNTRY MUSIC
Broke My Brain

GERRY HOUSE

BENBELLA BOOKS, INC.

DALLAS, TEXAS

BenBella Books, Inc.
10300 N. Central Expressway
Suite #530
Dallas, TX 75231
www.benbellabooks.com
Send feedback to feedback@benbellabooks.com

Printed in the United States of America
10 9 8 7 6 5 4 3 2 1

Library of Congress Cataloging-in-Publication Data
House, Gerry.
  Country music broke my brain / by Gerry House.
    pages cm
  ISBN 978-1-939529-90-9 (trade cloth) — ISBN 978-1-939529-91-6 (electronic) 1.
House, Gerry. 2. Disc jockeys—United States—Biography. 3. Songwriters—United
States—Biography. 4. Country musicians—United States—Anecdotes. I. Title.
  ML429.H78A3 2014
  781.642092—dc23
  [B]
                                                              2013037796

Editing by Erin Kelley
Proofreading by Michael Fedison and Jenny Bridges
Indexing by Jigsaw Information
Cover design by Ty Nowicki
Text design and composition by John Reinhardt Book Design
Printed by Bang Printing

Distributed by Perseus Distribution
www.perseusdistribution.com

To place orders through Perseus Distribution:
Tel: 800-343-4499
Fax: 800-351-5073
E-mail: orderentry@perseusbooks.com

Significant discounts for bulk sales are available.
Please contact Glenn Yeffeth at glenn@benbellabooks.com or 214-750-3628.

This book is for Allyson, Autumn and Shane, Willa and Holland, Lucy and Desi, and Charlene.

Contents

Foreword

I'LL NEVER FORGET the first time I met Gerry House.

I was doing a radio interview with him in the '80s. He had on a white shirt and a bow tie. It was fairly early in the morning. I was wondering after a few minutes of talking with him, *Has this guy been up all night?*

After leaving the interview, I told my publicist, Janet Rickman, "That guy won't be around very long." Little did I know, not only did he stay in the radio business for many years, I would also be recording a fun, toe-tapping song he had written, called "Little Rock." And I certainly didn't know we would go on vacations together, us, along with Gerry's wife, Allyson, and my husband, Narvel, and surprisingly enough, we all became close friends.

Gerry is a very talented writer with a cool sharp wit. I love to listen to his stories. They can hold me captive for hours. When I hosted the *Academy of Country Music Awards*, Gerry helped me with my scripts. I couldn't have done it without him.

In 2003, he scared me to death when he had to have brain surgery, but I think it helped. I love Gerry—always will—and can't thank him enough for sharing his warped sense of humor with me, his lovely wife, Allyson, and their daughter, Autumn. They have always been a tight family—a great example for all of us to learn from.

I invite you to sit back and read all the silly, funny, heartfelt things Gerry has to say. I know you'll be thoroughly entertained, as usual.

Love ya,
Red (aka Reba)

Introduction

IT BEGAN IN KENTUCKY in 1958. I was ten. At the time, I was little more than a life-support system for freckles. Looking back at pictures of that era, I had the exact physique of a praying mantis. All I really cared about was the Cincinnati Reds' batting averages and my pets, Petey and Thumper—a parakeet and a rabbit. Both were lost in tragic freezing accidents. I do remember Petey being more fun postmortem than when he was with us on Earth. I could hop him around easier.

My father, Homer, was an electrician. My mother, Lucille, was an electrician's wife. Dad kept the Kroger Co.'s lights on. He was good at his job except at home, where, for some reason, our lights dimmed when Mom started the washer. I was always being instructed about the ever-present dangers of electricity by my dad. "Be careful, Hoss," he'd say, waving a pair of pliers around like a wild man. "Electricity is just like a snake. You never know when it will bite ya." One time during an electricity lesson, he accidentally touched some "hot" wires with the pliers, and a ball of fire shot out of the wall. It sounded like a cannon went off, and it blew both of us across the room. My dad's hair was steaming and his eyebrows were gone. Good job, Pop! Love the danger demo. Actual fire and smoke!

Technically, it began on a summer day in 1958. We were going to take *the vacation*—the one golden week of the year when my father wasn't avoiding electrocution. We would just "take off." It was planned and discussed for months in advance, but we would just "take off" to the same place every year—the Smokies. The Valhalla of tourism. Yes, that special land of dreams 300 miles due south on the Dixie Highway. Don't you love that name, the Dixie Highway? It just sounds like the road to heaven, doesn't it? Sweet jubilation chilluns, we done got on da Dixie Highway. I should mention the Dixie Highway was pre-interstate. It was also pre-restaurants, gas stations, and rest stops—just one tiny burg after another, like an endless stream of stop signs and yard sales. But still, we were on our way to the Smokies! Gatlinburg! *The* home of tiny motels and cheap food and "beautiful vistas of mountain peaks and verdant valleys" that all looked exactly alike!

Now, my father's main goal in life on every vacation was to *make good time.* It was all about beating the previous year's record of pushing the Chevy Bel-Air toward Mountain Mecca. Hurry up and whiz and get back out here. We're behind on last year's good time. Good time meant that you hunkered down. We never actually did the "coffee can" pit stops, but only because Mom flat refused. So it was Dad driving, Mom in shotgun, and me clinging to the back of their seat perched on the hump that ran through the car floor. Our first objective was to make it to Renfro Valley, Kentucky, in time for breakfast. One hundred and thirty miles of back-rattling road that meant we left at Dad's usual "gettin' up" time—four in the morning. We rolled into Renfro like conquering heroes and had the same annual meal around 8 A.M.—country ham, biscuits, and red-eye gravy. My father raved about how wonderful it all was. For those of you who don't know, country ham contains in one serving all the sodium you'll ever need for your entire life. The biscuits were usually lukewarm, and the butter, for some perverse reason, was kept on ice in little dishes. It's important to make sure the butter is like a tiny yellow brick in Renfro Valley. To this day, I have *no* idea what makes gravy "red-eye" other than that most of the people in the restaurant had 'em—I imagine from "making good time."

Because we always left on Monday, I will assume it began on a Monday in the summer of 1958. Dad turned on the radio. I saw his eyes light up as he lit up his fifteenth Winston of the morning. Here is how it all started:

Smoke was coming out of his mouth as he exclaimed without turning his head to me, "Hoss, *that* there is the greatest song and the greatest singer *ever!*"

Whereupon Mom chimed in, "Honey, that's Hank Snow." She sorta glanced back. "Your dad *loves* Hank Snow." I wasn't sure if she was in the fan club or not, but it was started now. I could feel it begin to tickle the back of my lizard brain. Something was happening (not as much as puberty that would later rock my world), but I was making a decision! And before I could stop myself, I blurted out the words, "Dad, turn that *down!*"

It was country music. It was the Singing Ranger and his huge smash "I'm Movin' On."

(Not to be confused with the Rascal Flatts song "I'm Movin' On," to which I would also have a connection years later.)

At this age, I was vaguely aware of Elvis and a few other songs, but this was definitely *not* anything I wanted played near me. The Hankster had a certain vocal quality that would make any goose proud. He had a bleating honk so pronounced that flocks of his fellow vocalists would follow the car if you turned the radio up loud enough. This was *not* for my ten-year-old taste. Homer House loved it. I did not.

I should explain my three musical influences up to this point.

First: Church. I played the piano every Sunday at the Banklick
  Christian Church, starting when I was seven and had to sit
  on a phone book. Across the aisle was Lily Mae Scott, a large-
  boned woman who wrestled with some contraption called a
  pump organ. She worked the pumps with her feet and forced
  air through the tortured instrument 'til the choir could kick
  in and really nail "Bringing in the Sheaves." With Lily Mae
  pumping away like Lance Armstrong and me struggling to
  remember what the dots on the music meant, we were a force
  to be reckoned with. I'm certain it sounded like a train wreck,
  but nobody seemed to complain. The choir was usually about
  half a verse behind us.

Second: Pleasure Isle. Pleasure Isle was neither a pleasure nor an
  isle. It was a massive concrete swamp that measured 100 yards
  long and 175 yards wide. The water was pumped right out
  of the creek beside it and was purified by the Iranian owner
  riding around in a motorboat pulling a bag of chlorine. In the
  '50s in northern Kentucky, it was the Riviera. *The* place to be.
  My mom and all the moms and kids went there every day.
  Now, remember, this was before they invented skin cancer,
  so we all slathered on baby oil and iodine and roasted in the
  summer sun 'til we looked like minstrels. Pleasure Isle had a
  jukebox that blared the same twenty-five songs over and over
  through the worst speaker system in America. Those songs are
  seared in my brain with a musical branding iron. Elvis. The
  Everly Brothers. "Volare." Ricky Nelson and something called
  "The Purple People Eater." I still *hate* that damn ditty.

Third: Mrs. Riggs. My third musical influence was my piano
  teacher. I don't remember exactly when I started lessons. I've
  blocked it from my memory like abductees and people married to Madonna do. All I remember is I could never play

my weekly assignment to her satisfaction. Mrs. Riggs was an imposing woman. She dressed in Early Librarian in a house that always smelled like mothballs. With her glasses on the end of her nose, she endured my keyboard technique and clucked signals of disapproval. I still haven't recovered from those sweat-filled afternoons. Grunt, hmmph, tsk, tsk, tsk. "Young man, did you even open your lesson book?"

Looking back, I'm certain Mrs. Riggs trained with the SS and had barely escaped through Poland to hide out in Covington, Kentucky, disguised as a piano teacher. To this day, I can barely read sheet music. The dots are connected to Mozart somehow, but it "don't come easy," as they say. All I remember was the "Eyetalian" musical word for slow was *lento*. I swear she said *lento* a lot when she talked about me to my parents.

Thusly formed, I decided that Country & Western music, à la Hank Snow, was not to be my musical preference. It didn't speak to me. I didn't "dig" it. It damaged me. My drain was bamaged.

Today? I love to hear a good Hank Snow record. If I do, I'm back to being a little peezer in the backseat of an old Chevy "making good time" with Mom and Dad on the way to the glorious Smokies.

Alligator Clip Radio

I'M NOT SURE what makes some people drawn to radio. The "golden age" of it all was before my time. I studied and was influenced by all that later in my career, but what really hit me was live/personality/Top 40/transistor radio. I have friends who even today ride around in their cars, listening to jingles and commercials from that era. I don't do that. That would be nutty. I just write about it.

I have two distinct memories of my early radios: the transistor and the Rocket. The transistor was from Japan. It had a distinct smell I remember, and still I have no idea what that is today. But I was always aware that when I took the back of my transistor radio off to insert a battery, it had a "Japanese/transistor-y" odor all its own. I carried my Japanese transistor with me everywhere. I actually expected Japan to smell like that when I visited Tokyo decades later. It kinda did, I think.

The Rocket radio was even more basic. Again, as usual, I have no idea how it worked. Even to this day, I don't understand how people speak into a "can" (*O Brother Where Art Thou* reference) and how it comes out the other end to a listener.

I am stunningly ignorant of what an actual transistor even is. I know when your cheap transistor radio died and went to radio heaven, you pulled out all the parts. It always had a flat piece of plastic with little things soldered to it. The Rocket radio had, I think, a diode. Don't even think of asking because I have no idea about that, either. I guess it's what the old-timers called a "crystal set." The antenna came out the top of the Rocket, and you attached the radio with an alligator clip to your bedsprings. It picked up powerful, 50,000-watt radio stations you heard through your earpiece. It was pure magic.

I was hooked. I listened to my transistor radio all day and at night plugged my earpiece into the Rocket, hooked the clip to the bed, and fiddled with the antenna 'til I got something. More often than not, I picked up WCKY in Cincinnati, which played country music at night. Shuddering, I started moving the antenna again. Please, *not* country music. Usually it was all I could get. I don't know why this was so fabulous: a skinny kid in Kentucky listening to music he didn't like at all, over an earpiece that made it all sound like it was coming from Mars. But it *was* fabulous, and I listened deep into the night.

It was exciting, adventurous, and, most of all, it was showbiz!

When I look back now, I realize I've spent most of my life attached to a radio. I've also done television, live stage performances, and movies, yet radio has always had a hold on me. It's really got a hold on me. *Baby! I love you and all I want you to do is just hold me, hold me, hold meeee.*

That's from a song by the Miracles, featuring Smokey Robinson. It was during an era when songs were played side by side, one after the other. Country songs, R&B, standards, big band, jazz, polka. You name it, and if it sounded like a hit, it got played. Patsy and Elvis and Chubby and Bert and Andy and Perry and Little Richard. There weren't specific "formats." It was all a big, wide-open sound. The BBC still does this today, but other than a vague

Top 40 moniker or "Beautiful Music" tag, the stations had a lot of leeway.

Radio footnote: I've heard all my career about the good ol' country music songs that no longer exist today. The Patsy Cline and Conway Twitty classics. How "pop" music has ruined country. In fact, the Patsy Clines, et al., were actually pop hits. People I met in Nashville, such as Brenda Lee and the Everly Brothers, recorded in Nashville and were accepted the world over. They were pop radio stars who happened to be in Nashville. They just did it. The songs and the vocals and the music were POPular all over America.

Nobody thought of them as "country"; they just made great records. Only later did the kvetching start about the downfall of country. In the beginning, Don and Phil were played right alongside Chubby Checker, Bert Kaempfert, and Dion and the Belmonts. *Nobody* ever complained except the folks who liked big band music, and they were certain this new noise was gonna ruin America.

It's been the same ever since. I often wonder if, when the first teenager stretched an animal skin over a hollowed-out log and began beating on it, his father said, "Turn that down and go kill something for dinner!"

It was also at this age when I noticed something else about radio, in addition to the music, the jingles, and the commercials. *People.* Guys with voices like gold who were joking, laughing, and talking to me. Talking directly to me.

It was *all* guys back then. Oh, there was the occasional TV weather girl who appeared as a guest, but it was a man's world.

In the '70s, I had a radio friend who announced one day, "I think the key to success in radio is to get us one of them animal names." I thought about it but stuck with my own. The airwaves were populated with animal guys: Wolfman. Coyote. Spider. Hoss. I had no idea people used fake names on the air. Later I heard stories about poor souls who had to assume a particular name because the station had already spent money having jingle singers record IDs with these names. If the old guy got fired or left, the new guy took that "paid for" name. I guess management thought the audience would think, *Wow, Clark Sullivan sounds like a different person today, but I like Clark, so I'll listen.*

Technology has changed radio a lot. Nobody hops in their car and hooks up alligator clips to the driveshaft to hear their favorite station. Today, you can get any station anywhere, anytime. But for all the techy stuff, quite often, it still comes down to a guy, or a guy, a girl, and a geek, talking to each other and to listeners and playing music.

I knew I loved it, but I didn't enter a radio station for ten more years. I was just a listener for awhile. Still am, actually.

The Fights

IF YOU DECIDE one day to revisit the house you grew up in, be prepared for the incredible smallness of it all. I don't know if it's a size/ratio thing or what, but everybody always says, "I couldn't get over how tiny the place we grew up in was." Do we expand the size as we get older, or did we just not pay any attention to things like square footage when there was a softball game to be played?

In a tiny house, you have tiny bedrooms. Even then, I felt there was a treehouse feel to the bedrooms in our original home—those bedrooms built in an attic space that wasn't meant for anything but storage. I loved it. On the front wall of both upstairs bedrooms were dormers. Dormers are little construction excuses to have a window sticking out of a roof. I spent many an hour crouched in my dormer. I think it's the reason for my posture today.

My parents had a dormer and two impossibly small twin beds with the world's chintziest chest between them. On top of the chest, I usually saw a glass of water for Mom's "partial plate," an ashtray, and a copy of the church bulletin. The bulletin always had the latest info about when a visiting missionary would return from the Congo and who was on their bed of affliction.

As a kid, I never went into Mom and Dad's bedroom much except for Friday nights. That was when Dad and I each grabbed a spot on one of the beds, and he fired up the little transistor. The *Gillette Cavalcade of Sports* started, and we were ready to listen to the fight that night.

I know what you're thinking. Listening to a fight is kind of like watching stamp collecting. It's not. When your pa is all fired up about the fight, it's exciting. Plus, you gotta be ten.

Come Friday nights, the Gillette boys sponsored another great match between somebody named Tiger and somebody named Sugar. Boxing on the radio is almost an oxymoron. You can't see anything in the ring. You can't watch someone get knocked out. You can't witness a champ raising his arms standing on the corner of the ring. But you *can* hear and feel and experience it all because of the announcer. The bell, the crowd, the music, and one guy or two recounting the action, blow by blow.

I didn't grow up in the golden age of radio, as it's now called. I heard stories about families gathered in front of the Atwater-Kent listening to Fibber McGee and Molly. I read years later about the fireside chats and the horrors of war being broadcast to America. I only know about two guys in silk shorts trying to knock each other's brains out in three-minute bursts.

Dad and I spent years listening to the Cincinnati Reds as Waite Hoyt "called" the games. It was, however, the Friday Night Fights with my dad that I loved and that drew me to the sweet science—the mystery that is radio. I knew something was special when it made my dad get so excited he'd leap up on the bed, like when his favorite boxer knocked somebody out of the ring. Usually Dad banged his head on the low ceiling and experienced a near-knockout blow himself.

I always say I grew up in the country. I look at maps now and realize I was about ten miles from downtown Cincinnati. "Over the river," we called it. Kentucky *is* the country, and I grew up in it.

We had a regular neighborhood gang. My friends all had nicknames like Frog and Moe and Birdie and Mudhole. Frog tried to get out of being drafted into the army by trying to get flat feet. He leaped off the roof of his house repeatedly in an effort to flatten his pods. Moe, his brother, kept me up to date on Frog's plan. I saw Frog hobbling around every now and then, so it seemed to be working.

Donnie was the neighborhood weirdo. Everybody has one of those guys. He was always laughing at a joke nobody else heard. Ours was the kind of neighborhood where you just walked in the front door without knocking. The kids were a kind of giant village blob, drifting in and out of houses and garages at will.

My good friend Mike and I once walked in on Donnie when he was about fourteen, hooked with ropes around his ankles. The Donster had this brilliant idea he could pull his legs over his head 'til he could reach his own manhood. We walked in just as Donnie was almost bent in half with his pulley system of ropes and the headboard of his bed. Since I knew zippo about sex at that time, and Mike didn't either, we just accepted this as normal. We stared at Donnie as he was about to achieve some sort of relief 'til he realized we were in the room. Most folks would be either embarrassed or angry to be caught in such a position. Donnie just slowly lowered his legs and asked if either of us had any bubble gum.

I still consider this as the ultimate in cool in handling what could have become a reputation-crushing moment. Not to Donnie. He acted like it was nothing, and so we acted like it was nothing. A lesson learned: pick yourself up, or in Donnie's case, lower your legs and pull up your pants, and move on with your life.

Life was nothing but one long float on an old car top made into a raft on the creek. A pickup basketball game or softball challenge. It was tramping through the woods and sleeping in lean-tos in the front yard. We had floods and power outages and a few shootings mixed in for excitement, and it all seemed completely normal. It was.

Cincinnati, Ohio, during my childhood was filled with media stars. If you were on the radio or television in the '50s and '60s, it was a golden time. I still see the influence of those early pioneers on David Letterman even today. Paul Dixon did a local early morning show and was very funny. Ruth Lyons was a legend. However, it was the radio jocks that got to me. WSAI, WCKY, WLW, and WKRC had talent for days. I was raw material absorbing how to do radio without even knowing I was being taught.

My high school was typical of that area—a country school that was no match in sports for the city schools. I hear people talk about the difficulties of adjusting to high school. Oh, the angst and pain of the teenage years. I'm sorry, but I reveled in every second of it. Band, basketball, clubs—it was all a total blast. Obnoxious, I'm sure, but nevertheless true.

Dusty Rhode was a DJ on WSAI, the station all the "kids" listened to every waking moment. For the embryos reading this now, I will explain how Dusty came to walk among mere morals. He had the coolest name in the world, he was young and good-looking, and he was on the radio. He was a star!

Dusty came to my high school for a sock hop. Sock hops were the hormone-infused dance parties from the early days of rock 'n' roll. There is nothing more valuable in the world than the gym floor of a high school. The wood is apparently some kind of rare African rosewood that must be protected at all costs. Walking on it in shoes would ruin this protected and highly polished collection of planks, and thus, "sock hops" were invented. Kids could hop around on the floor, flailing to music, but only if they were wearing their finest white cotton footwear. Shoes were verboten.

To celebrate a sports victory, be sure to have one of the biggest celebrities known to man in honor of the occasion. At the time, I never realized what Dusty Rhodes was required to do. Dusty drove the winding country roads to a hick-filled high school on a Friday night. He was by himself, so he had to haul in some old speakers and an amp to produce some noise. He had boxes of 45s and some radio station junk to give away. Dusty was probably in his twenties and getting twenty-five dollars for the opportunity to watch acne-ravaged, dance-challenged hillbillies leap to and fro. "Louie, Louie" blared from the speakers, and we twisted and shuffled in our stocking feet in what seemed like heaven. Dusty was amazing. He'd ask, "Are you all having a good time?"

Are you kidding, Dusty? What could possibly be better than this? Every fifteen minutes, he gave away another highly coveted station bumper sticker and asked if anybody had any requests. The guy was a born entertainer. Three hours later, we were exhausted, Dusty was out of stickers, and we were out of time. I had witnessed show business at its highest level.

I imagine the school principal slipped Dusty a five and a couple of tens outside. Mr. Rhodes likely hauled all the equipment to his car and drove home at midnight. Surely, he was as honored to have this chance as we were to have him there. Talk about a win-win for everybody. Years later, I learned firsthand how much of a thrill radio "personalities" get from going to a remote location.

But it was on that evening in a small high school in Kentucky when I knew what I wanted to do with my life. I never walked into a radio studio until I was in college, but it was always my plan...my dream...my future.

The other side of all my tomorrows was also there at the hop. She was blonde and beautiful and a dancing machine. Little did I know that I would still be married to the girl who agreed to a dance that golden evening. Love is a wonderful thing, especially if you can find it while saving a gym floor at the same time.

QUIZZICLE #1

Who did I hear say the following: "Pud me dine, Goh dim eet. Pud me dine"?

A) Mary Chapin Carpenter

B) Hunter Hayes

C) Michu, The World's Smallest Man

Don't Bother Me

DURING A LIVE TV show from the Tennessee State Fair, I did one of the most bizarre interviews in the world. Our guests were the geeks. My producer thought it would be "good TV" to welcome the sideshow people working for the traveling carnival. We had a guy who could pop his eyes out of his head. I just remember thinking how he probably used a gallon of Visine. He actually sort of focused and then protruded his eyeballs 'til he looked like me the first time I saw Sara Evans changing clothes backstage. (That's another story I may never tell.)

We also had Miss Nude Teenage America—a title to make any parent proud. I did the entire conversation with her while her "manager" held her by her bra from the back so she wouldn't bolt from the set. I felt sorry for her, and when she asked in a panic, "Can my mom see this in Jackson?" I knew we were in trouble. I hope the "manager" is in a small room somewhere with bars on the door.

Our first guest was Michu, "The World's Smallest Man." I'm talking small—Sleepy and Bashful small. When Michu puffed up,

he was two feet, nine inches tall. You may have seen him portray-
ing ALF on the network show of the same name. My cohost was a
lovely but slightly daffy girl named Valerie Lindell. She was fabulous
because she had no filter. Valerie rolled with whatever goofy thing
I had to say and asked questions of guests I wouldn't have touched
with a ten-foot pole...or one the length of Michu, for that matter.

We were instructed rather harshly by Michu's manager/handler/
gofer. In the thick Hungarian accent of Michu's homeland, the lady
told us how to talk to Michu. "He is a full-grown man. Do *not* treat
him like he's a child. Do *not* speak down to him [which was almost
impossible, I pointed out]. And above all, do *not* touch him." Got
it: man, grown, and untouchable. I was cool with that.

Now we're on live TV. We welcomed Michu, "The World's
Smallest Man," to Nashville, Tennessee. Michu scrambled like an
elf toward a waiting and very low chair, whereupon Valerie proceeded to pick him up and said, "You are *so* cute. Who makes
your little pants?" She then plopped the obviously enraged Michu
on her lap. The director, in a panic, cut to me while Valerie began
struggling to hold her cute, little, and extremely pissed-off prize. I
sort of said to no one in particular, "Michu is a full-grown man and
is from Hungary." That's when I heard his tiny, elfin voice going
out over live television.

"Pud me dine. Goh dim eet. Pud *me dine*. Air vas your miners,
beetch lady! *Pud me dine!*"

Slowly, Valerie and I began to realize what he, in near-Hungarian,
was actually saying: "Put me down. God damn it, lady! Put me
down!" He was spitting mad. I started laughing at the scene.

Valerie slowly began to unravel his mysterious noises as a string
of "cussin' like a sailor" in his thick accent. She handled it well.
Valerie leaned away from him and, with both hands, gave him a
shove off her lap. OK, it was more how you would get rid of a wild
monkey, which he kinda was. Poor Michu was propelled through
the air like a sack of small potatoes and landed six feet away.

And for the finale, an elephant from the carnival had recently left quite a pile of pachyderm "exhaust." Teensy Michu was not only insulted, he was also flailing around on live television, in his little silk pants, in elephant shit. He actually handled it better than I would have. If you need someone who can show class flailing in elephant shit, Michu is your man.

Always the pro, Valerie then turned to the camera and said, "We'll be right back with more from the State Fair. We'll get to meet a teenager who is famous for being naked."

We never did another live show from the State Fair.

Country Music
Causes Brain Damage

COUNTRY MUSIC CAUSES brain damage. Yes, I know what you're thinking: if this doofus can write a book, I'm certain it will prove his theory. You're right, of course. I am, however, writing as a field observer and battle-scarred veteran of the hillbilly wars. For more than thirty-five years, I've been subjected to country music. I've been immersed in it. I am the lab rat on the other end of the mountain music ray gun. When I say brain damage, I mean the usual things that I've seen people do or say that leave no doubt that a steel guitar and three chords will change the cerebral makeup of a person.

I'm talkin' about lyin' and cheatin' and drinkin' and smokin' folks. And those are just the religious ones I know who listen to country music. In fact, they are usually the worst. I'm talkin' about stealin' ideas, fistfights, drugs, divorces, car chases, cussin' and spittin', not sleeping for a week, ordering mail-order chickens, dying your hair prematurely jet-black, wearin' headgear you don't qualify for, murder, mail fraud, wacky 'baccy, liar's poker, bottles of Jack Daniel's, and pyramids of beer cans.

I specifically know that this blessed genre of hick art will eventually result in shoplifting, sex in convertibles, jumping out of windows, snake handling, potshots, bacon grease, illegal bus stops, immoral business practices, and peeing in the sink. If you'd seen as many backroom-dealing, wife-hugging, fake hair, three-timing, coke-sniffing, radio-bribing, carjacking, golf-cheating, mansion-buying, horse-trading, whacked-out cowboys as I have, you'd know I ain't lyin'.

I've always said that there are two things that cause the most grief in the world: somebody's gettin' somethin' I ain't gettin', and my God is better than your God. On a global level, that's probably true, *but* country music and brain disaster are a very close third, ahead of global warming, the economy, and today's modern radio.

I'm only here to serve as an early warning system. As the tornado siren of Nashville, I'm going off at full blast just so you can't say, "Why didn't you warn me?" So here I am. This is your final warning. It's singers and songwriters, publishers and managers, and record people and radio people, all interconnected like some giant dysfunctional family and all joined at the hip by their involvement one way or the other to what's been called "America's Music."

It's no wonder this country is in trouble. Country is more popular than it's ever been. Oh, sure, it's inspiring and touching. It honors God and family and kids and horses and riding around in a truck. That's all well and good. I'm just saying, from what I've observed with my own lyin' eyes, there's something going on between C & W and an MRI.

I also want to say I wouldn't have had it any other way. I love 98 percent of these people. Like Lot's wife, they are the salt of the earth. The other 2 percent I hope are abducted by aliens and have their buttocks probed.

So here we go. My story. My evidence. Country music causes brain damage.

Johnny Paycheck

BEFORE JOHNNY PAYCHECK left this planet in 2003, I had not seen him in a few years. He is a great example of "my country vs. your brain" theory. Johnny was a genius at singing and questionable at life. He truly was an outlaw. He actually went to prison. Johnny was old-school. I'm also fairly certain Johnny was no-school. His greatest recording achievement was "Take This Job and Shove It," a true two minutes and thirty-five seconds of blue-collar, frustration-busting music that nearly everyone felt in their soul and a one-finger salute to every bad boss we've all ever had. Johnny also could get slightly out of control.

In a bar in Ohio, he fired a .22 at a guy's head and served the same amount of months in prison for trying to give the dude cranial air-conditioning. Talk about brain damage. The guy didn't meet his maker, but it certainly put a crimp in Johnny's concert schedule. Early in my career in Nashville, while I hosted a morning radio show, I also occasionally filled in for the host on a local TV program and that was the first time I met Johnny Paycheck.

We were set up to do the show live from a bar in the downtown nightclub district of Printer's Alley. The place still reeked of the night before. Eau de Honky-Tonk was in the air. I squeezed onto the front of the tiny stage crowded with ancient equipment and a couple of microphones to start the show promptly at 9 A.M. The TV klieg lights had that little club percolatin' along at about 125 degrees. I'm gonna guess here that Johnny had not been home resting up the evening prior to this historic TV appearance.

I interviewed Mr. Paycheck several times in later years on the radio, and I've said in public that interviewing Johnny Paycheck was like interviewing a chimp—a lovely chimp. He was pleasant, but quite active, and prone to unexpected leaps, squawks, noises, grimaces, and bursts of maniacal laughter. That morning in a smoky honky-tonk, Johnny was in rare form. He was so wired I thought he was gonna burst into flames at any second.

It was forty-five minutes until we would go live on Channel 2. Johnny was bouncing around the back of the stage like a fly in a bass drum. Then one of his "handlers" sidled up to me and whispered, "We have a problem."

"What?" I worried.

"Johnny don't got his teeth."

I was sure I didn't hear that correctly. "Johnny don't got his *what?*"

He said again, firmly this time, "Johnny *don't* got his *teeth*. He thinks he left 'em on the nightstand at his motel."

(Maybe John did rest up a little before this show.) I took a stab. "Do you have someone who can make a teeth run for him?"

Not wanting to volunteer himself, the "associate" replied, "Johnny said he'd go, but I'm afraid he won't come back. I'll see if the drummer is up for it."

It was then that I waved at Johnny, who was back in the dark, bouncing around like a kid on a trampoline. He waved back and gave me the biggest, gummiest grin I'd ever seen. This was not going well.... There was only a half hour to go before showtime.

Finally, I saw the drummer sullenly walk out the swinging doors to retrieve Johnny's smile. I'm pretty sure he had lost a bet. Apparently, Johnny really needed his teeth. "He sings like Gabby Hayes if he don't got 'em!" the bass player said.

Once in Texas, on a particularly forceful version of "Take This Job," Johnny hit the word "shove," and his dentures took a flying shot into some poor lady's beehive in the front row. Spit his dentures right there, next to her bow.

I was a nervous wreck. My producer was a nervous wreck. Johnny was a hopped-up gummy disaster and didn't seem to have a care in the world. The drummer arrived at 8:57 A.M. with a red handkerchief full of uppers, and at 9:02, Johnny was in full-blown wail and smiling for all of Nashville to see. If you were considering taking that job and shoving it, this was your song.

Johnny was a sweet man and hung in there for a little extra run at country music. He came back from some scary tour of low-rent bars in Europe. He'd brought me a bottle of "foreign wine from one of them Swede-y countries," as he put it. I still can't hear that song without thinking of the magic of country music, the glorious wonder of showbiz, and that Texas lady's hair.

Glossary of Terms

BEFORE WE GET TOO far along into the business of country music and radio, I think I need to give you some definitions of words that are thrown around a lot. I hope this glossary provides you with a backdrop of understanding to help you slog through the rest of this. Therefore, and calypso facto, here are the words you need to know:

Advance: Money given to a writer or an artist before they've done anything to deserve it. Usually takes several careers to pay back.

Airplay: What kids do with invisible guitars.

Agent: Person who books you one night in Calgary and the next night in Peru.

Clearance: Music you record that you found at a yard sale.

Cloud: Where you store digital property, or what's over Willie's bus.

Deal: What two parties agree to that they totally disagree on later when there is a triple-platinum record.

Distribution: Formerly massive record stores, now on some kid's computer in India.

EPK: Ethiopian Pizza Kitchen.

Get Signed: Securing a record deal, or what Bill Engvall does to people.

Independent: Record people who don't have to listen to a mega-corporate vice president. However, they usually do have to report to some guy who owns a chain of Mazda dealerships.

Jewel Case: What Tim McGraw wears in his pants.

Jingle: What you give to someone when you want to talk to them on the phone.

"Key Man" Clause: Unspoken agreement giving you the right to hire somebody to break into an office to see how badly you're being ripped off.

Points: When an artist's manager gestures to other people when his act is upset. For example, "That dude right there in the T-shirt drank all your Jack."

Public Domain: Music that can only be played in parks and public bathrooms.

Recoup: Getting all your money back, or what you do when your chickens get loose.

Sampling: Those little pieces of food on a toothpick at Winn-Dixie.

Session: A three-hour time period set up for expensive musicians to noodle around for the first two hours and forty-five minutes.

Streaming: You know your career is in trouble if you see the audience doing this out the back door during your third song.

Americana: Folk music for geeks. Usually performed by artists who don't have a record deal anymore or never had one.

Mother Church of Country Music: The name of Garth Brooks' estate in Oklahoma.

Outlaw: Older artists who have actually been to prison, as opposed to new artists who didn't return a library book.

Set List: What roadies present to the star showing where the best hooters are in the audience.

Press Release: Lies sent to newspapers, radio, and TV. Also, how you open the bathroom door on a tour bus.

Backstage Pass: What you make at a babe backstage.

Pitch: What artists do out the window to songs handed to them by people as they leave the venue.

Publisher: Person who cashes the royalty check first to be sure the songwriter won't spend it foolishly.

Strat: Guitar, or someone who is both strong and fat.

Spiritual Adviser: Person who buys all the hooch for the tour.

Fitness Trainer: How a woman wearing nothing but panties and boots is introduced when she wanders off the bus in the parking lot at Denny's.

Music Row: The heartbeat of country music that needs to be shocked back to life every ten years.

DJ: Person who plays songs on the radio and is massively underpaid.

Air Personality: Person who talks too much on the radio and is massively overpaid.

Sidekick: Person who reminds hung-over Air Personality what he was talking about during awkward silences.

Pickin' 'n' Grinnin': With guitar, it's country music. Without guitar, it's often disturbing to watch.

Roadie: Person who hauls all the stuff offstage while the star has left for his jet.

Country & Western: What people from New York and L.A. call country music.

Dipshits: What country people call people who say, "Country & Western."

Hillbilly: Loving reference to rural types who have an underfunded dental plan.

Rednecks: Proud group who are convinced the world is a better place because of large trucks, country music, and women with tattoos.

45: Early vinyl music product or required breast size for redneck women.

33-1/3: Original speed of vinyl albums. Also, IQ of most disc jockeys.

Banjo Player: Person who has never said the phrase: "Wanna go for a ride in my Porsche?"

Steel Guitar: Country instrument mostly used to get prisoners of war to confess.

Manager: Individual who tells country music artist he's brilliant every day and then cancels *all* decisions made by artist.

PR Rep: Gets artist an appearance on a TV show he doesn't want to do after the artist has complained he never gets on any TV shows.

Meet 'n' Greet: How artists meet their second wives.

Groupie: Fairly attractive young woman who believes riding on a bus all night to Dothan, Alabama, is the dream of a lifetime.

Producers: Usually hit by a train because they can't hear anything.

Recording Engineer: Secretly produces the album when the producer passes out in the parking lot.

The Mix: One of several hundred variations of a recording. Each version is never liked by more than one person at any one time.

A&R Coordinator: Finds hit songs for artists who turn them down for a song they wrote last night with a groupie.

Promo Guy: Honest person who buys sixty-inch flat-screen television for radio program director, strictly as a token of love and respect.

Payola: Rumored under-the-table payoffs for airplay; have always been total fiction.

Arbitron Ratings: Radio audience figures, compiled with no basis in science or reason, used to fire Air Personalities.

Tracking Session: Professional musicians play instrumental parts of a record based upon a different song that sounds like the one they're recording now.

Radio Listeners: People who call and request the song the DJ is currently playing.

Radio Remote: Public appearances by radio personnel at car dealerships for purpose of giving away station bumper stickers and ruining the afternoon for nearly everyone involved.

Radio Engineer: Guy who smokes cigarettes and fixes broken equipment just by walking into a room and saying, "Let me try it."

Business Manager: Person who fails to convince artist that investing all his money in glow-in-the-dark condoms is a bad idea.

CD: Piece of plastic that never goes back into the other piece of plastic that has the title of the piece of plastic on the front.

Jukebox: Ancient record player found in bars that takes quarters and should never be rocked.

Honky-Tonk: Dive with music. Pickled eggs at the end of the bar usually a requirement.

Radio Sales Rep: Person who promises to client that Air Personality will do a remote broadcast every Saturday at car dealership for free.

MP3: Music file that is returned to sender because mailbox is full.

Songwriters: Unhappiest people in the world because the deck is stacked against them.

Songplugger: First person to arrange stacked deck against songwriters. Also second-unhappiest person in the world because writers turn in such crappy songs.

Fragrance: Endorsed odor of star. Actually smelling like star not a requirement.

Bus Driver: 50+ male with the patience of Job and the kidneys of a camel.

Hair Stylist: Young male who works five hours on artists' hair so they can cover it with a hat.

Clothing Stylist: Young female who explains to female artist that *all* stage clothes shrink on a bus and have to be made larger over time.

Radio Contesting: Way to give away concert tickets to listener who says, "I hope they're better than the seats I won last week."

Segue: Music with no space in between for Air Personality to do a "bit."

Bit: Joke that Air Personality heard last night on *Letterman*.

12-in-a-Row: Presentation of songs that radio programmers think is major genius.

Swag: Promotional items given away that wind up in yard sales.

Classic Country: Collection of ten to twenty songs played endlessly for people who don't like anything that sounds remotely new.

Hank: Artist referenced constantly by new artists who hardly know who he is. See also: Jones, Haggard, Waylon, and Hank Jr.

One-Hit Wonder: What failed artists would give their right arm to be.

Cowriter: Person who actually writes the song while the artist is on a cell phone to landscaper.

The Lid Incident
and Smoking with a Monkey

WHEN I WAS FIVE, a very traumatic thing happened to me. I was pretty small, and I took advantage of it. Whenever I had to take a leak, I would stand at the big porcelain target in our only bathroom and lay my pecker on the edge of the bowl. This freed up both hands, and I could just relax and go about my business.

One day I reached for a towel and, I guess, brushed against the back of the toilet seat. The next few moments happened in slow motion. All I remember is standing there with my male glory laid like a guilty Frenchman at the guillotine. I just froze as I watched the 400-pound solid oak lid come crashing down toward my favorite appendage. I heard someone screaming like he'd had a massive piece of wood smash directly on top of his willie. My mom (who'd been next door and still heard me) came rushing into the narrow bathroom and scooped me up. "Oh, my darling, you squished your weenie, didn't you?"

It was a pretty obvious observation, but I whimpered something that resembled "yes." At that point, my father heard the commotion and was roused from his giant brown easy chair by the police radio and wandered in to check on the situation.

My mother was grief-stricken. My father thought it was hilarious. I leaned more toward my mother's reaction. My father asked if he could view the damaged dingus for himself. Mom wondered aloud if we should go to the doctor. It was then I learned my dad was funny. He said, "Well, if you do, see if he can take away the pain but leave the swelling." At the time the humor flew right over my head, but for years afterward, it became known as the "lid incident." We laughed about it 'til he passed away.

The lesson that I take from that experience is that sometimes, in the midst of what is the worst possible situation, there might be something funny going on. I don't mean grace under pressure; I panic probably more than most people. But making fun of something awful, embarrassing, or painful can sometimes help the situation. Or get you punched out. You have to judge the situation case by case. Realizing you're at your lowest and learning to laugh at it is, however, a good quality.

One of my favorite singers in the whole world was able to do that. I don't want to reveal his name because he's had some difficulties, but he told me what had changed him. He'd had several major pop hits—big, wonderful, amazing records that made him a minor star. He then turned to Nashville when the pop thing started to slide a bit. I would go see him at The Bluebird Café or the Exit/In anytime he was playing one of his solo shows. We became friends. Not call-you-from-jail friends, but still, we shared some good talks. He told me this story:

He had moved to Nashville to start over, something he was quite good at. Before the move, he'd been drinking and taking other "additives," and eventually his concert dates got worse and worse. He'd fallen to the point where he was now playing in a hotel on the beach in Tampa, opening for an animal act. Yes! He went on first, and then this guy and his chimp came out to amaze the 7 P.M. and 10 P.M. dinner crowds. During the day, there was nothing to do but sit on the beach and smoke a joint or two. He waited all day for the sun to go down and for showtime.

It was just a typical day, and he was on the beach enjoying a little smoke when the trainer with the chimp ambled down and plopped beside him. Our hero, the trainer, and a monkey at the beach. Our hero took a hit and passed the joint to the trainer. The trainer took a long, smoky drag on the joint and handed it to the chimp. The chimp puckered up his lips and then, with a deep and satisfying sucking sound, "hit" on the community joint. They did this two or three times. They all got very mellow and just gazed out at the ocean. My friend told me the chimp was especially calm. So much so, they all fell asleep. They were startled awake by the hotel club manager screaming they were "on" in ten minutes.

Showtime! The trainer pulled the groggy chimp to his feet and half-dragged him toward the hotel. My singing friend stared up at the sky and started laughing uncontrollably; he couldn't stop. The manager just stared at him.

It was at that precise moment our singing hero stopped doing drugs and drinking for the rest of his life. Quit. Cold turkey. He's clean. How? He said, "Man, once you're smoking grass with a monkey on the beach, you know it's time to quit drugs and try something else."

QUIZZICLE #2

Who actually said this to me:
"I am the father of Madonna's baby"?

A) Johnny Cash

B) Jason Aldean

C) Roseanne Barr

Baby's in Black

WHILE I WAS ON the radio one morning, I answered the phone. The Man in Black was on the other end. Johnny Cash was at the airport and had run into the Judds. Apparently, Naomi explained to John that I was asking who the father of Madonna's baby could possibly be. Madonna had announced she was "preggers" and at that time wouldn't divulge who made her that way.

After some prodding from Mama Judd, Johnny decided to call and confess that *he* was indeed the Papa of the Madonna Love Child. Few people know what a wacky sense of humor John R. Cash had. Whenever I ran into him, Johnny Cash was imposing and bigger than life. It was *that voice*. But once you started talking to him, you realized he was a kind and normal guy. He was also very funny.

I remember having crossed 57th Street in Manhattan several years ago, and noticed beside me a man in white—white pants, white shirt, white hair. The packed New York City street crowd never had a clue that Johnny Cash was walking beside them. I said, "Hey, John, it's Gerry. What are you up to?"

He rumbled back, "Oh! Hi, Ger, I'm going downtown to visit Rose." (Rosanne Cash, his daughter, lived in New York. She's one of the smartest people I know and what a songwriter.) I also noticed that this older gentleman crossing the street was invisible...until he spoke. When he answered me, suddenly fifty people turned to see where *that voice* was coming from. It sounded like Johnny Cash, because it *was* Johnny Cash.

That was the last time I saw John; he left us not long after that. I didn't bring up his "confession" to being the father of Madonna's baby. It was just a fun story between friends. I remember seeing him wave and fade into the crowd. All in white and kinda fragile.

He was still the Man in Black to me. He was still Johnny Cash.

Garth Brooks

MY WIFE HAD AN AUNT who never wanted to meet anybody new. She said she'd "met everybody she needed to know," and if she met one more person, she'd have to forget somebody. That makes perfect sense to me. I notice now, when I shake hands with somebody I've never met before, I get a slight chill. It's because a person who was once dear to me or who worked with me or who went to school with me is leaving my memory bank. I can almost hear the door click behind them.

Like most folks, I also greet everyone as warmly as possible and say my name. They do the same and tell me their name. I then *immediately* forget it. I can't remember people's names even when they are wearing name tags. I can't remember the names of people I'm related to. I'm not suffering from any old-age problems; I've just been like this all my life. I hate it. I feel bad. I have very little celebrity, but people do come up and speak to me all the time. I feel like I should say, "I'm so glad to meet you, but next time I won't remember your name, so shout it at me when you see me."

The worst thing folks blurt out when they are walking toward me is, "You don't remember me, do you?"

"Of course I don't. I'm not even sure who that woman standing over there is who looks like my wife! How the hell am I supposed to remember you?"

I should be honest and tell them the truth. But I never do that. Instead, I say, "Of *course*, I remember you. How could I forget you?" Then I'll turn to the woman I think is my wife and say, "Honey, you remember Adolf Hitler here, don't you?" They laugh and nine out of ten times announce their name to what's 'er name. Then I repeat the new name and for the rest of the night call them "Pal" or "Buddy."

Now that I've admitted what a doofus I am about remembering people, I should mention a guy who apparently never forgets anyone. I *do* remember his name: Garth Brooks. In all my years, Garth is perhaps the most mysterious of all the people I've crossed paths with. He has charisma for days. He's lovable and quick-witted. And he seems to remember a guy who did his dry cleaning from thirty years ago. I'm certain it's a trick or a gift or that he has a "person" who works for him taking pictures, but he remembers everybody. It's a wonderful thing. I've probably had a hundred people say they ran into Garth at some affair or another and say, "Man, he walked right up and said my name and shook my hand." These people *glow* when they tell that story. To be honest, it always made me a little jealous. If I could remember one of the names of the people who've told me that story, I'd call them up and tell them it's a trick or something.

Garth is also a genius at marketing. That's part of his deal. He has figured out how to sell the same twenty songs over and over in different packages. I think that's brilliant. And he's a great singer, guitar player, and entertainer. He's not much of a dresser, but then who is? He has that Garth eye, too. Whenever I see the ads now for the movie *War Horse*, I always think of Garth. It's kind of scary, with the head turned and that Big Eye starin' at ya, sizin' you up. Rememberin' your name and useless stuff like that.

Over the years, I've seen and heard several versions of Garth sing—The "Aw, Shucks" Garth, the "Country" Garth, and the "Barry Manilow" Garth—and there's nothing wrong with any of them. "Aw, Shucks" Garth can self-deprecate himself into a tizzy. "Country" Garth can wear old boots and jeans and sell out Vegas. "Barry Manilow" Garth stands in a dazzling spotlight and belts to the stars. There have been recorded versions of all the Garths: "Friends In Low Places," "Two of a Kind, Workin' on a Full House," and "Somewhere Other Than the Night" = "Aw, Shucks/Country/Barry" Garth. It's brilliant!

Garth also has had the benefit of one of those music guys with a magic touch: his producer, Allen Reynolds. And good record biz people. I think Garth deserves everything he has, including the fabulous Trisha Yearwood.

One of the weird things that happen to famous people in the press is how the public absorbs certain moments: "He's gay." "She hated her mother." "They aren't really the kid's parents." Some statement that's usually lifted from an interview or a story that may or may not be true.

I saw it happen to Garth. When he was preparing to jump ship on the artist life, he did an interview. Talking with that "can you believe it" line of thought, he said one quick off-the-cuff thing. It wasn't meant the way the public accepted it. Garth said, "I've got more money than my children's children can spend." It was one of those typical self-effacing, "Dude, am I lucky or what?" moments. That's all it meant. But over and over, that comment has come back to me in various forms. Listeners, fans, and friends all think it meant, "I'm rich, so back off." Nothing could be further from the truth. Or so I read it. Yes, he *is* rich; we all know that. It's just odd how resentment rears its ugly head on so many things. In other words, "He's gettin' somethin' I ain't gettin'."

I can't imagine how many times the guy who said those words has been confronted with them. I guess it becomes part of the lore, and unless you want to spend all your energy fixing it, you just shrug and know in your heart it isn't true. That is, if you're normal and secure. Me? I'd be out there every day going, "People of Earth: I am one of you. I was *not* born on the Planet Ignoramus, as you have been told. Don't believe what they say about me. Don't make me come out there!"

There was a moment in time when Garth had his own record company. His own personal little business dealio was called Capitol Nashville Records. I'm certain there were many other acts on that label who also think they were on that label. They were, but they were just tick birds on the rhino. Garth was the gorilla in the room. The promo department, the press department, and the executive department worked for Garth. He was *that* big. I also know he spent a lot of time taking care of people. He called them back. He listened to their songs. He paid overdue bills for people. He did (and does) a ton of charity work.

Remember that horrible incident where a congressman from Indiana or someplace criticized Garth for not meeting with a cancer victim? I vaguely remember it myself, but the point is that Garth didn't ignore anyone. Like *all* artists, they are supposed to drop whatever schedule they have and run immediately to handle something somebody else wants them to do. They do this a lot. They hold concerts, they go to hospitals, and they meet sick people.

Vince Gill, who spends most of his life doing so much charity work his friends call him "Benefit," once told me, "I was rushing to the car to catch a plane, and a woman yelled for me. I just had to put my head down and keep going. She said, 'Wait! I have *cancer!*'" What is anyone supposed to do at that point? I was furious when Garth got raked over the coals for meeting or not meeting somebody somewhere.

Most of the time, recording artists don't even know their own schedules. My journalist friend Robert Oermann said it best: "Since when is it the sole responsibility of artists to meet with the sick?" I guarantee you that lame-ass congressman doesn't spend his days running to be bedside for somebody he doesn't know.

Yes, it's disappointing when the artists can't meet you. You hurt for your niece or cousin, who is an enormous fan of the star. These fans don't have much time and are literally dying to meet the artist. I get that, but try to remember these artists are trying as hard as they can to get it *all* done, to shake hands and hold and kiss and nod with tears in their eyes at as many people as they can. Often, people will promise an artist's presence, and the poor singer doesn't even know about it. And don't even get me started on how much these people do for our troops.

I wish I had a really funny Garth story here, but I don't. That's because, even though I've been with him many times, I don't really know him—or any of the three Garths, for that matter. I'm not sure *anyone* has much of a bead on the guy except those that know him really, really well. And they all have glorious things to say. And as I said, he got Trisha Yearwood.

I remember when Bruce Hinton at MCA hired Trisha to make albums for his record label. Bruce is a quiet, unassuming exec who ruled Music Row for years. He is the human Zoloft. Bruce is one even-tempered dude. He makes Don Williams look jittery. His idea of a riotous evening is putting on an Oscar Peterson piano album and having a glass-*and-a-half* of wine. Party! He's also one of my close friends.

Bruce is a numbers guy. Not the mob numbers, but the accountant/business numbers. He told me, "I've just signed a singer who is gonna change the world. She's so warm and so fabulous and such a wonder that I can't wait for people to hear her." That singer was Trisha Yearwood. In 1991, "She's in Love with the Boy" was her first hit and launched her career. Trisha always had that big-moment, white-hot-spotlight, operatic finish to her songs that I just love. I often thought she'd just explode at the end of one of her concerts and that would be it. Trisha would hit that last note with all that power, and boom! Good night, Ms. Yearwood.

Trisha, who loved to hear the late Luciano Pavarotti sing, did an event with him, and he had all his costars over for a small, casual twelve-course dinner. Even though it meant a lot to her, Trisha gave me the invitation he had sent her for that night because she knew I loved to hear Pavarotti sing Puccini's aria "Nessun Dorma." Later, I went to see him in concert and watched him "brace" himself for the big note that was coming. I think he *did* blow up one night in Italy.

But it was just nice she sent that to me—a special memory from another evening in a long night of special evenings she wanted to share. I know she's doing a cooking show nowadays, and I'm certain she can still peel the cover off an onion with her voice. I think she's Garth's greatest accomplishment.

I once suspected Garth of quitting the business as a stunt. He did a lot of events as a stunt. I still love the moment on an awards show when David Bowie (the original musical chameleon) introduced Garth as Chris Gaines. Ziggy Stardust gives us Chris. Garth wore a wig and sang songs from his movie that hadn't yet been written. A lot of stuff going on there. But quitting as a publicity ploy? Boy, was I wrong. Wrong-o! Oh, sure, he does Vegas a bit, but he got off the rocket ship. Just opened the door, tipped his hat, and said, "Fellas, I'm outta here," and he stepped off into the unknown. Or maybe the very well known—his kids and his fam. I know for a fact that you've really got to be secure and know who you are to do that and do it successfully. Garth did it.

I bet Trisha is whipping up a peach pie for him right now. I hope so.

Gay Country

I DON'T EVEN KNOW where to start when talking about the gay influence on country music. I really don't have any gay agenda. In fact, I'm not really sure what a gay agenda is. I never understand the phrase "flaunting their lifestyle." Doesn't everybody flaunt their lifestyle? You are who you are and that's your lifestyle. Right?

I have friends who are gay. I worked for years with gay folks. There is a surprisingly large family of gay (openly or not) men and women in Nashville. It's no big deal to me. It's as if you whispered to me, "You know, he's French." OK. Although I also firmly believe most French are also gay. They are openly French and flaunt their Frenchness without letting up. Them and their words for stuff we can't understand. Damn French Flaunters.

I do know that if you landed here from another planet and saw pictures of the *Opry*, you would also conclude nearly everyone in country music is "playing for the other team." I've never seen such a fussy, bedazzled, dyed, primped, gussied-up, outlandish collection of humans in my life *not* to be all gay. Seriously, you mean you dress like that and you don't live in the East Village? A suit with lips all over it, and you're not a hairdresser? Rhinestones, darling, and you are actually straight? Really, George? George *Straight*? You're kidding, right?

My gay-dar is pretty good, but I am still shocked by some dudes who, I learn, prefer men. I always thought my friend Harry had the best response to learning of someone's sexual preference. I was sitting with Harry when an old cowboy at the table referenced a well-known publicist and outed him. I had suspected as much, but Harry just took a swig of his vodka tonic and calmly pronounced his feelings about the situation. "It's his mouth...he can haul coal in it if he wants to." That says it all for me. None of my business.

I've only known one person to use gayness as a career crutch. She was a slightly successful singer/songwriter who came out as a lesbian. *Cool*, I thought, *she's probably more comfortable now.* However, Chely Wright contended that her "career" had been ruined by the Music Row community when they learned she was gay. The unfortunate part of her argument was that her career never really got that big to begin with. Chely was not exactly Carrie Underwood at any point. Besides, it had been years since she'd had a hit or anyone had even thought of her. It was like getting a note in high school from a girl you once dated in the ninth grade, announcing she was through with you. You could hardly remember her last name and now you were dumped? Oh, *no!* The agony, the pain...then "Who is she again?" I do hope Chely is happy, but I've always sort of doubted that happens much.

The truth is, I think hardly anyone on Music Row would punish you if you're gay. Hell, *they* might be gay. Nobody cares—or at least the people that matter don't care.

I just realized in the past few minutes I've written the word "gay" 1,000 times. Gay, gay, gay, gAY, GaY, GAy, GAY.

I've heard the rumors about some of country's biggest stars being "that way," as my mom used to say. I remember being quite young and my mom asking me, "What do they *do* when they're gay?" Try explaining the "gay birds and bees" to your naïve fifty-year-old mother. I submit, if you can do that without causing her to have a heart attack, you should apply for the United Nations. She also summed it up for us when we'd talk about guys who "never married or seemed to date much." Mom said, "In my day, we just called them bachelors." Life was simpler then. I'm glad times have changed, but times were simpler then.

I've heard many, many people repeat the same old stories about how so-and-so was most certainly a queen and everyone knew it. I also know I've actually been sitting beside the "rumored to be gay" star and witnessed firsthand their attraction to a passing female fan. I can only say if they are gay, they have mastered the art of covering it by flirting, buying drinks, and inviting babes on the bus for a quick overnighter to Peoria. The same target of the rumor mill is also one of the biggest and most consistent Casanovas in history. Somehow, night after night, they manage to contain their gayness by chasing cuties on the road. Having their roadies pick out Bambis for special backstage passes and even being given "Hottie Alert" locations in the audience so he can wink at them during the concert. Protesting too much is one thing, but *nobody* can keep up appearances *that* much. Oh, I'm certain there are closet cases, but if these guys are in the closet, they are also in the witness protection program. It's impressive.

It's the clothing styles of country music that amaze me. Not so much anymore, but the early stars who really dressed like they should be in the Village People. I know Manuel, designer to the stars. He is one fabulous human being. His clothes are works of art, but you gotta be pretty secure to walk onstage in a lavender jacket with red roses on the lapels and white leather boots. Truly, a lot of Porter Wagoner's classic outfits could easily be reused for a local production of *La Cage aux Folles*. Visit the Country Music Hall of Fame sometime and see if you don't think those costumes weren't made for Marty Robbins but Martina Robbins.

And the hair. Let's not forget the hair of the ages. Puffed and buffed and shaped and whipped and teased and bullied into positions that don't normally occur in nature. I'm sorry, but I think there *is* such a thing as Gay Hair. Ridiculous, to be sure, but it's another of my theories. It's not the length—sometimes it's a buzz-cut to the scalp—but it's a giveaway.

Look, I'm as gossipy and nosy as everyone else. I'm a total hypocrite in light of all my "none of my business" pronouncements. It *is* none of my business, but I still sit around with songwriting buddies and wonder out loud, "Who's *he* trying to fool?" I'm sorry to fans and hope you won't take it the wrong way, but I have long suspected there are several major Hillbilly Twang Slingers who ride Side Saddle.

I am also on record as endorsing gay marriage because I believe gay people should have to endure marriage like the rest of us.

On another separate note, I also want to announce here in public that I once kissed Keith Urban. Just a peck on the lips. At the stroke of midnight on New Year's Eve. From what I recall, there was a substantial amount of wine reported missing the next morning. My wife was off in another room when the big midnight celebration moment arrived. I puckered up for the nearest person in order to honor Auld Lang Syne. It just turned out to be the guy who married Nicole Kidman. Also, I should tell you that he never writes. He never calls. He treats me like yesterday's newspaper. I have spent many nights standing in front of the fridge, eating ice cream out of the container with a scoop because of it.

Gorilla Glue

ONE eye opened. It was cold. Damn, bone-chilling, "shrinking" cold.

I have got to get up, he thought. *I don't know where I am.*

That's when he discovered that he couldn't get up. The queasy realization that he was immobile washed over him.

I've had a stroke. Oh, my GOD! I've had a stroke. I'm paralyzed. Oh my God, I'll never bowl again. Oh, my GOOOOOOOODDD, he shrieked silently in his head.

He tried again, and slowly through the fog realized it wasn't so much his body he couldn't move, but that his body he couldn't move from the cold floor. It was some kind of tile.

Wait, I know this tile. It's in her bathroom.

He focused his eyes and saw the bottom of the hideous green commode, the shower curtain with mermaids, and the plunger with dog bones painted on it. He grunted and stayed there like a walrus on a cold rock.

What the . . . ?

He tried to move again. He had to get out of there, and right now. What if she came home and found him. She was already pretty P.O.'d about things. Some women just don't understand life with musicians. It's tough out there. It's hard.

There are so many requirements and rules, meet 'n' greets, recordings and lyrics, and drinks and concerts and women. And wives. Or, in this case, wife. As in, *the* wife. Some women just can't get it through their heads that some men don't wear wedding rings and can still be married. Hell, country music is all about drinkin' and cheatin'. What did she think they'd been doin' for three years? Drinkin' and cheatin'—in equal parts and usually in that order.

In fact, now that he thought about it, that's what they had been doin' last night. He remembered the drinking part. Whose idea was it to try Tequila Sangria anyway? You had to be Mexican to drink that stuff. Couple of beers, couple of Jacks, she's dancing on the chair, a pitcher of that tequila wine grape juice, and whammo! He made a note to slow down one of these days with the tequila.

She's the one who said, "Baby, let's go back to my place," he thought.

He tried to move again. Nothing. He could rock back and forth a little, and yet he couldn't seem to scoot toward the shower. He noticed somebody had been selling purple Buicks on the big white phone, too. It was all stained. Then he vaguely remembered he wasn't feeling so good earlier. He also remembered her screaming something at him through the bathroom door about what a lyin', cheatin', washed-up bastard he was. Something about calling her the wrong name. Washed *up?* Who's washed up?

He took a deep breath and tried to clear his head.

Let's go over this again. I'm naked. I'm in a bathroom. I'm stuck. I'm STUCK!

That's it . . . he was stuck!

Wait a minute. I'm not stuck, I'm . . . I'm glued! I am glued to the goddamn floor. I'm naked, and I'm glued to the goddamn floor.

Be calm.

He was calm.

Breathe deeply.

Then he saw it. There, in the corner by the dead plant. Nausea and panic fought for control of his stomach. Panic was winning on points. The panic had started from somewhere deep inside him. It was true. It wasn't just glue, it was Gorilla Glue.

Jesus!

That batty woman had Gorilla-Glued him to her bathroom floor. He felt like "The Fly."

I have a gig in Jacksonville tomorrow night. Go panic! I can't sing Gorilla-Glued to the floor. I've sung drunk. I've sung high, I've sung on mushrooms, I've sung half-asleep, but who the hell can sing SUPERGLUED TO THE BATHROOM FLOOR OF SOME LOONEY I'M CHEATIN' WITH?!

They rescheduled the Jacksonville concert, although the promoter said he was taking it out of his hide. Actually, a good portion of his hide was already missing. His manager had received a call from a woman telling him where the fallen star could be found. Her story was that a couple of thugs had broken into her apartment and overpowered her. The thugs then thought it would be funny to attach our star to the floor with Gorilla Glue. She had somehow "managed" to escape, but was afraid to call the police on account of the bad publicity and all. She was only trying to protect his reputation as the moral and righteous country singer he was. Why, if it hadn't been for her, he might have been found months from now, layin' there like a country ham.

His manager had to call an ER buddy and a carpenter to get him loose. His wife didn't really buy the "attacked by glue-wielding thugs" story. Or his later tale that he'd actually slipped while doing a charity visit to an old-folks home and had fallen into a pile of denture cream—the kind that's super-powerful and grips tight to help you eat corn on the cob.

The wife was spotted two days later driving a new pink Porsche 911.

His girlfriend—correction, ex-girlfriend—sent a message that she had pictures and her lawyer was holding them in case anything happened to her. She told his manager that in one of the shots her ex looked like 200 pounds of Spam on a barbecue spit.

His manager quit.

He had to wear women's panties for three weeks because he was so raw. He also had to ride the bus sitting on one of those kid's inflatable swimming pool tubes. He swore on his great aunt's eyes that he'd never drink or cheat again.

That lasted 'til Saturday night in Lubbock.

His great aunt's vision is fine.

When the waitress reached back and grabbed his ass, the pain was so intense he shouted his wife's name.

Grand Canyon Reba

HERE'S HOW LAME I AM. I got bored with the Grand Canyon. I have a grandeur limit. I can only take so much fabulousness, and then I start to glaze over. We drove from Phoenix to the Grand Canyon, as excited as could be. Just an early glimpse through the trees of the very edge was like seeing Marilyn Monroe get her skirt blown up. After about five or six pictures and some oohs and aahs, I was over it.

I started looking at other people taking pictures and wondered exactly how many gawkers a year fall backwards smiling for Grandma. Isn't that awful? One of the wonders of the world, truly, the Grand Canyon is, as canyons go, really, really grand. But when it's all said and done, it's really just another sinkhole. Or massive dent in the earth, made by a river. They have trails where you can walk to the bottom of the Grand Canyon and see its grandness from the bottom up. I opted out of that little jaunt.

The most exciting part of my visit to the Grand Canyon? In the restaurant, where you can have wine in case you're not dizzy enough, I saw Davis Love III come in, look around, and dash out.

I was more impressed at spotting a pro golfer than I was looking at the magnificence of Momma Nature. Some things I just get bored with.

However, Reba McEntire is not the Grand Canyon. Oh, she's grand all right. She's a wonder of nature, and she's from out west. I never get bored staring at Reba McEntire. I believe she's also the same age. I may be off by a few years.

Let's just call her Reba for now and forever. I think she left her last name somewhere on a bus outside Tulsa. Reba is one of the grandest things in the world, right up there with the Pyramids and, pardon the redundancy, Dolly Parton.

I met "Red" (or, as we often use between each other, "Ruby Two Shoes") about thirty years ago at some event. She was with her Mercury record execs, and I actually met her three separate times, introduced by various guys. The third time she laughed and said, "I got it. His name is Jurry and he's on the rayjoe." That's how it sounds to me when she talks. Jurry on the rayjoe.

She has not changed one iota from the first time I saw her—same sense of humor, same voice, same kind way of listening, same direct replies. She's tough as nails but gets misty-eyed at things people say or do. She writes personal, handwritten notes to people to thank them. We're friends. We've traveled together, had dinners together, and worked on TV shows together. I have written a lot of jokes for her over the years when she hosted the *Academy of Country Music Awards* or some other showbiz deal. Make a note: there is nobody tougher on a "line" than Reba, but when she loves it, you can rest assured it's going to be knocked out of the park. She commits to everything. If you've never seen her onstage, she just takes over. It's wonderful to watch. Such poise is rare. We all know how amazing her voice is. And that hasn't changed a bit, either. To me, she still sounds exactly like she did on her first record. Before this gets too icky, let me just say Red is one of my favorite people and leave it at that.

When you write jokes, at least in my case, you stare out the window a lot. Or you keep a little recorder by the bed and sort of drift off and think of things. I've done that my whole life. I'm terrible onstage myself 'cause I get nervous. I can, however, write funny things for other people to say. I write better for Reba than anyone else. I wrote some stuff for Roseanne Barr early in her career when I lived in L.A. Roseanne's husband, Bill (at the time), would call and say, "Rose is going on *Letterman*. Write some jokes about her trying to quit smoking." So I did. Then I'd turn on *Letterman* and Roseanne would spout the lines I wrote, like she had just thought of them. She was good. This is all I want to say about Roseanne because she's *not* one of my favorite people, and it's taking up Reba talk.

Getting jokes past managers, wives, producers, and publicists is tough. Everybody has an agenda. *Everybody* is paranoid the public will hear something about their act or singing or whatever. It's always easier to just say, "No," than it is to say, "That's funny." All I know is Reba's husband, Narvel, sent me a script with a note that read, "Wanna take a whack at this?" I did and have done it many, many times since.

If there's anybody who should take up some Reba time, it's Narvel. Supposedly, he's her manager, but he's a lot more than that; he's also her best friend. He's one stellar human being. How do I know? 'Cause we went with them to one of her concerts in St. Louis or Cleveland or someplace. The place was sold out, as it usually is. Reba was off getting ready, and Narvel, Allyson, manager Trey Turner, and I were just roaming around this massive stadium.

We came around a corner, and there was a blockade set up. Security. NOBODY GETS PAST THE GATE. The ferocious security person eyed us as we walked up. She was probably nineteen, and in a shaky voice said, "Do you have all-access passes? Because no one without one is allowed past this point."

Now, we didn't have all-access passes because I was with the guy who was in charge of the whole concert and the building and the security and the roadies and everything else. *Nobody* had passes. Over the years, I've seen small people act big. I've watched as people were berated or belittled by some jackasses who thought they were being disrespected in some way. Do you know what Narvel Blackstock said to this nobody security guard who had stopped us?

He said, "You know, you're doin' a great job. Is there any way you could perhaps call the head of security or check backstage to see if somebody can get us in. We'll wait right here 'til you give the go-ahead."

She scurried off and in five minutes some embarrassed security guy who recognized Mr. Blackstock came flying out. "Oh, my God, Narvel, I'm sorry." Mr. Blackstock just waved it off and said, "No problem. That's what's she's supposed to do, and thanks so much for helpin' us out. I really appreciate it." What class!

Can I mention the Dixie Chicks here? It's because when I think of Reba, I think of the George W./ACM/Dixie Chicks/"We're ashamed that the president is from Texas" stuff. I don't know exactly what Red thinks of the Chicks. She was hosting the *Academy of Country Music Awards*, and all that Dixie Chicks stuff was exploding.

I know I was probably a little hard on them. They could say what they wanted even though I didn't agree with it. I've only met Natalie Maines a few times. I always got the feeling she wanted to shoot at me or something. Nothing overt, it was just that she always seemed a little "tense," if you know what I mean. I thought the other two Chicks, sisters Martie and Emily, were part of the background and that Natalie was the star. Plus, Natalie chewed gum when she was doing interviews, and I think that's reason enough right there for imprisonment. Wearing headphones while somebody smacks away into a microphone is maddening.

I think the Chicks could have survived the whole "W" comment if they'd left well enough alone. Instead, they got angry. I get that. I do the same thing. They probably felt P.O.'d that people thought they were against the troops, and I'm positive they didn't think that at all. In fact, I've yet to meet anyone who is against the troops. Natalie and the girls started firing back at country music, Nashville, and everyone in their line of sight. It cost them dearly in the music biz.

Now, I will admit that I wrote the joke that Reba told about how "People in Vegas will gamble on anything. They're now taking bets on the chances the Dixie Chicks will perform at the next Bush family barbecue."

Reba said it, and I thought it was really kinda harmless. As the storm clouds gathered over the Chicks during the following year, it was time for another Reba-hosted ACM show. The Chicks, especially Natalie, had really carpet-bombed Reba, Toby Keith, and others. It got pretty nasty out there. Do you remember seeing George Bush, the President of the United States, getting off a plane and being asked about the Chicks' comment? You should know Reba likes George W. Bush and especially his father, George H.W. Bush. Red and Narvel took a cruise with George the Dad, and she was as excited as I've ever seen her.

So, you take a whack at Red's friend, *then* you take a shot across her bow, and guess what? You get fired back at. A lot of times I sent stuff to Reba thinking, *There's no way she'll do* this. Those are usually the jokes she does. I wrote something down that was funny to me. It was funny to Ruby Two Shoes. Toward the end of the nationally televised broadcast, Reba McEntire said, "Boy, I don't know why I was so nervous about hosting this show this year. I mean if the Dixie Chicks can sing with their feet in their mouth, *surely* I can host *this* sucker."

Narvel told me later, "That went off like a bomb in the audience." People were jumping out of their chairs screaming and applauding. I remember that John Rich shot out of his seat like a cannon. I doubt any of the Chicks will ever speak to me again. They didn't talk to me much anyhow. I like Natalie's haircut.

I got an e-mail from Reba not too long ago that read, "Ger, do you realize it's been twenty-five years since I recorded 'Little Rock'?"

Yikes! That song, which I cowrote with the great Bob DiPiero and Pat McManus, helped pay for my kid's braces. Twenty-five years? Has it been that long?

Time sure flies when you're not staring at the Grand Canyon.

John Rich Gatlin Boxcar

I JUST CAME FROM the studio with John Rich—the Rich of "Big &" fame. The John Rich who won *Celebrity Apprentice*. He tweets with Donald Trump. He tweets with Donald Trump's hair. John knows a lot of people.

"Mt. Richmore" is on the front gate of his house. It's a concrete palace he had built atop a quiet neighborhood, over nearly everyone's objections. John does that a lot. I mean, he does a lot of things over people's objections. I really like the guy. He was a second-banana singer in the band Lonestar. Richie McDonald was the usual lead singer of that band. I think it drove John a little nutty, and he quit. I'm pretty sure half the town wrote him off after that.

Oops. He formed the Muzik Mafia, came crashing into people's radios with Big & Rich, and never looked back. It became a rolling-thunder review of singers and midgets and diamond hats and loud guitars. Hey, it's still like Chet said: "If it's recorded in Nashville, it's country music."

John is one of those people who make Nashville fit them. His grandma still makes his special jeans. His daddy is a preacher. He's got a rhinestone saddle in the massive bar upstairs at his house. He calls his old friends to come write a song. That's how I got to the studio today with John Rich. Larry Gatlin was coming in right after me.

In the old Combine Music Publishing building, there was a grubby little studio in the basement. A lot of hits were made there. Some started out as demos and just got released. "I Can Help" by Billy Swan got cut there 'cause Billy had just bought that cheap little organ you hear on the record. There is a blackboard next to the john downstairs. Folks wrote things there that I never forgot. One of my favorites said, "There's a cat mask in the bottom drawer, please don't make me wear it."

The other line that stayed for years and never, ever got erased was, "Will Rogers never met Larry Gatlin." Ouch. Larry Gatlin is perhaps one of the most amazing singers and songwriters this town will ever see. "All The Gold In California," and "I've Done Enough Dyin' Today" still give me chills. I was such a groupie that I went to see him sing before he ever made it big. The Gatlin Brothers—Larry, Steve, and Rudy—are just magic together. There goes that brotherly harmony thing again. Larry also developed a propensity for sticking white powder up his nose and darn near lost it all. He's fine now. I see him every now and then on Fox Network. Larry's a smart guy but can be tough sometimes. My cowriter Tom Shapiro described a guy we play golf with as "one of my hard friends." We all have them. You love them and you'd also like to make them wear one of those Hannibal Lecter masks all the time.

Larry would stop singing and berate the audience if somebody talked while he was warbling. I saw him stop and ask a chatty group what they did for a living. Turns out they worked for Otis Elevator. Larry then announced, "Great. If you won't talk during my songs, I won't pee in your elevators." He was right, of course. They were distracting, but it makes you a hard friend to root for.

John Rich wrote a song with Larry Gatlin, and I bet it's a smash. I feel like the "new" Larry is an easier version. John also called me the other day and said he had cut a song we'd written together. That thrill never loses meaning for me. I hope it's a hit, too.

Big Kenny, who is the "Big" part of the Big & Rich brand, is quite a story himself. He was knockin' around town going broke, from what I hear, and landed on his feet beside John. The Peacemaker and the Hell Raiser. John Rich keeps a massive Mason jar of authentic bootleg liquor in his bar upstairs. You haven't lived 'til you try to finish a song after a couple of belts of that kerosene.

There is something endearing about someone who just keeps going. Just picks it up from wherever they get knocked down and walks on. I admire that in a person. Sometimes this Crazy Town, as Jason Aldean calls it, will allow you to move along.

I worry sometimes about new little baby chick acts—people who become stars from a TV singing competition and are suddenly thrust into the middle of the circus. They have a few hits and then *wham!* Brick wall. The ride is over. If you sift back through the singers who made it to the top three or four *American Idols* in a season, you'll probably remember a couple of them.

Then there are stars who just come out of nowhere. Anybody remember Boxcar Willie? Yes, Boxcar Willie. What a story *he* was. He got famous from being in some commercials for singers who were kinda well known in Europe but obscure in America. I am not sure *how* you become a star in Europe and remain obscure in the States, but he did it. He dressed up like a hobo and sang nasal, old-fashioned songs about railroadin', ridin' the rails, and generally being homeless. I've never been a big fan of not having any indoor plumbing, but Willie had a knack for making it sound glamorous.

Boxcar had lived a pretty good life before he became famous. Believe it or not, he reportedly sold 100 million records. I think that's probably a little exaggerated, but I'm certain he did sell a trainload.

My favorite Boxcar quote came during a brief radio interview. I asked him if he'd like to appear on one of our charity shows later in the fall. As his faithful/manager/wife looked on, he replied, "Oh, you'll have to ask Mrs. Box about that."

By the way, John Rich ends his e-mails with, "That's the thing about salted possum. It's just as good the second day." That makes him good by me.

Kinfolk

COUNTRY MUSIC AND RELATIVES, hereafter called "kin," have a long and sometimes successful but mostly troubled history together.

There have been several successful brother acts: two guys from the same mom, who usually wind up with one breaking his guitar over the head of the other—typical brotherly love. For some reason, people like hearing brothers sing together more than sisters. The Everlys, Don and Phil. The Louvins, Charley and Ira. The Bellamy Brothers, Howard, David, and Ralph.

David Bellamy, who wrote "If I Said You Had A Beautiful Body Would You Hold It Against Me?", exemplifies one of the great uses of a joke in music of all time. David once called me for a long conversation about what exactly scallops were. I wasn't sure and he wasn't, either. He likes them, but he's a little sketchy about them. I feel the same way. What the hell *are* scallops anyway?

There have been sister duets, sister trios, and even sister quartets, those foursomes of DNA that sound like angels, but in country music, there hasn't been much success. Most of the family singin' thing has faded in the past couple of decades. Donny and Marie even recognized that they had to each choose a format for their personalities, hence, "She's a little bit country and he's a little bit rock 'n' roll." It's that "Hey! If you hate rock 'n' roll, she'll be singing country right after I'm done" plan.

The father/daughter duos are few and far between and, frankly, always gave me the creeps. It's one thing to sing with your off-spring in the kitchen, but there's something else about cheatin', drinkin', and heaven songs while staring into the eyes of Daddy. It's a little too West Virginia for me.

The Kendalls, Royce and Jeannie, were a father-daughter duo. Their big hit was "Heaven's Just a Sin Away." They seemed to handle it fine, but it sounds like massive therapy down the road to me. I know singers are playing a part. I know some who won't sing a lyric because they think the audience will assign them that part. Reba always said, "I ain't no hooker, but 'Fancy' is one of my favorite songs."

Pop and the Kid, however, can get uncomfortably close to being downright weird if you're not careful. Jeannie Kendall always wore a little hat, too. It gave her a sort of '40s movie/gun moll look that made it even more disturbing. I mean, wantin' to hold some-body tight and be with them tonight is *not* what I want to hear from Daddy and his little girl. Think about it: "Heaven's just a *sin* away?" With Daddy? I'm pretty sure there's a book of rules against that.

I've also seen a father and his teenage son and daughter take a shot at stardom. I think the problem is, the kids hated him and he loved them. All teenagers think their dads are dweebs. Who wants to watch "eye-rolling with banjos" onstage for an hour? Most teen-agers can barely tolerate Dad for the fifteen minutes he asks them about their day. Imagine the soul-searing resentment of riding on a bus 24/7. Sure, it's fun for *us* to watch, but it has that same uncom-fortable feeling you get when you watch a preacher's wife stare at her husband who is holding a press conference to announce he's gay.

All this aside, however, *nothing* beats the toxic combination of mother and daughter as a loving hillbilly couple. It's that wonderful mix of twang, grandpa, beauty, and seething, boiling, red-eyed jealousy. Which, of course, brings us to ... The JUDDS!

If you *really* want to kick things up a notch, be sure and make the *mom* a stunner. A heart-stopping looker who demands to be in the spotlight. Then create a shorter, wider, full-backier daughter who can actually sing.

The joy that particular mom and baby girl duo have brought to me over the years is incalculable. For off-the-charts drama and soap opera histrionics nothing beats *As The Judds Twang*. Mom twirls and sashays around onstage, dropping one-liners and life advice as if she's Rodney Dangerfield and Dr. Phil all rolled up into one red-haired package. The daughter wails and moans and thrills and channels Elvis. Give her a biting sense of honesty and a battle of the bulge, and, friends, you've got yourself a hit-and-hate-making machine.

For those of you taking notes and looking at your little sweetie singing like a bird in the kitchen, I beg of you, please don't do it. Be a stage mother. Be a taskmaster. Be Joan Crawford, but for all that's holy do *not* rent a bus and sing harmony with your kid in front of people for money. It's not part of the normal order of things. It's against the laws of nature.

I see that comedienne (who's had so many face-lifts she looks like a Picasso) with her daughter on TV, and I think at least they can spit at each other if they want to. Singing together requires some semblance of a loving relationship unless you're in a church choir. Actually, we all know the ratio of choir rehearsals and affairs, but that's for another discussion. I know it's none of my business, but I recommend either quilting or Greco-Roman wrestling over singing together as mom and daughter.

I've often heard doctors say that estrogen, ovaries, and a steel guitar are as deadly together as hard liquor and wing-walking. There are some things you just don't do.

However, if you go against all the good advice and common sense in the world and do decide to embark on a warbling career with one of your units, here's what you do to keep the wheels turning: pick hit songs. Hit songs are always good because flop songs tend to make you more likely to stay at home a lot.

Choose a hair color carefully. If you can't make your music bigger and louder, then, by God, make sure your hairdo is. The most popular is something the color and consistency of molten lava—orange-red and flowing.

And when things slow down a bit and nobody is paying as much attention as they used to, throw in a couple of near-death experiences. Choose one of you to tell how you "like to have died." Then set out on a well-planned, eight- to ten-year *See 'Em Before They Croak Tour.*

Fight offstage as much as possible. Do a lot of TV talk shows where you have dueling interventions. If somebody in the family starts telling the truth about some tragedy, always interrupt and say *you* had that first and it was much worse.

The public is nothing if not a sucker for paying to see what can go wrong during a concert. Demolition derbies are popular for a reason, you know.

I actually did a live, nationwide radio show with Wynonna and Naomi the Sunday night before Naomi announced she had hepatitis. She seemed good the night before, but that's an insidious disease and dangerous. The timing did make it difficult for folks to not at least "wonder" if it was all on the level.

Allyson and I actually went to that "final" concert of the Judds'. Last time together. Final moment to see them. They passed out little electronic candles so we could wave them good-bye. I did indeed seem to have the feeling they did a "good-bye" tour about every ten years. I'm confused and, frankly, quit keeping count after awhile. Every family has troubles; they just happened to make it the family business. The TV show on Oprah's network was hilarious. Each week, they would end with a cliffhanger. Will Wynonna shove Mom into a concrete mixer? Tune in next week for *The Edge of Nut.*

I think Wy called me a nut in one of her books. I had dinner with her the other night at a table full of showbiz types during an awards event. She and her new husband, Cactus Moser, had plopped down beside Allyson and me. Cactus was a member of a great group called Highway 101. A lot of hits came out of that band. I loved 'em and Cactus. Just two months after he and Wynonna got hitched in 2012, Cactus had a terrible motorcycle accident and lost a leg. Just horrible.

Here's the side of Wynonna I love: when Cactus' name was announced to come onstage and receive an award, they called for her to join him. While helping Cactus slowly make his way toward the stage, she said, "Nope, this is his night." With tears in her eyes, she stood by the side of the bright lights as her guy beamed like the Hollywood sign with his songwriting award.

Underneath all that glamour and cool and "Juddness" beats the heart of a loving, caring woman and wife. And Lord, what a singer!

Ashley Judd is amazing. I just remember her head bobbing around at press parties and gold record celebrations. She was gorgeous, smart, and lost. It was like watching a thoroughbred colt run 'til it gave out because the little thing never knew where the barn was.

Finally, be sure and throw in a life coach. (Whatever the hell that is! Do normal people have a life coach?) Also, announcing you are no longer speaking to anyone in your family is a nice touch. If things slow down, have a pow-wow with Oprah and go on tour!

Oh, and have a little "work" done. Nothing too extreme, you know, to where your family doesn't recognize you anymore. But,

over the years, do a little tweakin'. Believe me, I have no problem with getting some work done. However, for the best possible
outcome, have Mom slowly look younger than the daughter, if
possible.

Great Love Stories

THEY HAVE RELEASED the "new" version of *Titanic*. Leo and Kate are on the ship's bow, and "king of the world" is shouted to the open sea. Film buffs always declare, "It's the greatest love story of all time." My wife always laughs at that. She contends, and I agree, *Titanic* is more like a quickie on *The Love Boat*. Greatest love of all time? They hardly knew each other. I know love at first sight and all that, but the *greatest* love story of all time? They met and fell in love that deep, that quickly? What about *the* love story of Loretta and "Doo"?

Loretta Lynn and "DooLittle" Lynn's story was made famous in the film *Coal Miner's Daughter*. Loretta is hilarious. She just tells you what she thinks, and it always comes out to somehow make you laugh.

I once got lost in the Opryland Hotel with Loretta. If you've never been to the Opryland Hotel, you should go gawk at it at least once. It's immense. It has a "conservatory" in it, which is sort of a rain forest/hothouse under glass. I think most of the rooms in the Opryland Hotel are taken up by people who can't find their way out of the damn hotel. It's a maze with curtains. You can check out, but you can never leave.

Late one night after some event, Loretta and I got on the same elevator and then wandered for hours down one dead-end hall after another. She was typical Loretta. Laughing about what dumbasses we were for not being able to get out.

She married Doo when she was just a teenager. You all know the story: coal mining, Butcher Holler, and the struggle to get her songs heard. Years after she was a star and things sort of calmed down, I used to have a drink or ten with DooLittle Lynn at the Hall of Fame Motor Lodge. Of course, we all cleverly called it the Hall of Shame. DooLittle was also a hoot. He was pure country. He was smart, but not the college smart kind. Usually, he was in some kind of feud with Loretta—not showin' up, not comin' home on time, not rememberin' their anniversary, not not having one more high-ball—the usual stuff women don't seem to be able to understand. Women are just unreasonable.

I am positive that "Don't Come Home A' Drinkin'(With Lovin' on Your Mind)" was a direct response to Doo. Doo was also called Mooney. Mooney was short for Moonshine, and I have a nagging suspicion it was more than a nickname.

Allyson and I went to the premiere of *Coal Miner's Daughter*. It was a grand night for Nashville at the Belle Meade Theater. I didn't go to Belle Meade much. It's the rich side of town, and alarms still go off whenever I drive through. You have to have that deep, genteel Southern accent to live in Belle Meade. I was once standing in a hardware store when one of the grand matrons of Belle Meade announced to anyone within earshot, which included people in the parking lot, "I have *got* to have a hammah!" Even I started to look for one for her.

On this one night, the hoity and the toity had to mingle with the riff and the raff. I represented the riff. I saw the director get out of a Rolls-Royce limo and sweep into the theater wearing a cape. I didn't know anybody except Batman wore a cape, but there he was. Strictly by chance, Allyson and I sat directly behind the real-life stars of the movie.

I liked the movie, but all I can remember is Loretta and Doo getting into some kind of fight *during the film*. For a brief moment, Sissy Spacek and Tommy Lee Jones were fighting on-screen, and the people they were playing were fighting in front of me off-screen. For all their fussin', however, I think they had a love story to be told. It deserved to be a movie. Reba and Martina absolutely worship Loretta. Just the other day, Reba was telling me she called Loretta to check on her. It was a scorcher in Nashville, and Reba said, "Loretta wanted to go outside and pick some 'maters, but she told me it was too hot and them 'maters wasn't worth dyin' fer." That's how Loretta talks.

Sometimes, when you hear old songs by the Coal Miner's Daughter, they sound so dated and simple you don't appreciate them. Lots of music is like that. Upon closer examination, you hear what's going on underneath the words. The fury in "You Ain't Woman Enough (To Take My Man)" is palpable. This is one ticked-off country hellion who is about to send a girl to Fist City. These songs are hilarious and shocking and twangy and honest to the bone. So's Loretta. I think Loretta and Mooney went around every iceberg in their path.

Minnie Pearl, Hank Jr., Phil Walden, and Me

I SAT ON THE SET of *Nashville Now* with her during a commercial. She leaned over and said in a stage whisper, "You're doin' a great job, honey. Keep it up."

It was like being blessed by the Queen.

Filling in for Ralph Emery on his nighttime *Nashville Network* show was nerve-racking. Television is a touchy thing. It's like the camera can sense the inner soul of a person. Time slows down sometimes when you're on the tube. It took me awhile to learn that a pause or gathering my thoughts only took a blip of time. It *feels*, however, like you've gone mute and that a tiny pause is forever. I really never got very good at TV. I was better off in a quiet studio with just a microphone and nobody staring at me.

Minnie Pearl, however, became electric in front of a crowd. As she said, "If you love them, they'll love you back."

I adored the stories that Minnie shared with me. I'm certain she made everybody feel like they were part of her inner circle. Sarah

Cannon (Cousin Minnie's real name) wore the Minnie Pearl hat with a price tag and matronly dresses like the pro she was. She also gave me one of the best life lessons of all time. This from a woman who wrote the great joke, "Marriage is like a hot bath. Once you get used to it, it ain't so hot." Isn't that classic? Since I write jokes, we talked every chance we got about construction, timing, and performing. For twenty-five years, I called it "doing a Minnie." She told me that her husband, Henry, stood beside the stage nearly every night when she was on tour and afterward gave her input on her act.

"Why do you do that joke?" Henry would ask. And here was the lesson part.

"Because I like it. It makes me laugh. I look forward to it."

"But," he argued, "the crowd don't seem to laugh at it very much."

The Minnie: "I don't care. When you do comedy or anything, you've got to do something for yourself. It's my little joke. It's inside, but the folks who get it *really* get it. If I ain't havin' no fun, the audience will know I ain't, and they won't have no fun, either."

Good advice, eh? Do something just for yourself every now and then.

Minnie often told me about the "old days." I mean the really history-making, rough-and-tumble *old* days. She swore that one of the reasons she was slightly bent over was from riding in the back of Hank's car with a bull fiddle in the window behind the backseat. Hank is Hank Williams. The original Hank. Picture this: a 1945 Buick. Long and sleek with a long slope toward the back. Cars in those days had a "hump" that ran all the way through the car's interior. If you sat in the backseat three across, somebody had to put their feet on the hump. Minnie was the shortest, so she drew that seat. Hank Williams drove. Hawkshaw Hawkins rode shotgun. Hawkshaw died in a plane crash years later with Patsy Cline. Ernest Tubb on one side in the back and a bass player on the other. Minnie in the middle with that giant stand-up bass behind her head, stuffed in the rear windshield. What a glamorous tour it was…sometimes driving for thirteen hours to make the next show. But it was all worth it so she could stride onstage with that smile and holler, "Howwwwdeee! I'm just so proud to be here."

Hank Williams, considered the godfather of country songwriters, died when I was five years old. I have two "Kevin Bacon" connections to Hank Sr.

First, I did a play with George Hamilton, who had portrayed Hank in a biopic called *Your Cheatin' Heart*. George is a *movie* star and always will be. Tanned like an old wallet and dazzlingly handsome. I was in a play in Florida with him for six weeks, and every time he came through a door, I felt like I was in a scene out of *Gone with the Wind* or something.

Second, Hank's son, luckily enough called Hank Jr., recorded one of my songs. I bumped into Bocephus a lot over the years. His son, Hank III, we call Tricephus.

Hank Jr. did what he could with the hand dealt him. He continues to beat the "Hank" song drum and sing songs about himself and his pa. He was dressed up like his daddy and plunked onstage as a teenager. I don't know how some people handle what life gives them.

Even when he was in the spotlight, Hank Jr. was always in his father's shadow. But Hank Jr., of course, became a huge star on his own. The rough-and-rowdy friend shouted, "Are you ready for some football?" every Monday night. We all know Hank Jr. stories—except maybe this one.

Here's how showbiz works. Just like Bocephus, you go with what you got. I wrote a song called "Diamond Mine" with Devon O'Day and Michael Bornheim. I liked it, and so did Barry Beckett. The famed Muscle Shoals producer and groundbreaking studio piano player called me. "Hey, son, I like that song 'Diamond Mine.' Who's playing that guitar lick on the opening of the demo?" I nearly fell over. Not only were they gonna cut this song on *the* Hank Jr., but they were gonna copy my friend Chris Leuzinger's guitar lick. In fact, they had Chris come in and play it.

Now, I was already buying new furniture and dreaming of a boat when I heard this was gonna happen. It's what songwriters do. You know you should know better than to plan on any success, but this sounded like the road to No. 1 to me.

We got a call from Hank's new record company that the album was "in the can," and we should come over and hear the latest smash from Rockin' Randall Hank. Mr. Born to Boogie. Devon and I got off the air and made our way to the offices of the recently reformed Capricorn Records. Phil Walden was the owner, president, and one of the most amazing characters I ever met.

Phil Walden was a skinny white kid touring the segregationist South with a black singer named Otis Redding. That story alone is a movie. Phil Walden talked a million miles an hour in that south Georgia accent. Phil Walden always had plans. Phil Walden launched the careers of the Allman Brothers and Wet Willie and a ton of Southern rock stars. He managed Percy Sledge and Sam and Dave. I met Phil for lunch one day at the Sunset Grill in Nashville, and a skinny-bearded dude was at the table with him.

My daughter, Autumn, was tagging along. She was about twenty and home from college for a few days. She's as beautiful as her mother, which is somethin'. Phil started in the middle of a sentence, as he always did, about a screenplay of his life story, his tour with Otis "Dock of the Bay" Redding, and how exciting it was. The other guy at the table only seemed interested in Autumn. He flirted, laughed, and invited, all within about fifteen minutes. I wanted to kill him.

Phil was oblivious to the drama, and he spoke of how big the movie was gonna be and how probably Kevin Costner or somebody would play him in the movie. The Romeo at the table with us turned out to be the screenwriter. He glanced at me and Phil for about ten seconds and agreed it was quite a story, and then returned to asking Autumn about her plans for the evening. He didn't get very far with Autumn House. She's as cool as a cucumber. She was not gonna go out with *this* guy. Are you kidding?

Later, however, he did manage to marry Angelina Jolie. I just remember watching Billy Bob Thornton go down in flames that day. (I've said for years Billy Bob and Lyle Lovett, who was married to Julia Roberts, should write a "How I Married Her" instructional book.)

Phil also told me how he "saved" Jimmy Carter and got him elected president. Carter apparently was running out of money during his campaign. The guy worked for peanuts, remember. Phil got all his acts—The Allman Brothers, the Charlie Daniels Band, the Marshall Tucker Band, et al.—to host a series of concerts. The money went to Carter's campaign and kept him going 'til eventually he became leader of the free world. Phil said Carter was forever grateful and invited him and a lot of his pot-smoking buddies to the White House. Phil fired up a joint on the roof of the First Residence, and the Secret Service just pretended they didn't notice a guy with a doobie. Isn't that amazing?

Phil went bankrupt but kept a lot of his art. I picked up an old tomato soup can once in his kitchen and asked why he didn't clean up his garbage. He said, "Be careful with that can. It's an original Warhol Campbell's Soup can. Look, it's signed by Andy. He gave it to me at a party." That can was probably worth more than his house, and it was just sitting in the kitchen.

So Devon and I made our way to Capricorn Records. Phil had been on top of the world and had the pictures in his office to prove it. All the rock acts and a beaming Jimmy Carter posed with the guy who helped make their careers.

After so much success, Phil went under. Lost it all, but he was back this time, bigger and better. Phil Walden had plans. He'd just signed a new singer and was pretty hyped up about the young kid who had "a voice like liquid sex. Just like liquid sex, I tell ya. He's gonna fill stadiums, this kid. His name is Kenny Chesney." That's the way Phil talked. We listened to a few cuts from the new singer and agreed he was pretty good. In fact, I agreed to have him on the radio and promote the guy to help him get launched. What little I could do, I would.

Phil then said, "OK, now let's listen to Hank's new smash. Boys and girls, this is gonna be the record of his career. It's amazing. Makes me wanna just jump straight up. This song is *it!*" He explained this to the writers of the song as if he didn't remember who we were or why we were there. Above all else, Phil was a salesman.

He cued up "Diamond Mine." The Chris Leuzinger guitar lick came blaring out of the speakers. Hank started in his unmistakable voice. It was our song. It was a record. It was just plain awful. Out of meter and tuneless and just awful.

About halfway through, the pressure got to Devon, and she started to cry. Not heaving sobs, but she could hear her hopes and dreams going down the drain with every melody-free note Hank Jr. let loose. I don't know how it had happened, but somewhere along the line they'd missed it.

Now, in the country music business, *one* small doubt, one wrong word, one look of, "Gee, I'm not sure," and the project is dead. Phil was reared back with his eyes closed. Devon was now in a full crying jag. Phil leaned forward and said, "Hey, honey. What's the matter with that girl?"

Here is perhaps one of my greatest moments as a song saver and a showbiz vet. I put my hands on her heaving shoulders and said with a straight face, "Phil, she's just overcome with joy at the absolute genius of you and Hank and this record. Thank you for what you've done for us." Devon sort of let out a wail at this point, a hideous moan of loss and disappointment. Phil understood the excitement and patted us both on the back as we left with joy in our hearts and tears in our eyes.

We went to the video shoot. We watched the ad campaign come out. We talked to Hank Jr. about the excitement and Phil and the big plans.

"Diamond Mine" died in the mid-'80s on the charts after about three weeks. Years later, I think I got a check for twenty-seven cents.

Phil Walden became my manager.

My Wife Is Cheerful

MY WIFE IS relentlessly cheerful. She's also the most beautiful woman in the world. Really, she is. She always laughs easily, smiles at just about everybody, and is carefully polite to every jackleg stranger we meet. It's really profoundly irritating. I tell her all the time she's makin' the rest of us look bad.

We have a phrase we use at our house. On the old *Bob Newhart Show*, Suzanne Pleshette would be sitting in the kitchen, sulking and sullen over her coffee. Bob would bounce into the kitchen, singing and as chipper as a new puppy. He'd chirp a few "Good morning, sweethearts" and "Ain't it a beautiful day?" until Suzanne had finally had enough. She'd then send out a warning shot, "Knock it off, Bob."

Allyson thought that was hilarious, and I do, too. I'm not angry in the morning or even in a bad mood. I spent thirty years talking to people, so I had to be reasonably reasonable. But there is just no reason to be too damn happy. You understand my pain, don't you?

My wife is also hilarious, on purpose and not on purpose. I hate the word "ditzy" because it's not accurate. She knows when she's being ditzy. You can't qualify for ditzy if you recognize the symptoms of ditziness. She does, however, say or do things that sometimes give the impression of the ditz. She wears the ditz crown with ease and dignity.

One afternoon I thought she had a fly on her forehead. I looked closer and thought it was a seriously dark mole that had appeared. I asked her about it and she said, "Oh, that's Magic Marker." Right. She had made a good-sized dot on her forehead on purpose. And why? (I truly wanted to hear this one.)

"Well, I had my hair styled this afternoon. I paid $175 for this haircut and I'm about to shampoo my hair. I'm not paying $175 and not have it look the same after I wash it. I put a mark there so I'll remember where the part was." Always with the logic.

I am certain you have one of these in your family. Al, which is what I call her, has said things like that to me all of my life. She's been there practically all of my life. We went out when she was fifteen. I think I was twenty-seven at the time, but, hey, it was Kentucky. Seriously, I am a year and a half older. Same elementary school, middle school, high school, and college. She always says we've been together so long neither one of us can lie about the past because we were both there. She once ordered a cheeseburger but told the waiter to hold the cheese. She's also a worry-wart but that gets less and less as the years go by.

She's my best friend. I don't like to be away from her for very long. I don't take many golf trips because of that. Golf trips are, as my daughter calls 'em, "sausage fests"—all guys in some high-rise condo next to a couple of courses for five or six days with no wives. I don't like that... too long without my girlfriend.

Keith Urban says he and Nicole have a three-day limit. No matter where one of them happens to be, they find a way to be with each other after three days. I think that's a good rule. When I quit radio, I often said, "Who wouldn't want to spend more time with Allyson House?"

You haven't lived until you have dinner with Keith Urban and Nicole Kidman, by the way. We've done that a lot. We're friends. It's like walking into a restaurant with two aliens who glow like neon signs. Nashville is great for celebs because, for the most part, nobody attacks the stars. People are just so nice and let the aliens enjoy their salads. A lot of waves or "walk-bys" during dinner, but I understand how fans feel.

I want to stand up and announce, "Good evening, everybody. I'm over here having French fries with really big stars." I don't. But I'd like to.

Keith Urban is whip-smart. He's up to speed on almost anything you want to talk about. I've known him for quite awhile. He struggled for years to break through, and when he did, it was an explosion. I also once told Keith how much I admired him for facing up to his "problems" and doing something about 'em. I can't imagine how difficult that must have been. He worked hard to get his priorities where they should be, and that takes an enormous amount of courage.

Keith's also got a wacky sense of humor. I'd be on the air and he would start calling around 6:05 A.M. on the hotline. I think he'd had way too much fun that night.

He once called me six times in a row to announce he couldn't talk because he was on voice rest. He'd hang up, call back, talk for five minutes, and then say he couldn't talk anymore. Then he'd call again.

Nic is so calm, balanced, and normal that it's almost shocking. We have a house in north Florida, and she once said, "Oh, I love a road trip. Let's go." I'm trying to picture stopping at the Giddy-up Go in Andalusia, Alabama, with Nicole Kidman. Buying beef jerky and a Mountain Dew like your typical tourist. The looks from people would be priceless.

Don't ya love being with people in love? It's reassuring. That stuff actually works!

Once I played The Bluebird Café with Keith Urban in what's called an "in the round." He wasn't a superstar yet, but everyone knew he was crazy talented.

He always says, "You stared at me like you were angry." Actually, I was dumbstruck. Watching him play, I felt like I was playing guitar with boxing gloves on. I swear, I thought he had "tracks" hidden some-where and was making all that music with electronics. Nope. It was just him and the git.

I quit performing after that. Turns out I actually was wearing boxing gloves, and it cramped my picking quite a bit.

If you ever want a Woodmont salad from Bread and Company in Green Hills, Tennessee, Nicole Kidman will bring you one. If you ask nicely.

Al says, "Being nice is the easiest thing to do." I guess she's right if it comes to ya naturally, like being able to run fast or squirt tobacco juice through your front teeth. Some people are just better at some things than other things.

Nearly everyone I know in the music business is nice. A few, however, just have that "extra nice" gear. I don't know what it is, but they make people feel better and more comfortable being around them. It's not like they "try" any harder; they're just nice. Quite irritating, those people.

Steve Wariner is like that. Steve is an amazing guitar player, singer, and songwriter. I've called him the meanest man in coun-try music for years. Everybody laughs because they know nothing could be more of a lie. I'm good at that. Steve had a lot of hits. He was a star for years, and I never heard anyone say one bad thing about him. That's why I'd like to drop the bomb now.

Prison straightened Steve out. After he embezzled all that money from the orphanage and ran that puppy mill in Texas and scammed those poor people at the Senior Citizens Center out of their life savings, Steve learned a better way to be. Eighteen years of hard labor does that. I'm glad he's nice now. I'm sure when he reads this I'll find out if he's still that way or has returned to his Sing Sing personality.

My favorite picture of Steve is him standing onstage at the Parade of Pennies gift party. Every year, our station bought Christmas gifts for kids who didn't have much. The American Legion boys handled most of the logistics. The party, if you wanna call it that, was at the Tennessee State Fairgrounds in some godforsaken concrete slab of a building next to the hog pens and chicken coops. It smelled exactly like you think.

Now, these kids were from poor neighborhoods. Mostly African Americans, and they broke my heart. The little peezers were in sandals or an old T-shirt, and it was December and freezing out. They gathered in folding chairs by the hundreds, with hundreds of parents trying to control the screaming mob who were their children. The whole auditorium seemed like it was being overtaken by a giant, crawling, twitching, crying, yelling alien blob. The parents all looked at me with those eyes that said, "Thanks for doing this, but I gotta get outta here."

Now picture my pal, Steve Wariner. The pale, handsome, gentle singer and songwriter had volunteered to show up with his band at nine in the morning and do a show. While we handed out gifts, one by one to kid after kid, Steve got up on a tiny wet concrete stage and started singing his songs. He might have just as well have been up there giving a lesson on optical astronomy in German. It was like performing during a riot.

Steve plowed on. I couldn't hear him, but I could tell from the bass part and his mouth moving that he was going to sing one of his gentle classics—a remake of Bill Anderson's "Tips of My Fingers." By now, about 500 kids have toys and are shrieking like banshees.

The moment? Steve throws his head back with his eyes closed and sings this mournful country ballad as the kids decide the stage is the best place to try out their new plastic toy trucks. So the squirts climb onstage armed with Tonkas and start a small construction site as Steve is singing. At this point, the parents look like they're making a hostage tape. They've lost all control. I'm just immobilized by the noise and the smells and the cold.

Steve Wariner finished his song and calmly thanked the audience. He stepped over a couple of kids and started putting his guitar away. The band disappeared like deer into the forest. Steve maneuvered through the crowd, stuck out his hand, and said, "Thanks for letting me do this. It's been a really good time."

Bill Anderson, who wrote many great songs, such as "Tips of My Fingers," "Still," and "Whiskey Lullaby," lived across the street from me for several years. He was a true performing singing wonder. "Whisperin' Bill," they called him. His vocals were more like somebody making an obscene phone call. He had many, many hits in the '50s and '60s, on through the '80s. His "whispering" voice has been much imitated in Opry circles. I used to watch him walk out in his front yard and yell for his dog. He'd yell in that soft, little sound he made, "Here, boy! Here, boy!" The dog would be twenty feet away by the garage and not move a muscle.

He couldn't hear his master's voice.

Billy Dean is as good as they get. He's always upbeat and concerned. He is relentlessly nice. "Knock it off, Bob." We wrote songs and spent a lot of time together. My favorite Billy moment was when he called me on the radio. We were discussing the topic "what's the best song for people getting a divorce?" We had a bunch of folks call with the usual and the funny and the disturbing titles. "D-I-V-O-R-C-E" is obvious. Several suggested "Take This Job and Shove It," which didn't work at all. Billy said he was driving in his car and called to laugh about the topic and how funny other people were. Billy said he'd been racking his brain trying to come up with a song.

I then reminded him of the classic "We Just Disagree"—the perfect divorce song if there ever was one. Two people who love each other but can't get along might be the ultimate great song about splitting up.

The best part about the whole conversation? *That's a Billy Dean song!* He laughed his butt off. He couldn't think of his own recording. Dave Mason had a hit with it in '77, and Billy made it a hit again in '93. Butterbean Dean is a nice, nice guy.

Allyson's sense of logic is beyond compare. It works for her, and when she says something it usually takes a second to think about it. (No, I did *not* use the word "ditzy" here.) When we were young and broke—I'm talkin' "countin' pennies you find in the glove compartment" broke—we lived in a trailer in Kentucky. This was before trailers moved up and became mobile homes. Don't you hate it when your house gets a flat?

We had dinner carefully planned out to the last scoop of macaroni and cheese. We also had a young couple of friends who just showed up at dinnertime. They were broke, too. I liked them a lot, but I didn't want to share my pork chop with Bob and his fiancée. But what are you gonna do when they are sitting there like basset hounds watching you eat, their little tummies growling? So, we split up the food. It drove Al and me crazy.

When I finally got a job in upstate New York, we packed up everything we owned in a tiny U-Haul trailer (there's that word again) and pulled out on our adventure early one morning. We were now free of the freeloading couple. It was here when Allyson said, with her logic working on all cylinders, "I can't wait to see their faces when we don't see them anymore."

See what I mean? It happens every day. But she's my girl and she's nice.

Linda Davis is a saint. You probably don't know Linda. She sang "Does He Love You?" with Reba. It was a *huge* hit and a great moment in concert. I met Linda years ago when I was doing a TV show with Jim Ed Brown. Her husband was a production coordinator, and she'd tag along. She's also beautiful.

Jump ahead years later, and we'd all go to Reba's house for holidays and dinners. I tell this because Linda's little girl was always running around and jumping in the pool and doing what kids do. That little girl is now Hillary Scott of Lady Antebellum. It makes

me feel like I need to be carbon-dated to find out my age when I
see little Hillary up accepting *CMA Awards* or *five* Grammys!

That TV show that I worked with her dad on was also one of the
worst TV shows in history. A precursor to American Idol, *the show*
was called You Can Be a Star *and ran on The Nashville Network. I'd*
already lost out on an earlier job on that network, as I was to be the
voice of a talking jukebox on a Bill Anderson–hosted game show. I
didn't get the gig.

Unfortunately, I did get the job on You Can Be a Star. *I was the*
"filler" of time between the acts. Jim Ed Brown, a kind and foggy man,
hosted. We taped five shows a day, thirteen days in a row. Jim Ed had
his clothes all laid out by his wife, with matching numbers so he'd
know what went with what. Yes, just like Garanimals. One terrible
singer after another performed, and three semi-celebrity judges passed
along their opinions. Then they cut to me in the audience to fill time
before the next act was let out of the chute.

You might think that it gets easier over time, chatting with folks
and generally passing the time of day. It was brutal. When people are
nervous or concerned for their singing brother-in-law, they don't want
to talk about space travel or clothing styles or whatever I asked about.
I actually had several older, sweaty women say, "Leave me alone, I
have to pee," during the taping sessions. Hey, it was a paycheck.

We bought a farm a few years back. It's got lakes and three little
chalets, and it's a chunk of heaven. It is way out in the sticks. As
the Rascal Flatts song says, "You drive 'til you hear banjo music."
We love it there on weekends. It's also Command Central for the
world population of ticks and chiggers. Poison ivy can be found
if you walk near the woods. Nature is a cruel mistress, and something is trying to jump on you all the time. Allyson went hiking
and came back stung, bitten, and poison-ivied. I've seen coon dogs
scratch less.

We've all been there, and you feel sorry for anybody covered
in calamine lotion. One afternoon, she went off to her "Woman

Cave" for several hours to watch television. When she emerged, she had a look on her face I hadn't seen since our honeymoon. She smiled and said, "There's nothing like being alone with an itch."

I've had the itch for her since I was sixteen. And she's right. There's nothing like being alone with an itch.

QUIZZICLE #3

Who actually said this to me:
"You can't sue me. My business manager
says I can't afford it"?

A) Darius Rucker

B) Luke Bryan

C) Warren Buffett

You Never Give Me Your Money

WHAT A CAREER this dude has had. Darius is, of course, Hootie. As in, And The Blowfish. Mike Dungan at Capitol believed enough in the songs and Darius' charisma to let the Hootster make a country album. Smart decision. Mr. Rucker has had a truckload of No. 1s.

I like him a lot. I like his songs, I like his demeanor, and I like his sense of humor. I do *not* like the way Darius Rucker drives a golf cart. He's a menace to society and anyone within two fairways of him. When DR plays golf, he's a man on a mission. He's a fabulous swinger of the club and is ready to get on with it. If you happen to be along, please buckle up 'cause The Ruckster is gonna play some golf and move on.

I wrote songs with Darius (and renowned songwriter Tom Shapiro), and Darius is very patient. He sits there with his hands in his leather jacket and tosses off great lines. He sings and sounds just like Darius Rucker.

On the golf course, he likes to drive—the ball and the cart. This is where the trouble starts. I was barely in and he floored it. I just remember being tossed skyward and actually turning over while airborne. The cart propelled me into space. It was that surreal, "I'm floating upside down" moment. I landed on my head on the side of a hill.

Darius: "Come on, man, stop fooling around."

Me: "Ohhhhh, I think I'm dead." I shuffled, bruised and shaken, into the passenger seat.

Ever the businessman, Darius then announced, "You can 't sue me. My business manager says I can't afford it." Says it all, doesn't it? There is no problem, and if there were a problem, he can't afford to pay for the problem. He's right. We laughed about it. I wasn't actually hurt all that much, except for the permanent neck damage and the ruination of my game, not to mention my irrational fear of golf carts. I still suffer from Cartophobia Extremus.

Besides, who sues anybody named *Hootie?*

Mysteries of Life

THERE ARE A LOT OF THINGS in the world that I just don't understand. Perhaps it's because country music has robbed me of all my reasoning abilities. The mysteries of life we've all pondered remain unsolved. Perhaps one day we might learn why Alan Jackson sings so much about fried chicken, why Garth Brooks gives that google-y eye when he's singing, and why Bruce Springsteen sings like he has fire ants in his Fruit of the Looms. When will Wynonna Judd haul off and cold-cock her mom? How did Tim McGraw land Faith Hill? How much does Ernest Hemingway? What makes Bud wiser? Who put the Ram in the Rama-lama-ding-dong? How much is left in Dolly Parton's shoes? Which smells better, Luke Bryan or Buffalo, New York? Where's the rest of Carrie Underwood's dress? Did the same person make Conway Twitty's shorts? Will we ever see Hunter Hayes go through puberty live on TV? Will there ever be another country song without the word truck in it? Is the hot new word in country music "hick-wad"? What are video directors on? Does Eric Church sleep in sunglasses? Will there eventually be a country awards show every week?

I'm certain you've thought of these same things yourself. Or what about these:

Why is it nearly impossible to get someone on the phone at a phone company? It's an enterprise dedicated to making sure we all are in constant contact with the world. A corporation that spends millions in advertising urging us to reach out and touch somebody, anybody, and do it on a phone. Then why can't we just pick up the phone and talk to someone on the other end at a *phone company?* I just want to ask a few reasonable, simple questions about my phone bill, which last month was around 600 pages. If you call, you get an automated voice machine. If you go to their website, they give you a list of questions the poor souls who tried to get answers before you asked.

I also don't really understand call waiting *and* caller ID. Are these to make sure you don't actually ever talk to *anyone?* And I am certain that once I leave their phone store, they get a call from the president's office, saying, "Did the idiot who bought our newest high-tech phone pay full price?" Once that's an affirmative, they immediately issue a newer phone and start offering the phone I just bought for free if you own a pair of shoes.

And while I'm at it (I'll get to country music in a minute. Calm down there, fireball!), when you call the cable company 'cause your internet is out, the recording tells you, "Calling is not necessary. You can just go to our website and get everything you need." Thanks for that. But I can't go to the website *because my internet doesn't work, you idiots!* If I could go to the damn website, I wouldn't be calling you! It's just cruel, I tell ya. I realize Brad Paisley said he's a whole lot cooler "Online" (I told you I'd be back), but *I* am not online!

Oh, there are a lot of things that stupefy me. Why does my wife keep that old oven mitt with a hole in the thumb? I thought the idea of an oven mitt was to avoid turning your thumb into a "lit'l smokie."

Why do people going to exercise at the Y drive around for ten minutes looking for a place to park right by the door so they don't have to walk very far? They are going inside to get on a treadmill and *walk very far!* Couldn't they just as easily park ten blocks away and not even go in?

Quite possibly the biggest mystery of life to me is over my head. In fact, it's over nearly everyone's head, especially in country music. It's the hat.

Why do so many country singers wear a cowboy hat? Granted, there are a few cowboys from Texas or Oklahoma who might have worn a hat growing up, but not many. Do you know anybody who actually wears a hat? I mean a big-cowboy-swaggering-"get along, little dogies"-bona-fide-Stetson lid?

I submit 90 percent of the singers of country songs have *never* been on a horse unless it was on a merry-go-round or a pony at the county fair.

So, what is with the hats? We've even had women wearing cowboy hats. If you are a woman and you wear a cowboy hat, you had better damn well be in a rodeo at the moment. It's been this way for the thirty-five years I've been in Nashville.

I know it says, "I'm a country singer," to anyone who might be wondering who you are, strolling down the sidewalk, but is that necessary? Judges don't walk around in their robes. Doctors take off their scrubs. Ballet dancers don't go to church in their tutus. Even people who work at McDonald's take off their paper lid when they're off duty. But if you are even *thinking* of singing something twangy, the rule is, *Put on a hat!*

I know, I know. Some guys need a hat for a reason (see Dwight Yoakam). I'm cool with that. I could use a cover-up myself. Ball caps are passable, but I also don't understand actual artists who have their press shots made with a ball cap turned around backwards.

Why go to the trouble of hiring someone to take an expensive picture of you looking like the guy who unloads bananas at Kroger? There's nothing wrong with unloading bananas at Kroger, but girls don't scream at concerts for the banana boy. (That didn't come out like I planned it, and could be wrong.)

It's been the state of music for decades, the eternal argument—to hat or not to hat. And while some guys look damn cool with it pulled down low over their eyes, most singers look like something out of *City Slickers*. Here's the bottom line: if there ain't something in a saddle in the parking lot, take off the hat. (At this point, I want to extend an apology and issue a hat approval release to George Strait and Alan Jackson.)

I hope during the next few hundred pages to answer all these questions and more. But mostly, I blame country music.

The Oaks

WHEN I WAS IN HIGH SCHOOL, I was in a singing group. It was actually one of my first shots at a singing career. I'm still workin' on that. I can sing, but I have one of those "Broadway" voices. You know, the type nobody really wants to hear for very long.

I was in a group with three other wads of testosterone called the Comedians. We thought we were the greatest vocalists ever. Our name was actually a little too accurate. I introduced the songs and told a joke or two. We did a lot of wonderful gigs: before dramatic readings at the Masonic Lodge (Allyson did the dramatic reading), opening for guests at the high school fund-raisers, and...I think that's it. We actually had two performances.

Because of my membership in various groups and bands, I've always felt a kinship with country groups. Being in a band is hard. I find it very similar to being on a chain gang. You *have* to be with people who smell odd and you often don't like very much.

I always find it weird to interview bands. You find yourself usually talking to the lead singer. The lead singer is the de facto leader of the band. This typically makes all the other guys in the band upset except the bass player. The bass player in the band is just happy to be there and is often the most laid-back musician. Drummers are a little wacky, while the piano players are the intellect of this configuration.

But that's a *band*. What about the Comedians? Or even more to the point, what about those pure vocal groups like the Oak Ridge Boys? I have known the "Oaks" for more than thirty years. They are each and unto themselves unique and wonderful people—gentle, caring, and fascinating. And they are stunning showmen. It's hard to stand beside three other guys night after night and shine. But all four of them do.

Duane Allen is the "lead" singer, I guess. Duane listens when you say something. He's a great talent and wants the best for everyone. Joe Bonsall is the firecracker tenor of the group. He sings lead also and has been a friend for a long time. Richard Sterban is the unearthly bass singer. He's quiet and smart and has to walk behind a wheelbarrow to carry his testicles so he can sing that deep.

Then there's William Lee Golden. William Lee is the "Mountain Man" of the group—the one who is most identifiable with his long, long, gray hair, and leather-stocking pants, wild jackets, and, yes, a cowboy hat. His beard is a forty-year effort and a work of art. I once saw a tourist bus screech to a halt on Music Row, and all the sightseers inside rocketed to the front. William Lee was crossing the street, and these people streamed out of that bus, snapping pictures and screaming like they'd spotted Bigfoot.

Now that I think about it, maybe William Lee Golden *is* Bigfoot. I know you never see the two of them together. He's got a sweat lodge in back of his house. If you've never seen him, this will tell you about his appearance:

I remember William Lee once excitedly (or as excited as he ever gets, which ain't much) telling my friend Bob and me about how he'd just been to Reelfoot Lake in Tennessee. In that slow,

Southern drawl, William Lee Golden said, "Guys, it was amazing. There are bald eagles all over up there—beautiful majestic animals flying right over our heads. I'm telling ya, they sat there on those tree limbs, and we floated right up *next* to them, so close we could almost touch them!"

Bob listened and said, "Hell, Golden, you got that close 'cause they probably thought you were a *nest.*"

I love the Oaks. They were one of the first artists to ever record a song of mine called "Old Time Lovin'." It was their first album, and I couldn't have been more excited. I remember getting that first check—that first "mailbox" money—for probably $1,500. Al and I opened it on the porch and hugged and jumped up and down like kids.

We got a washing machine and some carpeting.

The Oaks Elvira'd and Bobbie Sue'd their way into the hearts of America. I know that George Bush the Elder (doesn't that sound like he was King of Prussia or something?) always had them perform at the White House. The Oaks have entertained everyone and anyone from leaders of the Western World to drunks to Boy Scouts

Full disclosure: when I was around twelve, I was in the Boy Scouts in Kentucky. Our Scout leader got us a gig washing airplanes. There was a private airport near our old Kentucky home and we little peezers would load up in a big truck and spend all day washing some rich guy's Piper Cub. It was hard work, but we did it for the Troop. Our Scout leader urged us on and praised us mightily for such great diligent work.

We were Scouts of the finest order. We eventually piled up several thousand dollars from airplane cleansing and other odd jobs. Later that summer I was shocked to learn our Scoutmaster had left the county. Something about being caught with a woman he wasn't married to and his clothes being found burning in his front yard. I also learned that our great leader "borrowed" every cent of our Troop cash assets before he left. It was my introduction to cheating and embezzlement at the same time.

I was deeply upset about the situation and went to my dad for solace. I told him what had happened. In his usual no-nonsense manner, he summed it up for me: "Hoss, what is the motto of the Boy Scouts?"

I stood straight and spoke, "Be Prepared."

Dad: "Well, you wasn't. Next time, you'll know better."

That was the end of Boy Scouts for me.

Right now, I bet the Oaks are on a bus headed to some State Fair or casino stage or Boy Scout Jamboree, ready to knock another audience flat-out. I hope Richard remembers his wheelbarrow.

Paranoia

I LIKE PARANOIA. Not the "talkin' to the dogs on the woods" type of paranoia, but the "what did you mean by that?" paranoia. The best example of great paranoia is from my lawyer of thirty years. Malcolm Mimms said he refuses to stick his hand down in the garbage disposal. We've all done that if something has fallen in there, and it's making that horrible "jar lid on metal" sound. Mal won't stick his hand down in there because, and I quote, "I'm afraid my other hand will reach over to the wall switch and turn it on while my hand is in there." Isn't that beautiful?

I feel exactly the same way. I don't like to sit with my back to the restaurant. I want my back to the wall in the Mafia seat. Allyson says the woman is supposed to sit against the wall. I think this is a social rule she made up so she can get the Mafia seat. It's called the Mafia seat because mobsters sat with their back to the wall so they could see people coming in who might shoot them. Actually, that's not paranoia, that's common sense.

I don't like to be standing on anything where I could accidentally but immediately plunge to my death. Some call this paranoia a "fear of heights." Not to be confused with acrophobia, which is a "fear of circus performers." I also don't like clowns because I know they have metal teeth and want to kill me, but that's a whole other discussion.

When I was ten, my mom, dad, and I went on a vacation with some neighbors. I have pictures of the Wright family and our family camping out on a small patch of stony land near a creek at Natural Bridge State Park. We look like something out of *The Grapes of Wrath*.

I've never understood why people go camping. The tents leak. The food is half-cooked. It's boiling hot during the day and freezing at night. Rabid bats can fly in and build a nest in your hair. There is *nothing* to do.

We did nothing for about three days. Stanley Wright smoked Pall Malls and wore a Speedo. That image alone is worth years of therapy. We sat like Polish refugees on the rocky shore of this godforsaken trickle of a river and waited for Dad to light a fire. He'd always say, "We'll rough it for a few days." My idea of "roughing it" is slow room service and no HDTV. I don't rough, at least not anymore.

The highlight of Natural Bridge State Park is...drumroll...The Natural Bridge—a tiny sliver of archway over a deep chasm that is minutes of fun. I have a fear of heights and gymnasts because of that damn bridge. My dad made me walk over it. As I recall (probably not with any accuracy), I think it was about thirty miles to certain rocky death below. I started across and eventually sat down and actually scooted toward the other side.

Paralyzed with fear and embarrassment, I actually left fingerprints in the rocks as I made it to the other side. My dad scooped me off and said, "See, it wasn't so bad now, was it?" He gave me a hug. Yes, it was *that* bad. Because of that scary adventure, I won't even change a lightbulb on a stepladder for fear of plunging to my doom.

I am paranoid. By the way, at the end of our vacation, Stanley Wright lost his job because he didn't have permission to take off from work. His job was Chief Bottle Washer. You've heard of the Chief Cook and Bottle Washer—that actually was his job. Stanley washed bottles at a dairy. He did the little jugs. (Insert own joke here.) I think his family wound up "roughing it" for real after that. That's why people should never go to state parks and camp. You wind up permanent campers.

The reason I bring up paranoia at this juncture is because it's rampant throughout Nashville in the radio business, in the music business, and in the business business. A wise old publisher once told me, "Son, don't worry about taking a chance in Nashville because they don't remember your failures in this town." I thought that was good stuff and cheerfully stumbled ahead into Chanceville.

Turns out people remember failures like they remember the first time they got the clap. They carry pictures of people who bombed at something. Seminars are held with speeches about disasters folks have had taking a chance. They publish Loser Guidebooks on Music Row. Monks in underground tunnels write all the mistakes in giant ledgers with goose quills and ink. That's why paranoia hangs over Music Row like smog.

I once had a song recorded by a movie star–lookin' singer named James Bonamy. James was sweet as could be, and he was a beauty. He sang great, looked great, and had that "thing" stars have. The song was called "Dog on a Tool Box." I wrote it with legendary tunesmith Monty Holmes. The record guys did a dance mix, an extended mix, a radio mix—it got *all* the stuff behind it. It hit the charts, and I was ready for the good times to begin and the mailbox cash to start bein' delivered. It was just a fun song with no agenda and no great social statements.

The second week of the record's birth, they had a massive national meeting of radio disc jockeys and radio bosses in

Nashville. They've had it annually for thirty years. Some big-shot programmer stood during a big meeting and said, "Country music is in trouble. We've lowered our standards too much. Why, there's even a song out now called 'Dog on a Toolbox.' The *last* thing we need is a song about dogs and trucks and country and toolboxes. People will think we are idiots."

The record died an instant death. Everybody was so paranoid and unsure about what they really liked, they accepted this piece of flawed logic as gospel.

I tell this story not so we could all learn a lesson, but so I could tell how I got screwed out of a hit by some doofus who didn't know what he was talking about. I feel better now.

A lot of artists control their image and their careers down to the smallest moment. Others don't really care all that much. I've seen both work. I also have learned that the bigger a star gets, the more they are on time, the more they have success, and the more you can depend on them to do what they say they will. It's not the big stars who are prima donnas, it's usually the middling singers and pickers who are a pain in the ass to deal with. It's because they are paranoid. Hey, it affects everyone. I have had acts show up an hour late, others chew gum and talk into the plants instead of a microphone, and some even bring their dogs or bring their kids who leave dirty underwear in the studio. I've had actual recording artists refuse to say anything more than "Yes," "No," and "Huh?" for thirty minutes. Paranoia strikes deep.

A great singer once told me he was doing a tour with Travis Tritt. I won't mention Joe Diffie here because it would embarrass him. Joe is one of the all-time traditional singers. Joe Diffie doesn't have a pretentious bone in his body. Travis is and always will be a rock star doing country songs. I think he got a little blown-up when he was on top of the charts.

Joe said they were about to start a show, and he was walking down the hallway. He saw Travis go into a room backstage.

He went in to speak to his costar before the show started. But there appeared to be nobody in there and nothing else in the room except a big road case on wheels in the corner. He looked around for Travis and couldn't find him. Then Joe decided to lean down and speak into the air holes in the top of the road case. "Travis?"

A whispered answer: "Yeah, man."

"Travis, are you in there?"

"Yeah, man."

"Travis, why are you hiding in a road case backstage?"

"Because, man, they have to wheel me onstage in secrecy or the fans might mob me."

Joe said there was no one backstage except musicians, a security guard, and a couple of people cleaning up.

Travis Tritt is a great guy, and I'm certain he's not paranoid. But I think when lightning strikes, and people start to react wildly to your presence, it makes you get wheeled onstage inside a road case. Don't get wheeled onstage inside a road case.

My mother was afraid of a lot of things. Everybody always says a child of the Depression is like that. She'd told me many times that, during those rough years, she'd been sent to live on a small farm in Kentucky with her aunt because her mother couldn't support her.

Mom said Aunt Lou also was broke, but she had three chickens. Those chickens laid six eggs a day. Three in the morning for breakfast, three in the evening for dinner. I never pointed out to her that mostly a hen will produce one good egg a day. She probably romanticized those super-chicks. I know they also struggled with the egg vs. fried chicken dilemma.

It was also during the Kentucky era that my dad said he saw a young girl walking down the dusty street in the town of Falmouth. He said, "I drove up beside her and offered her a ride." She just turned and walked away. She was the most beautiful creature he'd ever seen. I'm here because of that little introduction.

My dad wasn't paranoid. He was a blue-collar workin' guy. My mom didn't always trust the goodness in people. She unfolded her Mexican food to make sure nothing bad was hidden inside her burrito. Dad was one of those guys everybody loved. I never really saw my dad and what he was truly like 'til I started working with him.

From ages fourteen to sixteen, each summer I rode half asleep in the early morning in the back of his truck. I racked out on some coiled-up wire while he sang Hank Snow songs at the top of his lungs. We rode by Summit Hills Country Club, where the moneyed and upper class belonged and played golf. I stared at them like the total strange animals they were. Dad said, "Look at 'em, Hoss. They ain't happy." I always thought these people, in their crisp golf clothes on a sunny day, riding little carts over perfect grass, were the happiest-looking people I'd ever seen. But I never argued with him. My mom was funny, but slightly dark. My dad was funny and slightly sunny. I guess I got parts of both of them.

On the front seat of Dad's truck was a piece of wire. I think it's called BX cable. It's angry-looking wire, thick and covered in metal. On the end of this foot-and-a-half piece of BX cable was a melted mass of copper, an accident of electricity from some construction site. It was a weapon, primitive but effective.

I sort of tested it by hitting my leg, and gave myself a bruise. "What's this for?" I asked, twirling it around.

He said, "I go into some pretty rough neighborhoods [he worked at all the Kroger stores] and if somebody jumps on the side of my truck, I knock 'em off with that." He then said something I'll never forget. "Some colored folks are good, and some want to take your stuff." It probably sounds racist, but to him, it was just the way it was.

This was before the terms African American or black came into our speech. There were also other words in common usage at the time that, I must admit, didn't make me wince. It was just the way things were.

I didn't personally know any black people at all. I do remember being quite young and witnessing the most frightening thing I've ever seen. We drove past a burning cross and a bonfire. I saw the outlines of people in white hoods with the blaze behind them and somebody yelling a speech to them. I remember my dad saying, "Don't look at that, Hoss. Those people are mean and crazy." It was just the way things were.

I remember when we worked near some scary neighborhood in a run-down part of town during the winter, and this same man— my father—saw little poor black children walking in sandals or barefoot on the frozen streets, gathered them up in his truck, and took them to buy them shoes. It was just the way things were.

I guess if you're gonna talk about worrisome, paranoid people, you ought to end with somebody who is *not* that way. I pick Kenny Rogers.

We go way back. Kenny Rogers has finally been inducted into the Country Music Hall of Fame, and it's about damn time.

I've been all over the world, and when people find out I'm from Nashville, they always mention Dolly, Elvis, Johnny Cash, and Kenny Rogers. It's because those people are stars even in the smallest towns of the old countries of Europe. People there almost always say, "I want to come to Nashville and see Graceland."

I don't break the news that Graceland is in Memphis because I figure once they make Nashville, they'll figure that out. From what I hear, Graceland ain't "all that" anyway.

Back to the Kenmeister: Mr. Rogers and I go way back because I had gone to college. I'd never even been in a radio station 'til I went to Eastern Kentucky University. Allyson and I laugh about it now, but Eastern and Western and, perhaps, Morehead or UK were the choices we used for higher education. We were such hicks it never even occurred to either of us that we could actually leave Kentucky. I went to Eastern, and Al followed a year later.

College was the best thing that ever happened to us. I drank beer, and she got several degrees with honors. The lucky part was that during the radical years of '66–'69, I was a flaming liberal antiwar activist. I also was mostly an idiot. I went to sit-ins and candlelight vigils and heard the speeches. But basically, I was in a rock band and drank beer. It was sheer heaven.

That is, until friends of mine started coming home from Vietnam in body bags. Reality is harsh. Through one of my classes, I was chosen to go to the campus radio station and give a firebrand speech about the war and the world. After what was perhaps (in my mind) something to put Winston Churchill to shame, I walked out of the studio shaken but proud. I asked the guy listening to me, "What did you think of my editorial?" I had totally dismantled the military industrial complex and calmed the seas of war.

He looked me straight in the eye and said, "I think it was immature and idiotic, but I like the way you read."

I thought, *You* do? *You like something* I *did?* I totally forgot the very accurate immature and/or idiotic parts and went right for the amazing judgment of this learned professor. He said, "Why don't you come over, and we'll talk about radio."

Now, I'd listened to the radio for years and was a total goob for anything to do with it. I thought, *How tough can it be? I listen to it. I can do it.*

That day changed my life forever. I entered the radio world.

But you ask, "Whatever happened to Kenny Rogers, O Storyteller of yore?"

While I was a student there, Kenny Rogers and the First Edition came to EKU to do a concert. I think it was part of one of those *Dick Clark's Caravan of Stars* shows. (Full circle: in 2012, I wrote part of a speech for Reba to give at Dick Clark's memorial service.)

I was sent with my little tape recorder to go interview Kenny, who was, of course, the lead singer. I went backstage to do the Grand Inquisition. I was gonna ask the tough questions and break the entertainment world wide open. I was gonna get some scoop and be scooped up by NBC or somethin'.

"Hi, Mr. Rogers. Everybody, I'm here with Mr. Rogers, Kenny and his band, The Edition. How did you get started singing, Mr. Kenny Rogers?"

KR realized he wasn't dealing with just anybody here and proceeded to patiently explain for the 10,000th time his career and the New Christy Minstrels and on and on. He was funny, warm, and kind. I thanked him and walked away with showbiz GOLD. I still have that tape somewhere, but I'm too scared to listen to it.

When you interview somebody, especially your first, you feel a connection. I am certain Kenny doesn't remember the moment, but it's seared into my memory bank.

I also remember my second college interview, with the Imperials— an R&B vocal group led by "Little Anthony" Gourdine that had huge pop hits such as "Tears On My Pillow," "I'm On The Outside (Looking In)," "Goin' Out of My Head," "Hurt So Bad," and many others. I distinctly remember going into a locker room to see them after their concert. All of the Imperials were standing there in shiny red satin men's briefs. Anthony also had matching shorts and satin red socks. As I sat on a bench, they stood around me answering questions.

I was tough. The satin shorts didn't scare me. I looked right at "Little Anthony"(although, at this point, I'm not certain why he was called "Little") and asked the question everyone wanted to ask, "Do you ever get tired of singing 'Shimmy, Shimmy, Ko-Ko Bop'?" A ridiculous single they had early in their career in 1959.

Anthony's eyes rolled around and he said, "What the hell do you think?" He then walked to his locker and started putting on leather pants and black patent leather shoes. Another entertainment block-buster was going into the books.

Over the years, I've seen Kenny Rogers many times. We once did a live, hour-long show from New York for national broadcast. He was funny and very kind. We went to Tavern on the Green in Central Park afterward for dinner. I think he even paid. Rare, but I think I'm right. I say this because if I had paid, I would still be paying off the bill.

Kenny is a great judge of songs. He has picked hit after hit during his decades-long career. He does duets. He does pop. He does country, romance, and rock. He didn't care what people thought because he knew he was right.

Fast-forward thirty years to one of the last live interviews I ever did. It was for some Country Radio Seminar confab, and the room was packed to see Kenny. The hour-and-a-half flew by. He once told me in private he probably made more money in his other businesses than he did singing. I also remember asking him about his opinion of the president. Probably Clinton, Carter, or Obama—can't remember—but he said, "Hey, if a guy is smart enough and tough enough to get to that Oval Office, he doesn't need my opinion on how to do things. I just wish him the best." Greatest answer ever for a sure-fire political landmine.

However, I have talked to Kenny for hours and never asked him the stuff I wondered about. I never asked about how it became Kenny Rogers *and* the First Edition. I never asked him about the rumors of being caught with a certain blonde singer on his bus. I never asked him about his "work" and why there's nothing left in his shoes. I called him once at home to ask about his back surgery, but I never asked if his problems were from lifting his money. I never asked about the Roasters restaurant chain. What happened to all those chickens? I never asked if he ever got tired of singing "Coward of the County." And what about all the look-alikes?

I never asked if he wanted to be in the Country Music Hall of Fame. All right, I *did* ask him that, and he gave his usual KR PR answer. "If those people want me in, then I'll gladly show up." The perfect answer, as usual.

What about his years with so many duet partners, his tours, his family life, or the way he had reinvented himself over and over? I never asked because of paranoia. If you really like somebody and respect them, you worry you'll tip over into that place you shouldn't be asking about.

So, I just think I'll leave it alone and am happy that Kenny has finally been inducted. He once sent me a nice note thanking me for raising hell over the fact that he hadn't yet been inducted. He was in my Hall of Fame thirty years ago, and I'm glad the Country Music Hall of Fame caught up with me and the millions all over the world who love him.

And what *about* all those chickens?

QUIZZICLE #4

Why did Tanya Tucker say, "Pretend you're skiing"?

A) She was telling a dirty joke about three rabbis in Vail.

B) She was giving instructions for a correct golf stance.

C) She was describing to another girl the best way to pee in the woods.

Norwegian Wood

TANYA TUCKER HAS NO EDITING BUTTON. If it occurs in her head, it's gonna come spilling out her piehole. I think she's hilarious because of that one fact. She's also hell on wheels. I see these little girly girls strutting around onstage pretending to be High-Heel Harlots. They couldn't carry Tanya's mascara case. In fact, Tanya can barely carry her mascara case, but that's another topic.

She was a star when she was thirteen. "Delta Dawn." Think about that! When I was thirteen, I was sitting in mud. I wasn't touring and missing school and recording and doing interviews and all the jobs that go with stardom.

Tanya did all that stuff at thirteen. It's a tough life; it kills ya or makes you stronger. It damn near killed Tanya. And from what I remember, she nearly took Glen Campbell with her. They were not exactly the couple made in heaven. There were recreational additives and they P.O.'d a lot of people along the way. They were fascinating just to watch because you knew the train was on one rail at all times. It's like they put the Mercedes on cruise control and then got in the backseat. Nobody was watching the wheel at any time. It's kinda funny now, but it was scary then.

Tanya had the one thing that's necessary for a star—she sounded like Tanya Tucker and no one else. My producer friend Norro Wilson calls it "The Throat." When you can hear a record start and know who's singing, that's how you get a star. Or someone who will never, ever be a star because people know who it is and hate the way they sing.

Tanya Tucker and I spent a Halloween together. I happened to be standing in a bar with my friend Jerry Crutchfield around 6 P.M. having a glass of wine. We did that a lot. I was leaning back against the bar, when, suddenly, the front door flew open and in came Hurricane Tanya. She screamed my name and rushed forward and threw both legs up around my waist. Then, like a crazed monkey, she scrambled on up over my head and stood on the bar. "Hello, boys! Where the #@$% is the party?"

This was the normal entrance for Tanya Tucker. She arrived like she wanted and when she wanted. It's known as "T" Time. She had a limo, so off Crutch, I, and several innocent bystanders went. We wound up out in the country at some Halloween party we weren't invited to, nor did we know anybody there. Not a problem for Tanya. It was here I heard her explain to some girl who'd had a *lot* of beer that if she had to take a whiz, "Just whip down your pants and pretend you're skiing." Then she threw in a little women's lib: "Men shouldn't be the only ones who get to take a leak wherever they want." Happy Halloween!

Tanya also said something to me so chilling and so honest I've never forgotten it. Being onstage is like a drug. I've experienced it in a minor way a few times. It's a feeling you want. It's *very* addictive. Tanya Tucker said, "People have *no* idea what it's like. One minute, you're onstage in front of 5,000 screaming fans. The love is overwhelming. The feeling of power is amazing. The next minute, you're in the back of a bus alone. You are off to some new town, and you gotta stay on a schedule. You're pumped full of adrenaline and excitement, and there's nobody there to share it with." She looked at me with those eyes and continued, "That's how I got into trouble. Something—anything—to either keep that feeling going or to make it go away. There you are in a bedroom on a bus, bouncing down the road, and you turn to something else."

Tanya wasn't making an excuse or justifying anything. She was just explaining, from one friend to another, what it's like. She wasn't a star whining about the rigors of the glamorous life. She was just honestly telling me that some nights it's tough to do it alone. I gave her a hug and drove home to my darling as grateful for my life as I could ever be.

I just saw T. Tucker at a Hall of Fame event, and she was doing just fine. She's got it all back on both rails now. She also screamed my name and grabbed a glass of Champagne from a passing tray and said, "Have one on me, Hoss."

People Who Call

BECAUSE I GREW UP LISTENING to the radio and then wound up being *on* the radio, I always feel a friendship with people who've listened to me. I also believe there should be a little more quality control for people to call a radio station than owning a phone and a radio.

The overwhelming majority—I'd say 80 percent—of these people are wonderful. The other 20 percent are just nuts. Just in case you've never been "on the air," I'll run down the drill for you.

The radio personality/DJ/host/jock, etc. is figuring out the time, trying to catch up on the news, grabbing some music, writing a joke in his head, and answering the phone. If you have a producer, you are lucky. Later in my career, I demanded a producer. I remember having the discussion with management about it. The GM said, "You don't need anyone extra." I replied, "OK, next time you're in a sales meeting, answer the phone every time it rings instead of letting your assistant get it." I got a producer. Actually, over the years, I had *two* fabulous producers—Devon O'Day and Richard Falklen.

To this day, I can't just let a phone ring. I *have* to answer it. I think it's important when you're on the radio to have someone actually talk to your customers. I've called stations myself, and nothing is more frustrating than hearing the phone ring and ring, and then have to hang up in disgust. Tragically, most stations are now like this. The dirty little secret of radio is that quite often, there's no one there. I mean *no one*. The guy you're listening to might have prerecorded the show that morning in St. Louis. Or he is syndicated out of Dallas. Computers and robots took over a lot of manufacturing jobs, and they also took over radio stations. I'm not saying it's bad, I'm just saying it's different.

Now, let's talk about answering the phone. Radio is immediate. They hear you say something, they call. You see somebody on TV, you can fire off an angry or loving e-mail/tweet, but you won't usually connect. P.O.'d at the editor of the newspaper? You e-mail or snail mail. You might catch them on the phone but probably not.

Radio dudes and dudettes? Unless they just won't answer the phone, you get the guy on the air. I answered the phone, so they got me. That's why we hired Devon and, later, Richard. I couldn't handle it because people only hear about half of what they think they heard. I did better when we could sort through the calls by having a filter—the producer. They answered the calls that said they couldn't live without me and loved me. They answered the calls from people who hated me and wished I would croak.

OK, that's the run-of-the-mill DJ stuff, but *now* let's talk about the fabulous people who called and I talked with *live* on the radio. People I will never forget. People who probably helped me win awards, paid for my blue suede shoes, and put my daughter through college. People I will never meet, get to thank, or learn about their kids. These regular, superior-quality radio listening types often left me laughing or amazed.

She said she and her daughter lived in eastern Kentucky. The mountains.

I've been to these areas and it is capital "R" Rural. I mean so far back in the woods, there ain't nothin' behind ya. This is the country where people think, when they die, that they're goin' to Atlanta.

Mountain People. I often said on the air that I loved Mountain Women. It usually got me several angry letters and one flirty one from a prisoner. The lady caller said she earned extra money by singing at funerals. I know. I thought the same thing: *What? A little fun money by singing at funerals?* Yes, often at funerals they have someone sing the dearly departed's favorite song as they are lowered to their final resting place. Mountain funerals.

She said it was near Hazard, Kentucky, for a Mennonite family. It there ever was a well-named city, it's Hazard. I know it's a lovely Southern town, but I used to travel through there when I was in college, and it gave me the willies. I'm actually an idiot when it comes to the Mennonites. I confuse them with the Amish, which probably gives *them* the willies. (People have died from the willies, don't ya know.) I am one ignorant boob for not knowing much about these good gentle people, but I don't. They are kinda like the Shakers in central Kentucky. I think *they* went out of business because of not having sex, for religious reasons. This makes it tough to keep the dealio going when they ain't makin' any new Shakers.

But let's get back to the funeral. This woman, in her forties, along with her twenty-ish daughter, went to the funeral on a cold and bleak January morning in Kentucky. As this solemn group stood before an open grave with their flat black hats in their hardscrabble hands, she quietly asked the apparent leader, "What was your grandpa's favorite song?" I imagine Gramps was ninety, tough, pure, and going to heaven, if anybody was. The grandson choked back a tear and said in a tortured voice, "Joy Bells"—an old Flatt & Scruggs song. She said she quietly backed away, stunned but respectful, and whispered the title to her daughter.

Here comes the problem. It was cold. It was rainy. The wind was howling. There were forty or fifty family members standing by to send Gramps to his reward. Hours later, at the wake after the funeral, she learned what the poor grandson had requested. She was close, but no cigar. The mother and daughter took a deep breath and then started singing in those high and lonesome Appalachian harmonies what they *thought* was the song requested for this solemn occasion:

Dashing through the snow, in a one-horse open sleigh

O'er the fields we go, laughing all the way, ha-ha-ha.

Everybody!

Yes, Mom and her daughter performed, in full voice at this graveside with bereaved family members clutching memories of their dearly beloved and departed grandpa, "Jingle Bells."

I still love the mom for calling.

Moms often figured into funny stories. My own mom was funny. She called me for years when I was on the air. People still mention her to me. Once I asked her what she'd been doing, and she said she had painted the toilet lid.

ME: "Great, I'm glad that got done."

MOM: "Yeah but in the middle of the night I forgot about it and sat on the wet lid. Now I have the Blue Moon of Kentucky."

I think my mom *wrote* that joke. I'm not certain, but it's still funny.

Another guy called to tell me how his mother came home quite distraught from a shopping trip. "What happened to her?" I asked.

"Well," he said, "Mom told me she was driving along and heard a terrible noise and stopped. Something apparently had fallen off the bottom of the car and she'd brought it home." Mom led him out to the car, and there, in the backseat, was a sewer lid.

Or the guy who called to say his wife had recently bought some 600-count silk sheets—the most fancy, expensive sheets they'd ever had. He said he wore pajamas to bed that first night, but didn't know she'd made the bed with the new sheets. He gave a little running start and dived into the sack. When he hit the headboard, he was doing eighty-five miles an hour.

Most of you won't know what this story means, but in the olden days, back when cars had engine parts you could identify, manual transmissions, and no computers, you could jump-start a car. You'd put the car into neutral and get a push on the highway. (This sounds like I'm talking about something in silent movies, but it's true.) Some friends would help you get the car moving down the road. You'd then "pop" the clutch, and that would turn the engine over and start the car. (With today's cars, I am not really sure how to open the hood, but I knew how to do this.)

So the caller went on and told me he needed to jump-start his car. He said, "Mom, I want you to give me a push in your car." He explained the process to her. "I'll need to get going about thirty-five to forty miles an hour, and then I'll pop the clutch and get 'er started. You get in your car and give me the push." He said he got in his car and prepared to "get 'er started." He looked in the rear-view mirror and, to his horror, here came Mom. She was doing probably forty miles an hour when she hit the back of his Buick. All he had time to do was brace himself.

Then there was the woman who called the day we were discussing "How did you break a tooth?" She said her father had had an idea. Dad also had hemorrhoids. Daughter spilled the goods. Dad was wondering how his hemorrhoids looked, so he got up on the bed to have a gander in the dresser mirror. When he bent over to get a better view, he lost his balance, fell forward, and knocked his two front teeth out on the nightstand. Some things you just aren't meant to see.

I once talked to a guy who painted houses for a living. I asked him, "What's your favorite color to paint?"

He didn't even pause. He said, "The same color it was before."

Or the guy who called and said he used to work at a rodeo. The owner of the rodeo thought it would be fun to have a monkey ride a dog around the ring before actual cowboy action started. It would warm up the audience. The guy said he found a monkey for sale (as one usually does) and brought it to the rodeo. They had a big German Shepherd they thought would do fine subbing as a steed. During a test ride, the monkey got scared and pulled the dog's fur, making the dog stop. So, the night of the rodeo, they decided to tie the monkey's hands to the dog's collar to hold them down. The announcer introduced them as "Cowboy Coco and his trusty dog, Bullet."

The crowd roared with laughter as Coco entered the ring on the back of Bullet. It was just so cute. The dog took off across the ring and did one lap. Adorable. Coco bounced from side to side. Then somebody on the other side of the arena, not watching the daring duo, slightly raised a gate. Bullet saw his way out of this situation. The monkey held on as the dog raced toward the barely raised opening. The crowd gasped in shocked silence. They knew the gate was too low for Bullet to go under with a tiny rider on his back. Then the monkey realized the gate was too low for passenger clearance. Coco let loose a high-pitched warning scream, "Eeeeeeee!"—monkey for "somebody raise the damn gate!"

With a resounding "bonnnnnggg!" Coco stayed with the fence and Bullet dashed to freedom. The guy said, "We kept that monkey, but he wadn't ever right after that. He walked sorta funny and jumped in your hair if he saw a dog."

I won't wear you out with too many stories, but I do miss those wonderful moments of reality and indescribable joy upon hearing things like that.

Hope Coco is at peace now.

Randy Travis
and Don Williams

MY WIFE LOVES reality TV shows. She goes to the Woman Cave—the back bedroom you read about earlier—to watch *The Real Housewives of* (insert city/county here). I can take about five minutes of these shows. I really don't care if Tawanda is upset that somebody spilled merlot on her newly dyed poodle. I know these programs are successful and a moneymaking machine, and I really like that Andy Cohen dude who is behind all of the shows.

Allyson watches these intelligent video documents armed with a phone, so she can send texts to her friend Lori and e-mails to others. There is a flurry of AT&T conversation that goes on for hours. If they had a reality show called *The Real Housewives of Gassville, Arkansas*, I might watch that. *"On tonight's show, Irene's husband, Cooter, discovers those commodes at Target are for display only!"* I'm certain that's only weeks away from actually being on the tube. I am also really looking forward to *X-Tractor.*

When my dad used to listen to or watch baseball or a boxing match on the radio or television, he'd jump up and call his friend Bob Requardt about every five minutes, and they'd agree or argue, and then return to the action. I think this is what Allyson does now when Shelly on *The Real Housewives* tells Caprice, "Bite me, bitch." (Or whatever they say on those shows.)

I have said for several years now, *Jersey Shore* is the third sign of the Apocalypse and that we should all get our affairs in order. The End Is Nigh. That said, if ever there was somebody custom-made for a reality show, it's Randy Travis.

I've known Randy for decades. We're not close, but he'd call every now and then and I'd see him at Music Row events all the time. Randy had a brief brush with the law when he was pretty young. He actually did qualify for the "Outlaw" brand of country, but now he's as far from it as you can get. He's a sweet and gentle soul. Randy is also pretty laid back. He moves very slowly. Randy Travis is so slow, he's got a younger brother that is older than him now. He never answers right away. He sort of looks down and usually chuckles a little bit and then, in that unmistakable baritone, gives a good answer.

The only human who moves less than Randy Travis is Don Williams. Don is actually nicknamed "The Gentle Giant." He's gentle, but he's not really all that big. Don has had an enormously successful recording career—way back from the folky days 'til he had hits on his own. My good pal Wayland Holyfield wrote classic songs such as "Some Broken Hearts" for Don.

Don Williams could be lapped by a Galápagos tortoise. You could tell Don, "Hey, Don, your pants are on fire!" and he'd get to that eventually sometime the next day. Whenever Don was on my show, I always felt like he was on a delay system. Sometimes when you watch the news, the anchor is talking to a reporter who's someplace like Tanzania, with his hand to his ear. The anchor asks a question and about ten seconds go by before the reporter answers.

That's a satellite delay. Don Williams is always talking to you from Tanzania.

The easiest job in the music business is working the "follow" spotlight at a Don Williams concert. Stars have people who man the spot as the star moves around the stage, following them. At a Don Williams concert, you turn it on. Make sure Don's in the light. Two hours later, you turn it off.

When Don talks, he's hilarious. Unfortunately, by the time his answer oozes out, everybody is home asleep.

I know Don has had back trouble, and I don't make fun of that, but I know he didn't throw his back out making any sudden moves. Don is also a huge star in Europe. They don't like sudden moves in Europe, either, so I guess it helps him.

If Don reads this, I'm certain I'll get a warm response eleven years from now.

"Hey, Don, you're about to be attacked by a rabid sloth! LOOK OUT!"

I never knew what the dealio was with Randy and his wife/ manager Lib Hatcher. Lib was considerably older (sorry, Lib) than Randy. It always seemed like a mom/wife/handler/manager/custodial relationship. Hey, whatever works for somebody is good enough for me. Sadly, I know they've broken up, and I hear it's not one of those "friendly breakups." Don't you love it when people announce they are separating and say they will remain the "very best of friends." I always think, *Yeah, they're good friends, but somebody wants to use rat poison if they get the chance.*

Randy Travis made some of the most wonderful records ever. He was authentic-sounding because he *is* authentic-sounding. Nothing more, nothing less. What you hear is pure Randy. "Forever and Ever Amen" was so simple and yet so endearing, heartfelt, and such a great song and record that people were drawn to Randy. As you know, I have a lot of theories. I've got my Randy theory, but

I'm gonna let you make up your own theory. You hear things, you sense things, and you let it go because RT is so lovable.

Randy and Lib had a place in Hawaii for awhile. They raised macadamia nuts. Yes, Randy lived on a nut farm. I'm just sayin' that's reason right there to have a theory. (Roseanne Barr was required by law to live on a nut farm.) There is nothing in the world like that Randy Travis voice saying to you on the phone, "Gerry, now don't go makin' fun of my nuts. I heard you were doing that, and I'm proud of my nuts." Lib would be screeching in the background in that unmistakable "Lib" voice of hers. He'd hold the phone away and say, "Lib, he's laughing at my nuts." And, of course, I was.

I always thought I saw somebody else behind Randy's eyes. Almost like someone else who wanted out, to say something or do something else. Just my theory.

I really like him a lot and I think we might see that Randy one of these days. He recorded a song called "It's Just a Matter of Time," and I believe it is.

THIS JUST IN: Randy Travis wins "Worst Police Mug Shot in History" contest, displacing previous winners Glen Campbell and Nick Nolte. As I write about Randy, he goes and gets arrested for being naked in the road and resisting arrest. I hope our guy finds his way. I think there is a decent human in there.

THIS JUST IN: Randy has had a serious physical setback. I truly hope he recovers and can sing for us again. Most of all, I want to hear that baritone laugh. A glorious chuckle that tells you he's truly finding something hilarious. The world needs that voice and that laugh.

As we go to press, "It's Just a Matter of Time" now has a whole different meaning.

QUIZZICLE #5

Who actually gave me the definition of torque?

A) Gene Watson

B) The Band Perry

C) Dario Franchitti

It Won't Be Long

GENE WATSON IS ONE of the "old school" country singers. For the first fifteen years of my radio career, most of the country singers I talked to were nice but rarely very educated. They were blue-collar guys who broke out of the factory line by singing. They were the real honky-tonkers.

You may not even know who Gene Watson is, but he had several great records. His distinctive tenor voice gave us "Fourteen Carat Mind," and, earlier, one of the most suggestive songs I ever heard get past the country audience, "Love in the Hot Afternoon." But his signature song was "Farewell Party." It's one of those songs that ends on a powerful high note. We all waited for it. At concerts, you could see people hoping he'd make it one more time.

So, you get the picture. When you interview people over and over again, sometimes once or twice a year, it can get tiring. Boring for the artist to get asked the same questions and boring for the audience to hear the same answers. I usually tried to work the guest into the conversation we were already having before they arrived. Almost all of them seemed relieved to talk about anything other than "life on the road."

It so happened we were talking auto repair when Gene arrived one day, and I knew he'd been a mechanic working in a Houston body shop. We jabbered away about auto work until he mentioned he still had his old torque wrench.

Torque for some reason is a funny word to me. I asked him what torque really was. He said he knew but couldn't tell me on the air. I had no idea what he was about to say and figured it couldn't be that bad. His eyes started darting around, and he was stammering a bit. I thought, *Uh-oh, let's take a break, and* off *the air you tell me what torque is. Then we'll come back and explain it to everyone.*

It turns out it's an old joke, but I hadn't heard it at the time. So it's a new joke if you haven't heard it, right? Off the air, Gene said, "A guy gets up in the middle of the night with an erection and has to take a leak. If he's standing in front of the john and pushes it down, and his feet fly out from underneath him, *that's* torque."

I laughed for the rest of the interview. And I spent the next hour and a half explaining to callers why I couldn't tell them *on* the air what torque was. I remember telling one kind little old lady *off* the air what Gene had explained, and she said, "Oh, that's a good one. Wait 'til I tell my bridge club."

Religion and Country and TV Preachers

THE BANKLICK CHRISTIAN CHURCH in Independence, Kentucky, was the social center of my universe for the first fifteen years of my life. It remained so for my parents. Dad was a deacon. Mom was in the Eastern Star. I know a deacon is a big deal in a small church. I'm still not sure what the Order of the Eastern Star does, but Mom did it for years. I remember it was mostly organizing suppers after church.

Everyone brought potluck, which meant you'd have thirty fried chicken legs, one small bowl of pork 'n' beans, and a whole lot of that Jell-O with an orange floating in it. I hated potluck and often asked my mom why somebody couldn't organize it so there'd be steak and mashed potatoes or pork chops and mashed potatoes. My mom used to say steak was too expensive for most folks. She bought cube steaks for us for dinner a lot. She had a silver hammer with square edges and pounded the cube steaks into submission. I knew we were having cube steak hours before dinner because of the massive hammering I heard from the kitchen. I'm not sure what cube steak is. From square animals, I guess, but this stuff could easily have been worn as a bulletproof vest in emergencies.

The church was your movie-set little white church— a 100-year-old building where about a hundred or so souls sought salvation every week. These were all good, decent, blue-collar people who were put through the wringer by a fire-and-brimstone preacher every Sunday morning. My electrician pop installed fans in the church that he "borrowed" from an old Kroger store, and it was probably the only time anything cool ever happened in that building.

We had a succession of preachers, but the ones I remember most vividly were Brother Carver, Brother Lemon, and...get ready for it...Brother Love. Yes, the guy's name was Love, and he was a preacher, so he actually *was* Brother Love. Neil Diamond song or not, we had a regular salvation show every week with Da Bro of Love.

Brother Carver was a seminary professor in Cincinnati. He was a diminutive man who was perhaps the meekest person on Earth. If "the meek shall inherit the Earth," Brother Carver will be first in line. He delivered a studious, detailed, and sleep-inducing sermon every week. This guy could give Xanax a run for its money. Heads were drooping moments after he hit the pulpit.

Snoring was a regular occurrence. The heat, the fans whir-ring, and that professorial explanation of what Deuteronomy meant to today's world knocked you out quicker than you can say Nebuchadnezzar.

When Brother Carver left (to become a motivational speaker, I imagine), we got Brother Love. He was a young guy, full of common sense and the spirit of the Lord. His wife was a babe, so I welcomed the Brother and Sister into our midst with open arms. I skipped the "lusting in your heart" part and, therefore, felt no guilt over wondering what Sister Love looked like in lingerie. They left when Brother Love got a gig in a church in Nevada. I know first-hand there's a lot of sinners in and around Las Vegas, so he had his work laid out for him.

Then we got Brother Lemon. Never a truer name in all of mankind. Brother Lemon was a gangly "street preacher" type. He could become possessed of the spirit like no one I'd seen before. Not even the guys who came back as missionaries from the Congo could match the Lemon Fervor. This guy could sweat and shout with the best of them.

Now, understand, this was the whitest church in America. Even a tiny bit of emotion got them riled up, but the Brother had the choir jiggling and people in the last pew listening. They were awake. No one could sleep, of course, through his shout-fest. This guy *wailed!* When he got to the end of his sermon, you just waited for somebody to come forward to the congregation singing "Softly and Tenderly." It's a sweet moment.

Only one thing was wrong with our Lemon De Brother. He suffered from a speech problem. I believe it's called Substitution Syndrome. At the very peak of his sermon, when everyone was listening with rapt attention, he'd deliver one of these "And so, my brothers and sisters, remember it is as the Good Book *stainly plates...*" followed by a pause, and then he'd plow forward hoping nobody noticed. This was when it got good for me. A few seconds later, a sweaty Brother Lemon would then drop, "His word is a famp unto my leet." If anybody knows me, I think I fostered my love of awkward situations in that little white church. The shaking shoulders, the squelched guffaws, and choked-back tears of laughter are still with me to this day.

He was a good man. He just had a little problem.

I know when Brother Lemon unleashed, "Don't cast your swearls before pine," I ran out the church doors to keep my head from exploding by trying to hold in the laughter. My mother was incensed and P.O.'d at me. My dad didn't hear it because he was with the other deacons downstairs, counting the donations and whipping up the grape juice and crackers. Later, though, he did think it was hilarious.

So began my lifelong fascination with men of the Lord. Oh, there are a couple of women in there somewhere, but mostly it's the Elmer Gantrys of the world I can't abide (biblical term).

Country music and religion are deeply intertwined. I like that. I like some kind of deep belief system reflected in among the twang. I know a lot of artists and songwriters who are deeply religious. I also know a lot of charlatans, which is French for out-and-out crook—a swindler of the highest degree.

Just as I've written songs with guys who have said grace before a lunch break or who have invited me to share some testimony, I have also worked with and endured the hypocrites who fake their religiousness and screw everyone who comes in contact with them.

I had a lawyer who quit lawyering and became the head of a Christian music label. He was not cut out to do the Lord's work. First of all, he was an atheist, and second, he is perhaps the most honest human on the planet. He finally had a nervous breakdown and left that world. He said he just couldn't deal with folks who said their chief negotiator was God. He'd offer, say, 4.5 percentage "points" on an album. The artist got paid a formula of album sales based on those points. He'd make his offering, and they'd say, "Let me pray on it overnight." They'd return the next day and say Jesus told them 4.5 points wasn't enough. God thought eight would be better, and ten would be just heavenly.

They would also say God spoke to them about their per diems and how they also had to be doubled and, if possible, God wanted them to receive a fifty grand advance for wardrobe and hair without recouping requirements. You get the idea. Remember, this was a tiny percentage of the whole music business. But these people know who they are.

I should also add my mom *loved* Billy Graham. "Oh, he's such a good man." I agree. There is something calming and peaceful about a good man of God. I wish there were more like him.

If you've heard as many Sunday-morning radio shows as I have in my career, you can just tell when somebody is a con man. Those Nashville folks who bought Conway Twitty's old place, Twitty City, drive me up the wall. I used to see them in all their gospel glory, chugging expensive merlots at area restaurants. I'd then see them on their TV show the next day, begging for some "donations" because they wanted to put up a satellite dish in Italy. You know, where Rome and the Vatican are? Those poor Italian heathens just don't have enough religion in their lives without these goobers from Twitty City delivering the good news over their new station in Eye-taly (as they called it).

Google them sometime and see how many houses and planes they have around the world. In my mind, the faith healers are the worst. Benny Hinn is the man who travels the world "healing" the bent and desperate people of this wretched Earth. I've never understood why, if a person has that "gift"—to touch somebody and make them walk again—do they have to come to some auditorium in Sioux City, Iowa? Doesn't Benny know there are buildings called children's hospitals, where parents would give their lives to see their baby walk again?

I watched him one night, and so many people were being given the "spirit" that he stopped touching them on the forehead. People get into a state at these events; I understand it. You get all worked up and go forward, and Benny taps you on the forehead and you keel over like a sack of rutabagas.

On this one special night, after awhile, Benny was whacking people with his clothing. I believe it was a lovely checked Botany 500 number. He was delivering people to the Lord through the use of his sport coat. A double turn, a whack of the jacket, and people fainted dead away. Put another one in the "saved" column.

Where do old faith healers go, anyway? If they get decrepit or sick, can't they just reach down and lift the arthritis out of their knees and keep goin'?

There's a guy on television in Nashville I see every Sunday. He's your typical TV preacher guy—motivational and slick. His only claim to fame before he became a religious man was that he killed some poor woman down in Texas and went to prison. How do those folks sit there and listen to him exhort them to do the right thing with that bit of personal history floating around the pulpit?

This is where Ray Stevens comes in. Ray, or "Moan" as we call him (short for RayMoan), took this whole business on squarely with "Mississippi Squirrel Revival"—a gentle and funny song about a lively rodent in a small church like the one I had attended.

Ray is a genius. He has recorded so many classic comedy songs and written such amazing other songs that he's in his own category. I've sat with him backstage at the old Desert Inn in Las Vegas before his shows. We've played golf. We've had tequila and have sat through many a long night at music business functions. I love it that he wrote "Ahab The Arab" and "Gitarzan" with the same fingers that he used to write "Everything Is Beautiful." He's so tight he squeaks, but he's a great friend.

He also played the piano on "Five O'Clock World" by the Vogues. I put that in for music trivia geeks like me. Ray is, above all, honest and direct. He says what he means and is somebody you can count on for the truth.

I wish more TV preachers were like Ray.

Roach

ROACH WAS IN HIS CRYPT. Or that's what he called it—"the crypt." It was the only crypt with a TV screen and a little fan in case it got hot, but it was a crypt. It was just like several others in the middle of a bus in the middle of the country, rockin' down the highway. Some folks called them bunks or beds...or home.

Roach always thought of it as his last resting place. This is where he'd like to go out. This was his last ride; he'd had it. El Roacho was done with touring and roadie-ing and everything. It really wasn't *his* choice, but the star he worked for was no longer gonna go on these grueling tours. Times were tough, and even in Roach's world, jobs were getting hard to come by. Country music was changing, and so was Eldon.

That's Roach's real name. He hates it, so don't call him that. His mother was the only one who could call him Eldon. He got the name Roach, as you can imagine, because he could crawl up under anything. When he was eight, he worked for an electrician who had Roach crawl into attics and "pull wire." He was good at it and getting into anywhere. "Roach, go in there and see if them wires is hot." Then, there *was* that one year in junior college when a roach meant something else. He sort of went along with the street meaning of "roach" at that point, when people had roach clips for the end of a joint. Either way, don't call him Eldon.

The final ride—it felt like a movie. He rocked back and forth and usually would be asleep by now. A bunk in a bus was the only place where he found he could really get some quality z's.

No road noises, no shake 'n' bakin', no snoring, no sleep. He'd been a roadie for thirty-eight years of his life, and it was coming to the end of the road. It was the life he loved, but he was getting too old for this shit. He felt the bus shudder and heard a little thump. Probably hit either part of a thrown tire or some poor animal. Probably a possum.

He'd seen a lot of "sail" possums over the years. And sail cat, sail dogs—you name it, he'd seen the sail version of it. When something gets run over enough by buses and trucks on a steaming-hot asphalt highway, it sort of bakes down into a flat shape. You can pick up a sail possum and throw it like a weapon. Imagine death by sail possum.

Speaking of death, he remembered the time he tried to scare that guy who was hitting on his girlfriend, and laughed to himself. Roach just wanted to see if it could be done, that's all. Death by biscuits. Roach and Wheezer grabbed this dude and told him he was gonna die by biscuits. A Pillsbury execution. It was a horrible way to go. Never saw anybody shake so much at the phrase "Death by Biscuits."

Neither Roach nor Wheezer even knew if it would work. Besides, they weren't really gonna kill the guy, just scare him gray. The idea is you get a small road case, about $300 worth of canned biscuits, and then you stuff the guy and the biscuits into the road case on a hot day. The biscuits heat up, explode from their containers, and slowly start to expand. Roach had heard that guys confessed to things they didn't do just to get out of a self-risin' execution. He laughed again, remembering the victim's muffled shouts as the biscuits rose to the occasion. Pop! Scream. Pop! Pop! Scream. Roach finally let him free and told him to stay away from his girl. He was pulling biscuit dough out of his nose. Good thing it wasn't Roach's wife, or he would have probably let the guy die by dough.

Somebody got up to go to the head. It was one of the first squeamish things you got over real quick on the road. Nowadays they got grinders so you can do more than whiz on a bus. Thank God! No more dashing for the can at a truck stop. There are places in Bangladesh that have better johns than some truck stops.

Roach could play guitar and bass. He also could sing and even once had a recording deal with a private label out of Texas. It was owned by a guy who'd made a fortune selling fake cow pies in a box. They looked as fresh as the real thing, and you could have them delivered to somebody you wanted to either impress or tick off. But Roach lost his deal when the owner went broke 'cause he got sued by a family who ate one of the cow pies, thinking it was a snack. They were likely to have died, and so did Roach's record career.

Roach played bass in a couple of bands. The most fun he had was with Manny Sanchez, the Mexicali Mover. Thirteen dudes onstage in big hats and sparkly outfits. Trumpets, accordions, and one of those giant guitars. Those guys were so much fun 'til the immigration police took them away one afternoon in a big black truck.

He gave up depending on a paycheck from a band when the "OK Chorale." broke up. The OK Chorale was a great band, and Roach thought they were on their way. Wrong again. The drunken lead singer took a swig out of a bottle of Liquid Plumr left on the bar. The poor guy sang like a dying cat after that, and Roach decided on a leave of absence from performing live forevermore.

He drifted for a moment. In that space between awake and asleep, he always thought of his third wife, Mylene. Who *wouldn't* fall in love with a woman who could open a beer bottle with her butt cheeks? *Oh my Gawd, Mylene!* She could dance. She could sing. She could cook. The only thing she couldn't seem to do was avoid dating the local high school football team. She was a world-class nympho, and it was tiring after awhile. Not for Mylene, of course, but for Roach. The last time he saw her, she was standing on I-40 with a sign that said, "Last Girl Before Expressway." Ahh, My My Mylene.

Roach woke himself up snoring. He did that a lot. The guys on the bus said he sounded like a chainsaw that needs oil.

This was it. The final ride to a home he didn't have. The end of the trail. The last round-up. He winced at the thought of his bank account. He'd made some decent money, but between the wives and his "business" investments, it was gonna be tough sledding. But understand, he *never* put his earnings into anything stupid.

The prescription windshield *was* a great idea. He'd met a guy workin' for Tim McGraw's road crew, and they'd partnered up. The guy would run the business, and Roach was to provide the operating capital. The concept was brilliant. If you wore glasses, you could have the windshield of your car made to your prescription! That way you could drive even if you didn't have your specs with you. So simple.

They were on their way to a fortune 'til some idiot stole the test windshield car. The new driver didn't need glasses at all and promptly drove off a cliff in the Smokies. Some people just don't have no sense.

Now Roach was upset and awake again. He started to calm down when he considered maybe being a roadie in his "extremely late fifties" was not such a good idea anyway. He was really sixty-two. Time to hang up the ponytail, although he'd actually ditched the ponytail years ago after the ceiling fan incident. That hurt like a son of a bitch.

Being a roadie was tough, especially that tour he'd done with the rich TV comedian. Roach's job was to play and guard a cowbell for forty shows. Good money, but he couldn't decide which drove him nuttier, the comedian or banging that cowbell every night for two hours.

What else could he turn to? He had a few years to go before he could claim Social Security. He'd certainly tried other honest ways to make a living. Blimp pilot. It had been a good job, and he would be on Easy Street now except for the flight incident. Sure, he'd sorta fibbed about being able to pilot a blimp, but it was like his mother had said, "What a stupid place to put a building."

Roach dreamed and rocked to the rhythm of the road. It was peaceful now. Peaceful was good. Things hadn't always been so peaceful. Lord, there was that tour with the rock star who had decided to go "country." What an idiot. They were doing fairs and "soft ticket" dates, and his old rock fans showed up with their kids to see him—a middle-aged, slightly pudgy white guy in Spandex, singin' his "country" songs. Oh, he had fiddles in the band, all right. But he just couldn't let go of the rock star moves. Country people get moody when you bite the head off a baby rabbit.

Brandy floated through his mind. Not the liquor, Roach's second wife. She always said, "My daddy said I was made 'cause of brandy, so he named me that. Good thing they wasn't drinkin' Kahlua!" Then she'd give that high-pitched scream of a laugh. She was a good ol' gal. He'd met her at a club, where she shot ping-pong balls out of her coochie into the audience. She had great distance.

He'd always enjoyed women with talent. They were in love right up until she ran off with that TV evangelist who had a private plane. Last Roach heard, she was strippin' for Jesus at the end of his tent revivals. Good for Brandy.

He had to get out of roadwork. It was a good, solid life with good friends, but he'd been at it too long. How many times can one man be shot in the ass with a nail gun? Or have a case of M&Ms dropped on his foot? Or get third-degree burns from a parrot carrying a lighted road flare? We've *all* been through things like that, but enough is enough. This was where he was getting off the crazy train.

Thinking of getting off made him recall the really good times. He'd had his share of fun with women. Yeah, it was quite a week with those deaf-mute Vietnamese twins.

That ended when he woke up screaming. They were breaking his fingers so he couldn't tell anybody about his "Bangin' on a Mirror" trick. His right pinkie still points left more than it should.

It was always easy to slip back to the good nights. The Cheese-Eating Contest on that Brooks & Dunn tour in Switzerland. The Moose in the Tent night. The Unlucky night. He'd been warned by his bunkmates, "Don't hold a fart-lighting contest with a welder's torch," which was almost as bad as the "scooting across hot coals" moment in the Bahamas.

Roach knew he wasn't gonna have any more kids. He'd met a couple of young peezers who sidled up to him outside a Reba concert and announced they were his offspring. He didn't buy it. People just lie to get backstage. He also knew his baby-making days were over after that nut-lifting contest anyway. You tied a rope around your nutsack, and the first guy to lift a truck rim was the winner. The moment he heard something pop, he knew his days of being a pop were over.

Why wouldn't somebody want the Roachmeister for one more tour? Sure, he'd left that star's attached microphone turned on before the show as the star went to the can battling Montezuma's Revenge. Sure, he'd accidentally opened the floor lift bringing the singer up onstage while a fan was kneeling in front of him. That can happen to anybody. And for cryin' out loud, what kind of a roadie job is putting police tape on the floor—from the bus to the stage—just because the singer was always so hammered he needed the tape as a guide to find his microphone? Come on, man, it was funny when Roach put the tape leading to a Dumpster out back. Who knew that cowboy would follow the tape right into the garbage? Is that a reason to fire a man?

Roach knew the rules. Roach was a team player. He *told* that bass singer not to inhale when you're practicing with a blowgun. Wasn't Roach the one who ran out and lifted the motorcycle off Travis Tritt when he dumped his Harley onstage at the Derby? I mean, it *was* hilarious. You don't fire somebody for laughing.

It's not like he cost the backup singers *that* much money when he started the company that specialized in potted chipmunk. He still had a lot of life and great ideas in him. False teeth for dogs was a killer concept. A golf course with ball returns like a bowling alley had promise written all over it. There was so much to plan and live for.

The bus groaned and started to slow down. This was it. They were back in Nashville. Suddenly, dreams and plans felt foreign to him. His bones ached. His back hurt. The bus smelled like a locker room in the Philippines. He waited for a moment. He was gonna rise from the crypt and walk away. Say good-bye to his buds and the driver. The star had gotten home seven hours ago on her plane. He'd send her a note. She was terrific.

This was the long good-bye. The boys always said Roach got out of his bunk like an octopus falling out of a tree. He stood, stretched, and headed toward the door. He stepped off and grabbed his duffel. He tried to remember where he'd parked his car.

He felt a sense of freedom and panic at the same time. Maybe it was time. Roach was turning the corner for a new road. There were some other drivers and buses parked nearby. He gave a quick wave. And he walked.

A voice called out over the early-morning parking lot. "Hey, Roach! ROACH! It's me, Brandon. Been out on the road with Blake Shelton. Hey, man, I know your girl's hangin' it up. You have any interest in takin' a ride through Canada starting Friday? We're gonna have a lotta fun and we'll drink Canada Dry!"

Roach smiled.

Roy Acuff and Opryland

THE KING OF COUNTRY MUSIC goes way back. He was a singer with medicine shows in the 1930s and was a true pioneer. I spent a year working at Opryland doing a morning radio show from the stage of the *Grand Ole Opry*. Roy showed up quite often because *he lived there!* Yes, you read correctly. He had a house right there on the *Opry* property. Every so often, he wandered over with a cup of coffee and watched me stumble around doing my radio show. Kind of like when you look up and discover your neighbor is watching you clean out a litter box, or catching you running out to get the paper wearing one sock and a pair of boxers.

I should interject that the show I was doing was called *The Waking Crew*. It was *live* radio with a *live* band and a *semi-live* audience. It was early, and they were usually sleepy or from out of town and had *no* idea what was going on. I found both true sometimes. This was a long-running and beloved radio show that went back to the 1940s, carrying the grand tradition of great live radio and entertainment. Look up "The Breakfast Club" or "The Arthur

Godfrey Show." A host, a band, an audience made the show. I hosted it for about a year and drove it straight into the ground. When I left for L.A., they canceled the show.

Now, to be fair, there were problems when I got there. The band had been the star, and some of them didn't want me to tread on their comedy territory. I didn't learn that for quite awhile; I thought they were just mutes. It was like I was the mother-in-law on a honeymoon—not a good fit.

I always like to think it was canceled because I left, but it's probably closer to the truth to say they were so worn out watching me struggle to keep it afloat (literally "afloat" because we sometimes did the show from their General Jackson Showboat) that they just couldn't muster up the effort to find somebody else to host it.

Each daily show had two live singers. Often, a beautiful blonde named Lorrie Morgan came in. Other times, a whip-thin guy named Alan Jackson from the mailroom shuffled in. I'll never forget seeing this gorgeous creature, Lorrie Morgan, standing offstage in full regalia looking like a movie star. We were in a commercial break, and I walked over beside her. She fired up a Marlboro Red and said, "Wow, look at all these sleepy sons of bitches. Is that an audience or an oil painting?" I fell in love that moment.

What was I talking about before? Oh, yeah, Roy Acuff. The Royster only sang once on *The Waking Crew* with me present. "Great Speckled Bird" was one of his showstoppers. He was a real pro and a man of the people. I got kind of excited when my neighbor dropped in to sing, which brings me to the Roy story.

One day, a security guard at Opryland told me what had transpired with the *Opry* Master. Now, understand that Opryland was a theme park and a tourist Mecca. There were people in sandals and black socks wandering around for days like mental patients. I don't need to remind you they *loved* country music and were thrilled to poke all over the park. Gawkin' and snappin' pitchers and generally taking it all in. They were good folks, but tourists. Country tourists are the only people in the world who will drive 700 miles to a destination and have their picture taken with their car.

One summer morning, a gaggle of them got loose and wandered into Roy's *house*. Yep, front door is open. Let's go in and gawk...through Roy's kitchen...down the hall to ol' Roy's bedroom...while ol' Roy was in it, asleep! They gathered 'round the bed and watched Roy snort and snooze. He was all tucked up in the covers, talkin' to the Sandman, and these folks from Michigan or Ohio were workin' the Polaroids and snooping through his sock drawer.

Now, *this* is what you call a *real* country music theme park. Not only do you see the stars onstage, but you can also view them with their mouth open, snoring in *bed*—a place where tourists and *Opry* legends share a special moment.

A guard noticed Roy's front door was open and went in to check. When he discovered the "visitors," he told me he was afraid "Mr. Roy would wake up and think he was dead with these people gathered 'round staring down at him." It would be like waking up at your own funeral, I guess.

Our security expert silently ushered and shooed the thrilled trespassers out the bedroom door. As they crept out, the guard said he looked back and Roy was still sawin' away.

I always wondered if these folks went back home and were showing slides of their vacation. How they must have described being in Roy Acuff's bedroom: "Oh, Opryland is just so wonderful. We rode the Log Flume and got all wet. We had a nice lunch at this little country place. And we went into Roy Acuff's bedroom and watched him catch some z's."

"I hope next year we can see Dolly all racked out."

I think if the Opryland powers-that-be had incorporated this into the tourist agenda, they'd still be open and doing big business.

Sake's Fur and George Jones

"SAKE'S FUR QUIT WORKING," Allyson announced one chilly evening in March. I'm used to her saying things like that, so I asked her how she knew Sake's fur had "quit working." "Look at him," she said, pointing to the obviously shivering little Japanese Chin. "He's just freezin'. I guess his fur just gave out and can't keep him warm anymore."

Makes perfect sense, doesn't it? Sake was a Christmas Eve panic purchase I'd made with Autumn as my endorser. We couldn't think of what to get Mom, so we bought Sake at some pet store in a mall. I know it's a terrible thing to do, but we'd had two glasses of wine, and it was getting near the gift shopping deadline.

I don't believe Sake ever actually came to me when I called for him his entire life. He was a sweet little guy, but he either slept or stared out the window. He was a deep dog.

You could hear him thinking as he looked out while things blew by. *Leaf. Leaf. Squirrel. Leaf.* I am convinced Sake was actually a $900 rabbit. Sake has gone to doggie heaven now, but I kinda miss him giving that thousand-yard stare and bumping into the furniture.

I think George Jones' fur just quit working. It was possum fur, to be sure, because that's what a lot of people called him. I always thought bringing up George's resemblance to one unattractive rodent was an insult. He never seemed to mind and even referred to himself as the Ol' Possum. I maintain actual possums look so horrible because, when panicked, they fall over and pretend to be dead. To convince something that's about to eat you that you're dead, you have to look like "death on a cracker" all the time. Thus, and ergo, possums are horrible looking—like they've been up drinkin' and snortin' cocaine for two weeks. Now that I've said that, I understand why George Jones was called the Ol' Possum.

I knew George when his fur quit working. He'd been the King for a long time and married to the most delightful woman ever, named Tammy Wynette.

Tammy Wynette's voice just killed me. Nobody had that little "heart tug" in her voice like Tammy. "Stand By Your Man," "'Til I Get It Right," "I Don't Wanna Play House," and dozens of others were due to Billy Sherrill, a true genius producer and songwriter. Ask anybody to name one of their favorite all-time classic country songs, and I bet Billy is involved somehow.

After George Jones, Tammy married a friend of mine, Mike Tomlin. That lasted about as long as some of my lunches. Then she married George Richey, a songwriter and music business guy. That's who I always saw her with. I was there the morning she did that weird TV interview with the networks. She claimed she had been kidnapped and beaten up. When I asked her about it, she wouldn't or couldn't look at me. I have a pretty good bullshit detector. Years of talking to strangers over the phone on the radio will do that for ya. It broke my heart because something didn't sound right. I hugged her and told her to take care of herself. She had big tears in her eyes when she walked away. She seemed smaller than I remembered. I think she sang "Stand By Your Man" one too many times.

George and Tammy made some beautiful music together. This was before the duck. When I saw George years after divorcing Tammy, he talked in a duck voice. Not every now and then as a joke, but all the time. There was the rare sound of George's actual speaking voice, but usually he responded in Donald Duck–speak. To be honest, it sort of became natural after awhile.

This was during his "No Show" period. He was hell-bent and hell-bound. George snorted up half of Peru, from what I heard. He went broke and Johnny Cash slipped him some Cash cash to keep him going.

I always feel sorry for people who are addicted. It's a downward spiral you can't get out of. You wake up one morning and talk like a duck. Don't wake up one morning and talk like a duck.

Sometime in the early 1980s, Jane Pauley, host of NBC's *Today* show at the time, came to Nashville for some excursion or another. As one of the "Music City Guides," I gave Jane the grand tour (to quote a George Jones song) of the "inside" Nashville: the clubs, the homes, the stars. Jane also had broken her ankle or foot, so she was on crutches. We started out one afternoon at Printer's Alley just for some camera shots and discussions of what a typical night in Nashville was like.

Printer's Alley, where I broadcast that live TV show with Johnny Paycheck, is a tiny street filled with several strip joints and bars. In fact, I *only* went there when people did TV shows. For some reason, whenever anybody comes to town, they go to the Loveless Café, the *Opry,* and Lower Broadway. It's the law. You have to go to these three places and then explain to your TV audience, "It's the insider's Nashville."

So I took gimpy Jane Pauley and a couple of camera guys to Printer's Alley. It had a long history of gambling and Lord knows what else going back as far as Prohibition. Every city has a section of town like that. A little dangerous, a little risqué, and usually a lot dirty—this was Printer's Alley back then. Jane loved it.

We stood inside the nightclub. Actually, it was really a bar. More precisely, a honky-tonk. OK, let's just call it a strip joint. Jane hobbled around and suggested a place she could do a "stand up" and shoot some stuff. I wandered off to the bathroom. It was about 5:30 P.M., and the place was deserted. A tiny stage, worn carpet, and sad pictures of horses on the walls made this your typical dive. I tried to open the bathroom door, and as I did, I whacked some guy in the rear who was bent over the sink. The guy was George Jones.

I am not gonna guess what George was doing, but I knew it was not examining the sink top for cleanliness. He stood straight up and said in that unmistakable actual Possum voice, "Well, hello there, son." I was dumbstruck. *And* he didn't talk like a duck.

I led George back into the club and introduced Jane to the King of Country Music. She looked puzzled, as she should have been, and asked what George was doing in that club at six in the evening. Then the most amazing thing happened. George saw the cameras and somehow through his foggy brain figured out he was there to perform. He mumbled a few things we didn't understand. And then the man himself, the Voice, the King of Country, got up on that tiny stage and started singing.

We sat there like we'd been hit by lightning. The camera guys started to film, and Jane, much to her credit, stopped them. George wasn't aware that there wasn't a band. He didn't need one. George Jones sang "He Stopped Loving Her Today" all the way to the end. It was breathtaking. The tiny crowd was his, and we clapped. George made his way offstage and banged his way out the door and into the street. The Possum was gone.

Jane Pauley went back to New York and the *Today* show after visiting the *Opry*, Lower Broadway, and the Loveless Café. She cheered how great their biscuits were. Everybody up with the damn biscuits.

George Jones married Nancy in 1983. She saved George's life and legacy, simple as that. George was a sweet man who had gone off into the ditch. Nancy got him started on the long road back.

She got the Possum's fur working again.

Songwriting and Songwriters

PROBABLY AMONG THE QUESTIONS I get asked most are, "Do you miss radio?" and, "Are you sick of being mistaken for Pierce Brosnan?" and, "How does songwriting work?"

The answers are "Kinda," "No," and "I don't know."

I do know I couldn't have been only a songwriter. I don't have the nerve to do it, I don't have the thick skin to do it, and I certainly didn't have the money to do it. Songwriters are out there on the fringes of actual employment. You can be a songwriter and do it once every time Halley's Comet goes around. Nobody knows. Your wife probably knows and so do your creditors, but otherwise, you can put "songwriter" on your passport and everybody nods in acceptance.

In my case, I had another career/job as a radio guy. It was a double-edged sword. I played the songs my friends wrote and got paid for, but I also longed to play my own songs. How ego-driven is that?

Songwriters are brain-damaged. Imagine working alone in a room or with another songwriter on a tune for hours on end.

Crafting the lyrics, honing the melody. Working the demo and pitching it to an artist. It bombs. *Nobody* likes it. Not *one* human being on the planet says, "I am going to record that." That happens in Nashville over and over and over.

Being a songwriter is like being a piñata for judgment. People will listen to ten seconds' worth, turn down the volume, and start talking about their hemorrhoids. Your heart and soul are still playing in the background. Whoever is listening rejects it within seconds, and without so much as a whisper of regret says, "What else ya got?"

Once I was standing in the outer office of a major record producer. A guy who could make a hit out of a song on a cassette. I witnessed a young, scruffy, scared songwriter walk through the door like he was going to his execution. He said, "Howdy, ma'am," to the receptionist/door guard/gatekeeper/executioner. "I just drove all day to bring you this song 'cause I heard they take songs, so I brung down a hit." Now, this was early on in my songwriting experience, and it sort of chilled me. Without looking up and without a word, Eva Braun stuck out her hand. The rattled songsmith handed off his hopes and dreams. She tossed it over her shoulder, where it crashed into a massive cardboard box on the floor that used to hold toilet paper. It slowly settled into the thousands of other songs to join the black hole of hits. He stood there awkwardly and then backed out the door. Welcome to Nashville, there, son. I never saw that poor guy again.

I got the whole picture in that twenty-second exchange. She wasn't really being mean. It's just that *everybody's* song is a hit. If only I had been paid a dollar each time I had to listen to somebody's latest unrecorded wonder. We all do it. Usually it's the last thing we wrote. *This* is the one. Usually it isn't.

Here is songwriting in a nutshell, which I am covered in right now—a thin nutshell. I arrived in town having written some songs. I didn't know anybody or anything about the music business (often referred to as the music "bidness" or the "leave me alone, I don't want your songs" business). I drove to Music Row. I saw a building with the words Combine Music on the front. Quickly, I cleverly deduced, "They must take songs in that place."

I had four songs with me and pushed the creaky glass door open. The receptionist listened politely and said, "Hold on. I'll see if somebody will listen to your stuff." I was *in*. She told me to go up the stairs, turn right, second office on the left. As I trudged up those steps, I saw awards plaques lining the walls. A BMI award to Kris Kristofferson. A Million-Air award to Dennis Linde. A Most-Played Song of the Year award to Tony Joe White. It was intimidating, to say the least.

Suddenly, I was in the office of Al Cooley. He was lighting a cigarette, and we exchanged a few words. He was busy. I was nervous. I gave him the tape of my tunes. He listened to about twenty seconds of all four. He then looked me straight in the eye and said, "These are the weirdest songs I've ever heard in my life. Man, I don't know what else to tell ya. I couldn't get these cut if I had a gun." He had shot me straight though the heart, but he was honest and direct. That was his opinion, and I liked that. (We later became friends and smiled when we saw each other. And I didn't *really* like it, but people always *say* they like honest criticism.) If you believe people love criticism of their work, check out the rejected singers coming out the door on *American Idol*.

Armed with the knowledge that I had four of the "weirdest songs ever heard," I walked across the street for a block and saw the MCA Music Publishing sign on the front of an old house. Most publishing offices were in old houses along Music Row. I was gonna try it again. Receptionist-songwriter words exchanged here. Go up steps. More plaques of honor on the walls in office. There sat John Ragsdale. Songwriter-publisher, awkward conversation, hand over tapes. John Ragsdale leaned back and blinked, winced, twitched, and listened. All four, all the way through to the end. He leaned forward and looked me straight in the eye. "Man, I don't know what else to tell ya. I *love* these songs. I think I can get these cut."

Same songs. Same day. Same Music Row. One man's junk is another man's treasure. John Ragsdale is Ray Stevens' brother. (I didn't know that at the time.) John Ragsdale put up his own money and some of MCA's to make professional demos of my piti-ful guitar/vocal versions. Two got recorded. *This is gonna be easy,* thought the kid with songs in his head and dreams in his heart. As they say in the commercials, "But wait! There's more!" And that is, it ain't so easy.

I guess as a songwriter, I'd admit, "Thank God for radio." I've had several actual hits and dozens of album cuts, but I've never had that enormous smash. I always thought that the late Van Stephenson from the band BlackHawk had the best definition of a true hit song. Van had been a recording artist on his own and had one big hit single. He said one day, "I wanna write a song I don't have to sing to anybody. I'll say the title and they'll already know it."

Usually I have to explain the title again, and the star who sang it, and then I sing a little...and give the era...and then sing a little more. And *then* people will say, "Oh, yeah, I sorta remember that one."

My friend Don Schlitz can say to a room full of strangers, "Hi, I'm Don Schlitz and I wrote 'The Gambler.'" Everybody applauds. Don actually made up the words, "know when to hold 'em, know when to fold 'em." I've heard that in movies and TV shows and political speeches a thousand times, which explains why I hate Don so much.

Country songwriters are deeply brain-impaired by the fact they are surrounded constantly by the C & W. It's just painfully obvi-ous. Consider this: I know a songwriter who kept a stack of pic-tures on his kitchen table. You'd go over, and they'd be there. Just photos of a big boom box. When asked, "Buddy, why the pictures of the radio?" he would delightfully tell ya, "Man, I took them pitchers at the exact moment George Strait was singing my song on the radio." The song *was* a big hit, and Buddy had confirmed this moment in musical history by taking a picture of the radio. Of course, he could have taken it yesterday and it would look *exactly* the same, but in Bud's country-ravaged mind, he could sense George was singing his song. See what I mean?

I paid the bills with radio and earned my "mailbox money" from songwriting. Some guys live on one hit. They get a single song through the "system," and it gets played and then goes into the giant cardboard box of forgotten records. No matter, it's their badge of honor for the rest of their lives.

I knew John Ims, who had two hits—one for Trisha Yearwood (her first) and one for Reba. I saw him while he was taking that glorious "hit songwriter" ride, and he told me, "Ger, I am moving to the Rockies. With my lifestyle, I can make enough now to last me for thirty years. Gonna take it easy." And he left. Couple of homers, and he's going to the showers. Good for him.

I know a gentle soul who was constantly at the bar I inhabited. Of course, *I* was there *all* the time, but I always thought, *He is here* all *the time*. It's like going to a country club and seeing the same golfers. Don't you people have homes? Bud (yes, another Buddy) was there drinking and telling stories and laughing. He was the sweetest man in the world. That afternoon, a producer friend of mine (Ron Chancey) said, "Come up to my office. I wanna play you something." I was pretty interested. Ron then proceeded to tell me, "I just paid off Bud's bar bill at Maude's" (a famous Music Row watering hole). "In return, he gave me his publishing share on this song." (I'll explain publishing sometime, but basically the publisher makes the same amount of money as the songwriter.)

Ron said, "Tell me what you think. Did I just blow a thousand dollars?" (I guess Bud had run up a good tab over a few weeks.)

Wow. A thousand bucks for some song some guy wrote that I didn't know. Pretty risky stuff.

Ron started the tape and a demo singer began, "Blame it all on my roots. I showed up in boots and ruined your black tie affair." For the price of a set of radials, Ron now owned half the publishing to "Friends in Low Places." I can't imagine the millions that song made. In many ways, it started a wave of new country artists led by a singer named Garth Brooks.

Nobody got ripped off. Nobody strong-armed nobody into that deal. Willie Nelson had sold the rights to "Crazy," the Patsy Cline masterpiece, for fifty dollars, so Bud actually got about the same, adjusted for inflation. It's just the way the town is—the game that is Music Row. Songs are like magic floating in the air and talked about and rumored and BANG! Hits are born, and lives are changed. Fortunes are made, and some guy walks in style up 16th Avenue.

You can, it's hoped, now see why some people get wacky from country music. I've known people who hit the jackpot and lost it all. One guy had an enormous hit and spent his first big check on a tricked-out Winnebago, left to explore America, and never came back. It's that wildcatting thing that does it to everyone.

It's sort of calmed down a bit nowadays. This is a factory town, with guys going to little song mills and hammering out a piece of art and hoping someone will like it. It's not a coincidence that Willie knew, early on, enough about songwriting to write "Crazy."

Songwriting is a mystery to a lot of people, including me. It can be joyful, and it can be a total slog. It's both magic and mundane. Songwriters are the same way. I've written with guys who have plopped down in the chair opposite me, fired up a doobie the size of an ear of corn, and then announced, "I'll be with ya in a minute."

I once wrote with a guy who never looked at me. He sat at the piano with his back to me for three hours playing what he called "Danny" chords (i.e., chords he was making up). He then suddenly stood and said, "This don't work for me today." And he walked out the door.

I once wrote with a tall, blonde babe who showed up at my office braless in a tank top with low-cut jeans that were tattooed on and a purple thong showing in the back. I didn't write anything like what I was thinking that day.

Songwriters also have their own schedules—not *your* schedule usually, but *a* schedule. To be honest, quite often sitting down in a room with somebody when it's beautiful outside is tough. You don't want to be there. They don't want to be there. You could be golfing or fishing, so it's sometimes painful. That's why songwriters jump at any excuse to be late or not show up. They also use the "check in" as a surrogate for the actual appointment time. If your songwriting appointment is for 10:30 A.M., they will *call* at 10:29 A.M. and say they are running a little late. They "checked in," so they get credit for being on time. Others you just plan on being an hour and a half late, and you show up accordingly. And others never show up at all. You wait, you pluck, you hum, you think, and, finally, you call, and they laugh and say, "Man, I'm in the Everglades. I can't write today!" As if to say, "You idiot, didn't you know I was going out of town to go bonefishing? How lame are you to bother me now?"

At one time or another, every songwriter has said, "I am gonna quit this stupid business." This means other people's lousy, crappy, tuneless melodies and words are being recorded and yours aren't.

Songwriters lie and smile and say, "I'd love to hear your new song." They really don't. It's either gonna be terrible or so good they get jealous. It's true. I'm that way. Everybody is that way.

Perhaps Layng Martine is the only songwriter in America who is truly happy for you when you get a song recorded. Layng wrote "Rub It In," which has been a hit record and used in commercials for years. He's a special person and probably under some medication to make him so nice. I appreciate a great song, I really do, but I don't want to hear it before *we* start writing *our* song together. That's like going on a date and the girl says, "Before we start, here's a picture of the hunk I went out with yesterday." Great. I want to go home now.

What keeps me from saying, "I'm gonna quit this stupid business" to nearly everyone I talk to is the response from my friend Wayland Holyfield. When I told him I was gonna quit, he just said, "You may already be out. They don't send letters, you know."

The greatest part of songwriting is having somebody look up across a table or a room and say something just brilliant. That gleam in their eye says, "I've got an idea that's amazeballs." It happens. And then you get folks who will say something so confusing or ridiculous you just sort of ignore it, and life goes on.

Then there are the comedy songwriters. (I learned early on *not* to do this 'cause it really drives some folks nutty.) In the middle of writing a heartbreaking love ballad, there's always the guy who sings a fake line that's funny and inappropriate. Usually you laugh and sometimes join in, but mostly you just try to get back to the business at hand.

Songwriters are also the gossip kings of the western world. *Any* excuse to not write and talk about other songs and other songwriters and how the music business is going to hell on a runaway train is always fair game. I have several friends I've met for a songwriting session and gabbed the entire morning away without writing one note of a song.

Some songwriters are *serious*. I'm talkin' stern nun/state trooper/librarian serious. They are poets and "there ain't no room for cuttin' up while we're writin'" serious.

Then there are the guys who used to fax lyrics (remember faxing?) and call and have an intern stand beside the fax machine to make sure nobody stole their genius out of the fax machine.

Where you write is also interesting. It's usually in a small office in an old house on Music Row—two streets just outside of downtown Nashville, filled with the ant-like writers who move from hill to hill, office to office, studio to studio, making the songs that part of the world sings.

There is a major publishing company that has a writer's room with no chairs, just an old, grungy couch and a broken piano. Then there are the rooms with coffee machines and snacks put out for the kings of melody waltzing in around 10:30 A.M.

I can't write if I can hear the duo in the next room also struggling to wrestle a song to the ground. A lot of these old houses have ductwork and heat registers in the floor so you can actually hear everybody in the building. One time we started at 10 A.M., and so did three or four other groups in the building. By 2 P.M., we were all writing basically the same song through the heating system.

I've never done it, but some writers do what's called "chasing the hillbillies," where a star/artist/singer takes writers on the road with them. You ride the road and the bus and hope to catch lightning in a bottle when the artist is not drinking from the bottle or playing "spin the bottle" with some "friends" he met at his last concert. It always sounded dreadful to me and, from what I hear, I'm right. One great "chaser" told me he rode in a bunk for six days, and when he got back to Nashville, all he had to show for it was a killer hangover and a misspelled tattoo that read "Born Too Loose."

Probably a thousand people have told me they'd like to do a radio show called "The Story Behind the Song." I did it when I started out 'cause every hit has a funny/sad/movie plot story for how that song was born.

And there are some good ones...maybe five in history. What you then get is, "Well, me and ol' Harley hooked up about ten that morning, and he had this idea, and I had this melody thing, and it sorta fell out." End of "The Story Behind the Song."

I also really love to hear people say, "I didn't write it. It came from God or Jesus or someplace other than me." That's fine, of course, but I think it's funny that rather than say, "Yep, I wrote that one. Good, huh?" they give God cowriting credit. I always want to ask if they send half the royalty check to one of the Lord's helpers. Maybe they do.

Guy Clark is one of the Texas songwriting greats. He's also a luthier. He told me that at a New Year's Eve party, and I thought, *Why would a man announce his religious affiliation while wearing a party hat?* Turns out that a luthier is a guy who makes his own guitars. Guy's theory is that most great songs are written by one person.

I know, I know. You can instantly name twenty-five great songwriting teams, but if you think about *all* songs, a lot of the truly great ones were from the mind of one solitary man. Or if it came from a "team," most of the song was written by one guy. That's why we know the McCartney songs from the Lennon songs. Cole Porter and Irving Berlin did it all by their little lonesome and that's why those songs are so distinctive.

Cowriting is just odd to begin with. Who wrote which part? Who gets the credit for what? Who gets the money for what? It's usually understood that if you cowrite, you split it in half or in thirds, etc. There are, however, famous stories of one particular guy who counted the words he'd contributed. *Counted the words.* He kept track during the session and then announced, "I wrote 54.5 percent of this song, and that's what I am claiming credit for." Of course, this is the same guy who handed out copies of his new album in the reception line at his own wedding, so go figure.

Some writers can hear what others can't. Particularly rhymes. They create a masterpiece of a rhyme with the words stove and horse. "Hey, sing it," they argue. "It works. I'm telling you, it's fine."

Others are more exacting. Top songwriter Gary Burr says, "If you want to be certain it rhymes, use the same word." Gary didn't do that—he's brilliant—but I hear songs all the time that do that.

I wrote several songs with Clint Black. Clint is funny and smart. He's also from the Planet Igmo. He has written some of my favorites and some I have no clue what he's talking about. That's Clint. If you get the chance, write with Clint. Do *not* play golf with Clint. He does not understand the concept of "picking up." When you are out of the hole, or when you're on your fifteenth whack at the little white pill on the same hole, Clint stays with it. If he's on his way to a record-breaking 19 on No. 4, he's gonna make his 19! He's the same way when writing. He's gonna stay with it no matter what.

My favorite Clint Black moment (and there are many) was when we wrote for one of his later albums. Clint lived across the field from my house. He and his fabulous wife, Lisa, were neighbors. When we met for dinner one night at a restaurant, I told her she looked much different in person than she did through a telescope at night. She kinda laughed.

But back to Clint. We wrote a song and he said he was gonna cut it for his album. One sunny day he called and said, "Wanna hear our hit?" Of course, I was thrilled, and damn right I wanna hear it. He drove the few feet to my driveway in his little black Porsche. I walked out and got into the passenger seat.

He then said, "I only have the track. I haven't put my vocals on it yet. But it goes like this." So he started the track and put his vocal to it "live and in person." It was fabulous, and I gave him a "bro" hug and said I'd see him later. When I got back inside my house, I told my wife about the song. She ooohed and ahhhed and then said, "By the way, did you realize to people driving by it looked like Clint Black was singing to you at the top of his lungs in a car in the driveway, and then you hugged?"

Songwriting as a career is painful, exhilarating, and hardly like any other. It's wildcatting. Punching a hole in the ground and hoping to strike oil. Everybody has a song in them. Most of the time, it's not anything anybody wants to hear. Buddy Killen, a great music publisher, told me, "In thirty-five years, I've only had one good song come in through the mail. I always listen, thinking and hoping it's gonna be great. It ain't never."

Songwriters, for the most part, live on hope. They dream and they take even the faintest of a hint of a connection to a "cut" as their comfort. Getting a cut is like a drug. My friend Bob DiPiero has written numerous No. 1 records, but it's always the "next one" that he really wants. Here's how songwriters really are:

Will Robinson is a great songwriter. We wrote one for Reba. Will wrote many hits for Alabama. He said he was standing in a hallway at a publishing house when the receptionist told him, "Tony Brown is on the line for you."

Now, Tony Brown has made hit after hit as a producer. Tony Brown played piano with Elvis. He produced Reba, George Strait, and Vince Gill. The list is astounding. Tony Brown recorded my (and Devon O'Day's) song for George Strait. It was called "The Big One." I was riding down West End Avenue when I heard a car honk, and Tony was in his Mercedes next to me. I rolled down the window and he shouted every songwriter's dream come true to me over the street noise, "HEY! GEORGE STRAIT IS GONNA CUT THE BIG ONE." Yes, I know. When you repeat that out loud, it sounds like George has gas, but it was still a heart-pounding pronouncement.

Back to Will Robinson. Danger, Will Robinson. This is how songwriters think. Will said, "Between the time I got to the phone and said hello and Tony answered, I imagined he was calling to tell me that he was producing an album of all my songs. George and Reba had selected ten of my songs for their new project, and he wanted to let me know." What Tony actually wanted was a translation of song lyrics into Portuguese, which, oddly enough, Will speaks. But we've all been through it. The rumor. The dream. The hope that somebody took one of my tunes.

A word about what I call "The Big Silence." The BS is the most painful part. This is where you send in a song for consideration. I've done it a thousand times. Multiply that by the thousands of songwriters, and you get the idea. You rarely get a call back. It's an understood part of the game, but it doesn't make it any easier.

Over time, the Silence gets louder and louder. It's with you all the time. "Any word on the song?" you ask the bartender or wife or whoever happens to be near. I don't know how to fix the system, but it seems that with technology that allows you to send a song with the push of a button, you could also post somewhere that your song is rejected. Although then you lose the hope of a song being recorded.

The hope doesn't really die until you're on iTunes listening to the singer's new album and you notice your song is not on the record. This is usually a good sign that it's not going to ever be on the record. I still sometimes hold out hope that there's been a drastic mistake and that somebody will fix the CD or iTunes, and the song will magically appear.

You get the Big Silence from friends and nonfriends alike. I happen to know a lot of people in the business who actually record the songs. They is de Stars. Some write back and some just don't say anything. They become part of the Big Silence, too. Martina McBride, who I truly love, once wrote a tortured note to me about how the song didn't work for her album. I felt her pain.

I have to understand, as every other tunesmith does, that nobody wants to tell somebody their kids are ugly. And trust me, songs are kids. *Oh, I still send songs to friends. After all, if you can't beg, gherm, arm-twist, or guilt a friend into recording a song, what are they friends for? What does hurt are publishers who ask you to send a few mp3s (songs) over for them to consider. The BS roars again.*

Let me conclude by saying definitively, without a doubt, and with no further discussion, that although I hate the Big Silence, I understand it. I'm now going to try to make that work when my wife wants to know my opinion of which shade of white I like for the kitchen cabinets (we'll discuss that later). I'll employ the BS to see if that gets me off the hook. How do you like my chances?

An engineer told a guy fixing the plumbing that one of *my* songs was on the list to be considered as a possibility to present to a guy who knew a secretary who worked for a manager's girlfriend. Yes, it's that easy.

You want to live on the 1,000 days of "maybe." You're in the "pile." So, what happens? You call to see if they got the song. Yes, we got the damn song and stop bothering us. In the world of Nashville, the Big Silence means no! If they are gonna record the song, if they like the song, if they are remotely interested, they call and let you know. If it's tossed like an old newspaper, they don't call. It was just a song and there are a thousand more to hear. *You* don't feel like that. *You* know *your* song is a hit.

But one word from anybody can kill it. Some casual doubtful word from the receptionist can cause people to drop a tune. Lewis Anderson told me he went to the Bahamas because Alan Jackson had recorded a song, and it was on his new album coming out. "It ain't final 'til it's vinyl" used to mean it's officially a cut. You made the deal. Lewis got a call while he was lounging on the beach as a newly minted moneyed maker-upper of hit tunes. He was told, "We're recalling all the 300,000–400,000 CDs we printed so far and are taking your song *off* the album to put on another. Sorry." That's ugly, ain't it? It wasn't personal against Lewis. Alan just had a song he liked better.

My daughter listens to songs for a living. She's the most beautiful A&R person who ever lived. She's also very tough. I'm trying to get an appointment with her soon.

She told me, however, "I learned watching you, Dad. I always take care to let people down as gracefully as possible because I have seen how it feels."

She has a lot of experience watching songwriters hear they didn't make the project. It hurts, but then moments later somebody calls and says, "Hey, man, I just got a call from the guy who washes [producer's name here]'s car, and he said he saw our CD in his player! I think we're in."

Showbiz Is Tough

YOU KNOW THE OLD JOKE: A man is walking behind a circus elephant, shoveling "fertilizer" for hours. A friend asks the guy, "Why don't you quit that job?"

Man replies, "What? And give up showbiz?"

Actually, showbiz usually quits you. A close pal of mine once said of Pam Tillis (the supernaturally talented daughter of Mel Tillis and hit singer in her own right), "Pam will never quit. She's an entertainer, and that's what she does. She'll be out there on some stage for the rest of her life" (singin', it's hoped, Don Schlitz's and my song, "The River and the Highway"). Roger Miller once said about a fellow singer's need to stay in the game, "He'd appear at the opening of a pack of cigarettes."

I don't think there's anything wrong with that. You're an entertainer, you get onstage somewhere. That's fine, although sometimes you gotta know when to get off. One of the great things about the *Grand Ole Opry* is that it provides a venue for the older performers. I haven't gone to the *Opry* much because of that. Sometimes it's painful to see some of these people struggle through a song. Others still have the stuff or have learned to keep it going with new tricks. Their voices might be gone, but they continue to deliver the entertainment goods.

While I'm on the subject of gone voices, how about voices that never were? I know he's one of the all-time great songwriters, but Kris Kristofferson cannot sing at all. He never could. It astounds me how we all overlooked that fact because he's so cool and charismatic. If he tried out for American Idol, *he'd be part of the joke "vocalists" they always show. I comb my hair and never look at the back of my head. I know there's an exposed area back there, but looking straight on from the front, it's fine. I totally ignore my "spot" and instead go with the "damn fine hairdo" scenario. We do the same thing with bad singers and funny-looking singers. If the song is good or the guy is cool-looking, we are willing to ignore the "bald spot" in the mirror.*

I also am puzzled why women go bonkers over a star that they wouldn't sit next to in a mall food court if he weren't rich and famous. Oh, there are some hunks out there, but there are also quite a few singin' sex symbols that don't keep George Clooney up at night. I'm just sayin'. . .

I keep rubbing my eyes wondering, "Am I not seeing what the screaming, panty-throwing women down front are seeing? What the hell?" He's five feet tall and has a face only a mother would cover with a bag. Yet his tour bus has so many women getting on and off that he's got a turnstile in the front. It's as if everybody says, "OK, we're all gonna pretend he looks like Brad Pitt." Even if the guy actually looks more like Icky Pit, women are crawling over broken beer bottles to get to him.

I'm not jealous. Good for him. Good for the babes. It's just so odd to me.

Kris Kristofferson is a totally cool-looking guy. I understand that. Even today, when he walks into a studio in that hat and long duster, with those eyes, he's a star. But he sings like a shovel on concrete.

The worst part of showbiz is seeing people almost get to the brass ring. They are on top for about five minutes and are then voted off the island. You won't know this name; I only knew the name thirty-five years ago. Snooky Lanson was a singing star in the late '40s and '50s. He was "on the TeeVee," as we say in Kentucky.

Snooky replaced Frank Sinatra on the show *Your Hit Parade*. They had a rotating list of singers who came out to sing the latest hits. This was back when the song was as much a star as the actual star was.

Come with me now to a small studio in a building on Murfreesboro Road in Nashville, where WKRN-TV (channel 2) still did some local programming in the mid-'70s. I walked in to do a show featuring musical guests and saw a stack of albums on the floor. Atop the heap was a worn copy of a recording by Snooky Lanson. I picked it up and said, "Snooky Lanson? I thought he was dead."

"Oh no, he ain't!" I heard someone say behind me. There, in living black-and-gray, was the Snookster himself. He happened to be on one of the low-budget local singing shows they cranked out during those days. I was shocked and embarrassed, to say the least.

He just laughed and said, "Don't give it a second thought. That's what most people think." He told me of some of the glory days: the national stardom, the grand TV productions and appearances with big bands—all in the past.

Snooky was now a Chrysler salesman at a local dealership. To make a living, he spent his days trying to slide customers into shiny new Imperials. He was just as dignified and warm as anyone could be. No bitterness. Me? I'd be somewhere in a shotgun shack in South Dakota writing my manifesto of bitter.

Snooky knew sometimes showbiz quits you. So did Barbara Fairchild. She had one giant hit back in '72 called "The Teddy Bear Song" and a couple of others that did very well. She was one of those gentle souls that you just loved to see coming. I lost touch with her, and her career fell on hard times.

One afternoon for lunch, I was in one of those "meat-and-threes" that permeated the Nashville dining scene in the '80s. Our waitress turned out to be none other than Barbara Fairchild. I could hardly stand to sit there and watch the people I was with ask her for some more sweet tea. I couldn't tell if she was feeling like I was or not. She had a lot of pride, not a hint of bitter. Me? *Manifesto of Hatred for Showbiz, Part Two.*

Doug Stone had a slew of hits. I'm not sure how many hits are in a slew, but it's a bunch. Doug has been in and out of showbiz—and in and out of trouble—for quite awhile. I like him a lot. I also think Doug is listening to a station other than the one the rest of us are listening to.

In addition to his recording career, Doug also starred in one of the all-time cinematic classics, *Gordy*, featuring "The Talking Pig That Made It Big." I think there was a reason they put Doug in a movie with a talking porkchop. I believe Doug could actually hear and understand what the pig was saying.

The last time I saw Doug, he was facing me, with microphones in front of us, while we were on the radio together. Doug laughed that maniacal cackle of his and returned to his main interest in our conversation—a car he wanted to sell. He wasn't there to talk about his career, his records, or his appearances. Doug had an old car that had broken down on an off-ramp somewhere, and he was ready to deal. I asked about how things were going for him, and he replied, "OK, but I'm tellin' ya, this car is a creampuff. Great mileage and real fake leather seats." Then he gave his phone number in case somebody wanted the Stonemobile for their very own.

I don't know if Doug knows that showbiz quit him or not.

Remember Charly McClain? I didn't think so. She was simply gorgeous—a stunner who could sing. She was one of those who I think of as part of "feeding the monster"—the music machine that *must* have acts to stuff into the pipeline to keep everyone occupied:

the promotion people, the production people, the record people, the road people, the songwriters, and the managers...it goes on and on.

Artists such as Charly are the pectin in the pie—part of the middle that holds the whole thing together. They make a good living and have fans. They do interviews and take pictures and sign autographs. They have fan clubs and a bus, or, in some cases, a van. They ride the country's highways and set up their speakers, plug in, and sing for the folks. God bless 'em. Charly was like that. I vaguely remember her hits such as "Who's Cheatin' Who"—a duet with Mickey Gilley, and then one day, she was gone.

What a funny machine Music Row is. You go in one end and come out the other, sometimes rich, sometimes broke...and then you're gone. Off to those endless nights of smaller clubs and county fairs. Sometimes, you get married or start selling phones in Texas. But it's all good. I hope it was a fun ride for Charly. I always looked forward to seeing her, even if she never said a word.

Mickey Gilley was Jerry Lee Lewis' cousin. He was a piano-playing original, just like ol' Jerry Lee. At a Playboy Records party, I once saw Mr. Lewis kick a beautiful, brand-new Yahama grand piano to pieces. He wasn't nicknamed the "Killer" for nothing.

Mickey was a gentleman. He recorded some slightly rockin' country singles and made a fine living. He had a gold-and-diamond ring that put the Super Bowl ring to shame. It was so big, it had a license plate. He was the namesake for the Gilley's nightclub in Texas. That was the inspiration for the film Urban Cowboy *about the "World's Largest Honky-Tonk." Some folks made a fortune just from that soundtrack.*

What a guy Mickey was. I never saw him not smiling. Except maybe when his cousin, the preacher Jimmy Swaggart, got caught layin' on top of women he wasn't married to at the time.

Jamey Johnson is an old-school singer/songwriter. He wrote a new classic a few years ago called "In Color." He used to be clean-cut and fairly normal-looking. Now he looks like a yeti. I don't think he takes a bath; he gets sprayed with flea powder. He called me one day and said, "Dude, I need some advice. They're passin' me around like a joint at Willie's barbeque. Meet me for lunch because I don't know anything about what to say on the radio."

We phone-tagged and texted for weeks to set up a time when I could give him the lowdown on a "radio promo tour." That's when an artist trudges from city to city and gets asked the same ten questions for weeks on end. It's a horrible way to make a living with late-night dinners and early-morning interviews—all based on hope.

Jamey was to meet me at 11:30 A.M. at Bricktop's. By 1 P.M., I sorta thought he wasn't coming. Now, I've written with Jamey and know the drill. He's a late person; I'm not. He gets up late, and he shows up late. My phone finally rang at 2 P.M. "Wingnut?" (He calls me Wingnut.) "I ain't gonna make it. I'm somewhere in Arkansas without my pants or my phone, and I'm not sure who I'm with. I'm really sorry, but let's reschedule 'cause I ain't gonna make it."

I don't think Jamey is gonna make it... to lunch or in show bidness. You have to show up to have people pay you money for singing. Ask George Jones about how being a "no show" affects your concert bookings. I know a lot of singers who have their own time. That's great for them, but bad for everybody else. If you're really, really big and talented, folks will put up with it. If you're on the edge, they'll drop you like a dirty shirt.

Last time I saw Jamey was on television singing "Roll Me Up and Smoke Me When I Die." He was standing beside Willie Nelson. I imagine Willie is about 90 percent cannabis at this point. He's eighty. He gets to do what he wants because he's Willie F-ing Nelson! Jamey Johnson is not Willie Nelson.

Willie shows up, by the way.

I knew a songwriter from England who lived in Nashville for awhile. Like so many others, he's drifted off into the ether. I only remember he was always late and struggled with American slang.

He told me that one afternoon he had taken his family to Krystal for lunch for tiny square hamburgers. White Castle's are better, but who am I to quibble? But White Castle's are vastly superior. I went there after my wedding reception, if that's any indication.

England and his family stood at the counter and chatted awhile with the Southern teenaged girl fixin' their Krystals. One of those "Y'all ain't from around here, are ya?" conversations. "Wow! England is way over there," she told them, as if they didn't know London was way over there. Then, as they gathered their bags and walked away, she said, "Hey, y'all come back now, ya hear?" So they turned and went back. She looked at them and said, "Did you need something?"

"No," the puzzled Brit replied. "You just said you all come back now. So here we are." I don't think he ever learned how to cope with Americans—especially Southern Americans.

Other stars learn how to roll with the punches life throws at ya. Lee Greenwood became "Mr. God Bless the USA." And rightfully so—he wrote it. He made it a hit. The amazing thing about that song is that Lee wrote it during a downtime to promote patriotism and pay tribute to our troops. At the time, there really weren't any conflicts of the size that make us all realize how lucky we are that brave men and women keep their eyes on the horizon.

I met Lee the very first day he was in Nashville. He was a singer, piano player, sax player, and songwriter. I remember hearing the first mix of the song. It killed me. I also wondered how it would do on the radio during those "peaceful" days. It became a smash, as did many other Greenwood hits.

Lee was a Vegas entertainer. He went to Fan Fair and wore a U.S. flag leather jacket and sang a James Brown song. And he'll kill me for this, but he wore what looked like a dead beaver on his head. Hey, it happens to all us guys. It gets a little thin up top, and you sometimes gotta improvise. And Lee went all the way, from wisps to a full-blown pelt. The pelt didn't last long, thank God, unlike the self-described "helmet head" of Bobby Goldsboro.

Bobby sang "Little Things," "Watching Scotty Grow," and many more. He's also a good artist, as in a guy who puts paint on a canvas. He's also a good artist, as in a guy who puts music on tape. Bobby's wig-hat was a wonder of the world. He laughed about it, and that sort of made it all right.

On a golf green on a particularly windy day, Bobby's hairpiece decided to become airborne. It didn't get away because of a sophisticated system of tape and glue, but it sure tried. He stood right in front of me as his toup prepared for liftoff. His entire helmet lifted two or three inches, and I was fairly sure he'd be swept away with it. But the wind subsided, his hair eased back down like a chopper onto a rice paddy, and it was over. "Wow, that was a close one," he remarked. I didn't say a word. I don't know if he was referring to losing his helmet or me almost seeing that he wore a helmet hairpiece.

I loved Bobby's records with the exception of "Me Japanese Boy I Love You," which is much more embarrassing than a lid made of yak hair.

I guess singers go searching for the spotlight. If there's an audience, there's gotta be a way a singer can find it. If, however, you notice a distinct echo because there's nobody in the seats, quit. I've had some guys tell me they want to die onstage. (I've done it many times, but that's a different dying.) Maybe going out performing behind chicken wire, with a couple of cowboys and girls shuffling around while you sing, ain't a bad way to go. It's the ultimate way to quit showbiz before it quits you.

Don Light, Mark Collie, and Jimmy Buffett

DON LIGHT WAS A MANAGER, and his firm, the Don Light Agency, helped the careers of several artists. I can still see Don, slightly bent over, with his silver hair, walking into a room and taking a Heineken out of his ever-present sport coat.

I met Don through his brother, Joe. Joe Light and I once tried to do a TV pilot. Joe rented some god-awful studio and hired a camera guy, and we tried to make history on television. It was gonna be a talk show, and Don persuaded Faron Young to be our "special" guest, along with a couple of other folks nobody had ever heard of, to round out this fabulous production.

A major star in the '50s through the late '70s, Faron Young was once known as the "Hillbilly Heartthrob." One of his biggest hits, "Hello Walls," which was written by Willie and was No. 1 for *nine* weeks, was one of my mom's all-time favorites. Faron had racked up a lot of hits next to his name before he died tragically in 1996.

He had been despondent and committed suicide. But while he was with us, he was one of the funniest, most vibrant entertainers that country music ever had.

The opening guest was an old songwriter named Preacher Bobby. I'd never heard of him or his songs, but I welcomed him like he was in the Hall of Fame. Preacher Bobby only wanted to announce one thing. He wanted the world to know he'd sell all of his songs for fifty dollars apiece. I was shocked and asked him, "Preacher, don't you realize how much money you could be losing?" He shot back, "Sonny, you don't know how many songs I got. I got 10,000! That's a lotta money." His logic stopped me cold.

Our second guest, Faron Young, once known as the "Hillbilly Heartthrob" and later as "The Young Sheriff," was now sitting on our rented couch in a warehouse in East Nashville, under lights barely bright enough to make out our faces and one camera. The director/pizza-delivery guy shouted, "OK, we're recording!" and I turned to interview Faron. There is no record of this magnificent moment in showbiz history because the camera guy didn't know how to actually turn the camera *on*. I do remember, however, in spite of all the lame conditions and my amateurish hosting and the nonexistent pay, that Faron Young was a star. He didn't know the camera wasn't on, I didn't know it, and neither did the dumbass running the camera, but we did a show. Great stories, laughter, and a little a cappella singing, and I was on top of the world.

After that, I didn't see Faron much, nor Joe or the camera guy, but I did see Don Light and told him how wonderful and generous Faron Young had been. Don agreed and said perhaps I should write a tune with his newest singer, Mark Collie. Since Don was Jimmy Buffett's first manager, I made a date with Mark.

Don knew a star when he saw one. Mark and I wrote two of his singles, "She's Never Comin' Back" and "Three Words, Two Hearts, One Night." As Mark often says to me, "We were the kings of the middle of the charts." Both singles zoomed to the upper twenties and died. Mark went on to have several hits, and last I heard, he was touring a bit and doing some great acting.

He should have gotten the Johnny Cash part in *Walk The Line* instead of that Joaquin Phoenix dude. Mark *was* Johnny Cash. But that's Hollywood, of course.

Speaking of Jimmy Buffett, which we kinda were, here's my Jimmy Buffett story:

I knew Jimmy a bit from Nashville. I'd run into him from time to time at Tavern on the Row and late-night establishments. Jimmy couldn't pick me out of a lineup, but I did have many a beer with him. Buffet is a moneymaking machine and one of the all-time good guys.

So, a very rich Texas friend of mine, Steve Hicks, decided to throw himself a fiftieth birthday party to end all birthday parties. Apparently, they do that in Texas a lot. I owe most of my career and my house to Steve. He's a genius. And he spends a lot on his birthday parties. I can't wait for the next one.

Steve and his wife, Donna, rented a cruise ship for a week and invited all his pals. There were about forty couples on this massive ship built to carry 400 people. It was beyond belief. We all got up for breakfast in the morning and voted for which island we wanted to see. At night on each stop, we had a beach party. Clint Black was onstage on the ship. Asleep at the Wheel played the next night. The Beach Boys met us for another night. It was really something.

The fourth day, we stopped for lunch on St. Bart's. If you've never been there, it's like Rodeo Drive with sand. They only have designer birds flying around, and the garbage men wear Ralph Lauren. You get the idea. Posh.

We were having Champagne and lunch at some wonderful restaurant right on the water when, off in the distance, I heard, "Eeeeeeeeeeeeeeeeeee." I could barely make out a small boat with one passenger. "Eeeeeeeeeeeeeeeeeee," the tiny motor sang out as the figure got closer. Holy shit, it's Jimmy Buffet!

He pulled up on the beach and got out of the boat with a guitar. Jimmy has a house on St. Bart's. People, you gotta sell a *lot* of margaritas to buy a house on St. Bart's. Jimmy walked up to a microphone that was wobbling on the sand and said, "Folks, I'm your lunchtime entertainment." Now, I happen to have a rough idea of what Steve paid the Leader of the Parrot Heads per song. You could buy a small car for every single performance. Let's just say it was worth it. Jimmy reeled off ten or twelve of his greatest singing moments. *"Wastin' away again in..."* I was calculating he was in six figures for the gig by now. He led us all in a "Happy Birthday, Steve." It was magic.

Then Jimmy B. said one of my favorite lines ever. "Steve, I know this has been a dream of yours for a long time. And believe me, it's been a dream of mine, too." Mr. Buffet hopped back in his little skiff and pushed into the blue waters of St. Bart's a whole lot richer.

Eeeeeeeeeeeeeeeeeeeeeeeeeeeeeeeeeeeee.

Trombones

AS LONG AS WE'RE TALKING about music, I thought I'd take a second to pass along vital, life-saving knowledge to the kids out there who might be thinking of choosing an instrument. It is important to remember the old adage, "You are what you toot." Or pluck or bang or squeeze. (The last is to warn anyone thinking of taking up bagpipes for the high school marching band.) In my opinion, this choice can determine the rest of your high school career; your entire reputation and safety may depend on it. Let me explain.

For some strange, unknown reason, when I entered the eighth grade and began discovering myself, I decided to join the high school band. I was really into sports, and the two usually don't mix. My saving grace was delivered because our high school didn't have a football team. Sad to say, as our band wasn't required to show up for games because the pigskin was not part of our athletic program, we actually loaded up the band bus and played for *another school's games*. For an ever-stranger, more unknown reason, I decided to take up the trombone.

Please listen and learn. There is no surer way to get yourself assigned to the Dork Brigade than by playing the trombone. It's really just a notch away from making music on plumbing. It is perhaps the unsexiest instrument in the world.

It took me nearly four years to escape to bands and lead singing and guitar and keyboards because I spent most of high school carrying a huge trombone case. This is just like asking people to kick you. The trombone sounds like a wounded moose. It's really only useful for a couple of stirring patriotic marches and/or stripper music—or to make that wah-wah-waaaah sound when a joke falls flat.

At the time, I never really considered that no man in history ever got chicks playing the trombone. I hear that, in his day, Mozart got the girls by tinkling out a couple of sonatas or a concerto. Every skinny dude who ever carried a Stratocaster knows sooner or later a girl is gonna fall for him because he plays guitar. I think even the bass drummer translated his bang-bang-bang into something more romantic. Artie Shaw played the clarinet, for God's sake, and as seemingly nonsexy as that is, he married Ava Gardner. The licorice stick got Artie laid by Ava.

You are, however, what you toot. Trombones and babes? Nada. Nothing. Zilch. As in *no action* for the seventy-six idiots in history and song who chose, in a moment of delirium, to play something brass that looks like it belongs under the hot water heater.

The single incident of any kind of attraction during my trombonist career was using the slide to poke Donna Stahl in the behind while performing a rousing version of "When the Saints Go Marching In" during band practice.

Walking the halls of high school as a freshman is difficult enough without carrying a large, gray, bulky, dorky, stupid, bothersome cardboard case. Everybody knows by the shape that a trombone is inside.

Quick! Name a marching song that helped any guy get lucky. "Oh," she sighed breathlessly, "when he plays 'Stars and Stripes

Forever,' I just melt. He's so sexy blasting some Sousa when we park late at night under the stars."

People, that never happened, and it never will.

I saw President Obama giving a speech on CNN in front of a bridge in Cincinnati. He was plugging one of his shovel-ready programs and was cheerfully pointing out how this bridge was falling apart. Soon, thousands would plunge to their death into the frozen Ohio River unless we gave him another billion or so. I stood on that bridge the night it opened, which explains why *I* am now falling apart.

It was twenty-five degrees out, and my high school band was "lucky" enough to be chosen to play during the celebration. (I always felt our bandleader had lost a bet.) We stood for several hours in the thirty-mile-an-hour Canadian wind to play one song, ready with our instruments prepared for the downbeat. I held the metal mouthpiece to my lips prepared to blast into musical history.

The downbeat came. We bleated and honked our way through God-knows-what song 'til, mercifully, it was over. The moment of celebration was complete. And we were frozen.

I prepared to pull my trombone from my mouth. If you've seen the film *A Christmas Story*, you know what comes next. You stick your tongue on a lamppost in icy weather, you got trouble. You play trombone below thirty-two degrees, you spend the next month with a raw, red, bleeding circle around your mouth.

Kids, just say NO. Take up the triangle or get a blue corduroy jacket and become a Future Farmer. No mas el trombono.

There is a reason you never hear trombones in church. It's Satan's favorite instrument.

Sleep, Gretchen,
and Charley Pride

I HAVEN'T REALLY SLEPT since Jimmy Carter was president. (I miss Billy Carter, by the way.) I have sleep apnea. Everybody I know has sleep apnea or sleeping problems. My problem was that when I could have been sleeping, I was up getting ready to work—every morning around 3:40 A.M. for thirty years. This is almost two hours before the chickens. I don't know why chickens are known to get up so early, but they'd be racked out when I'd get up.

I had an early job, just like a lot of people. I loved it once I was *at* work. I can also tell you *nothing* good happens at three or four in the morning. The highways are filled with nutty drivers and people coming back from having too much fun. I got pulled over by the cops quite a bit because normal people aren't out doing things at that godforsaken hour.

Sleep is a good thing and, overall, I haven't had much. So I went to a sleep clinic. A sleep clinic is where they attach electrodes and wires to your head and body and watch you sleep. You don't sleep normally when you have electrodes and wires stuck to your body and your head. And you have to have all the electrodes and wires removed if you gotta whiz. Then they hook you back up and tell you to have a good night's sleep. The next morning they tell you, "You have sleeping problems."

Amazingly, it turns out it's difficult to get any z's hooked up like a lab rat to some sleep gizmo. But they told me I needed to get a CPAP machine. So I got one. It's to help you sleep and works just fine if you don't mind sleeping with a vacuum cleaner on your face. I use it part of the time, and the rest of the time I think about jokes and world peace and lingerie models.

Most of the recording artists I know don't get enough sleep. I don't want to get into "life on the road," which is one of the most overdiscussed and stunningly redundant topics in conversation history. However, I will say that I've talked to my share of singin' stars who stand in front of a microphone and need a CPAP or something.

Gretchen Wilson is a fabulous chick. She is one hell-raising, singin' sumbitch. I love her. Gretchen was scheduled to appear on my show bright and chipper in the morning to discuss something or other. When Gretchen showed up, she announced she'd just spent the previous evening and most of the night "hangin' out with Kid Rock."

Gretchen was slightly green. You know the look—that "no sudden moves" look. Overserved. Have to get better to die. Just before we were about to start yakkin' (a term that has two meanings), she announced she'd be right back. She dashed from the studio. I felt sorry for her, but what a trooper. My producer told me later he could hear someone in the ladies room yakking 'til it sounded like her shoes were gonna come up.

Did Gretchen Wilson bail on the interview? No! Was Gretchen Wilson actually wishing to heaven that she could go lie down with an ice bag on her head? Yes! But she got through it. I meant to send her a lifetime supply of Alka-Seltzer afterward, but I didn't. It hadn't even been necessary for her to be on the radio that morning, but she was lovely and funny and pure Gretchen. I've had many worse interviews with well-rested, sober hillbillies, which reminds me of Charley Pride.

He is a star of the *Grand Ole Opry*, a Hall of Famer, and has made some wonderful records. As the Statler Brothers once said, "Get a gimmick like Charley Pride." Charley is an African American from Sledge, Mississippi.

Charley is also very cheap. We used to play golf together, and after an errant shot, he would look for a ball for two hours 'cause "that was an almost new ball I bought just a couple of years ago." You need a shave by the time you finish playing golf with Charley Pride.

Charley sang "Kiss an Angel Good Morning," and everybody in the world loves him. He's just a great guy. *However*, if you happen to be hosting a live, one-hour Sunday-night show across America, make sure you don't plan on filling the hour with any of Charley's history. I know; I did it.

The problem is that Charley is bored with answering the same old questions. I also get bored asking them, but if you're live on the air and introducing a legendary singer to a new generation, you gotta cover a little history.

When the guest doesn't want to talk, an hour stretches to eternity. You know the ticking stopwatch on *60 Minutes*? If the guest is monosyllabic, the clock sounds like this: Tick. Tick. Tick. Tick. It's flop-sweat city.

I asked Sir Charley about life in Sledge. He said, "That's in my resume."

"Charley, you played a lotta baseball."

"That's in my resume."

"I know you worked with Chet Atkins."

"That's in my resume."

Can you sense the exciting direction of this nationwide gab-fest? I got through the unending hour by asking Charley about his favorite golf balls. Because he still has them all, he chirped on and on about great Top-Flites he had known and missing a putt and losing a quarter bet. I just remember being in the weeds with Charley Pride for an eternity.

Then there's Mary Chapin Carpenter, probably the most intelligent artist to ever wander the streets of Music City. I know for certain she was doing calculus or pondering Greek literature *while* she was singing. We've had a long and wonderful friendship. For many years, we've exchanged back and forth at various birthdays and award events a velvet painting of a bullfighter. I think I gave it to her first, she regifted it to me, and so on. I'm not sure who has it now.

Chapin could have also been a great monk. She's not Ms. Yakety-Yak. I've seen a lot more excitement on a hostage tape. Let's face it, people, she's quiet.

Chapin has had a lot of great songs and made many hit records. I also know she nearly had a nervous breakdown because her record company *made* her record with Joe Diffie. Why? I don't know, but for some reason it didn't fit into her career plans. I can't remember the record. Joe probably doesn't remember the record.

In conclusion, I have some helpful sleep tips. These time-tested and easy-to-follow methods of dropping off to SnoozeTown will help if you're sleep-deprived.

1. Take an overnight flight to Milan from Nashville. Try to arrive about 8 A.M. at your hotel in Italy. Make certain your room won't be ready for five or six hours. Then just do as Allyson and I did. Lie down by the pool on those warm deck chairs for a quick nap. You'll wake up refreshed and peppy around sundown. You'll still be wearing your street shoes and a jacket. Your wife will have her purse clutched to her

chest. Italian tourists will be standing over you asking, in Italian, if you are dead.

2. Have two glasses of Champagne before going into the theater in London. London isn't as air-conditioned as America. The theaters are just below baby chick incubator temperature. Settle into your $250 seats. As the orchestra strikes the first note of the overture you've waited to hear, you'll drop off like a baby in a rocking chair. I've done this about ten times. I even once slept all the way through *Stomp*—the one where they bang on garbage cans for two hours.

3. If all else fails and you just can't get to sleep, do what Burl Ives did. Burl was one of America's greatest actors. *Cat on a Hot Tin Roof* and *East of Eden* made him a star. He also sang one of the most popular Christmas songs of all time. "Holly Jolly Christmas" still makes me feel full of the holiday spirit.

I think Burl was about 100 when he was on my *Saturday Night House Party,* a middling effort I hosted for several years to rev up radio on a Saturday evening. I had Burl on as a guest, on the phone from Los Angeles. I could hear his wife prompting him about my name and what he was plugging. We were ready.

I did quite a lovely and glowing introduction of Burl for the audience. I mentioned the movies and the writing and the singing. I said, "Ladies and gentlemen, say hello to Burl Ives."

Ten seconds of silence were followed by one of those snorts you give when you're so asleep you forget to breathe. You wanna get to sleep? Listen to me on the radio.

Ol' Burl had no sleep problems at all.

QUIZZICLE #6

Who actually said this to me: "I ain't scared. I once made love in a canoe standing up"?

A) Trace Adkins

B) Betty White

C) Carrie Underwood

Why Don't We Do It in the Road?

I WORKED, AND I USE that term loosely, for a couple of years on the biggest country station in Los Angeles. It was tough, a real slog. I won't go into detail, but some of the folks I worked with were great, and some were a royal pain. It was always fun, however, seeing the stars out buying groceries and having their teeth fixed. In Nashville, you are likely to see Keith Urban driving through Fatburger or Martina McBride buying asparagus at Kroger's. Betty White is one of the national treasures I saw several times in L.A. She was and still is a huge animal lover. Our little peezers who live with us, Lucy and Desi, are part of the family. Betty always turned up at any event to help a little stray.

I agreed to do my show live from the Palamino, one of the few "country" venues in L.A. It shut down a few years ago, but at one time, it was *the* place for up-and-coming country acts to visit. So, here I stood *behind* the bar at the Palamino at five forty-five in the morning. It was obviously a bar and smelled like it. I saw a little figure making her way toward the bar through the tables full of upturned chairs. She hopped up on a bar stool and grinned at everybody. It was Betty White.

All those TV shows, games, series, movies, interviews, and appearances sat on that little bar stool. We might raise a few bucks for the Adopt-a-Pet Foundation. She absolutely glowed. I handed her a microphone and said, "We're going live in a few seconds, are you scared?" Her reply was hilarious; it was vintage Betty White, and wasn't for anybody but me. As she said during the show, "I love dogs because they are just as excited to see you coming back from getting the paper as they are when you come back from Europe."

I jump up and down whenever I see Betty White.

The Woods and the Sticks

I LOVE THE WOODS. Heck, I grew up in the woods. OK, technically, I grew up in the sticks. The difference is that the woods are where chipmunks hop and frolic. You can smell honeysuckle and jasmine in the air. Soft modern jazz plays in the woods. Snow falls gently in the woods. The rain caresses the lovely green canopy of the woods. It's what you see in Disney films. Rabbits kiss and fawns nuzzle while bluebirds sing overhead.

The sticks are the rednecks of woods. The sticks are great but usually populated with guys pointing guns while takin' a chaw of tobacco. The sticks smell faintly of old socks. Nothing good happens in the sticks. That thing from *Alien* won't go into the sticks by himself.

You get slightly lost in the woods. In the sticks, you step into an old well or a huntin' trap. If the sticks were people, they would be that guy who catches turtles with his bare hands. The sticks have that same grin. Wild hogs come flying out at ya in the sticks. You never hear banjo music in the woods. Quite often while crashing through the sticks, you can hear the faint sound of *Deliverance*. Ba-da-BUM-Bah-BUM.

Here is the main difference between the woods and the sticks: in the woods, a young girl dressed in an L.L. Bean outfit, wearing a ponytail and ball cap, walks hand in hand with a guy wearing chinos and a white shirt. They pause at a stream. They can walk gazing into each other's eyes for miles and meander past a pond with lilies. In the background, you can hear "Wind Beneath My Wings." The woods are where you picnic. The woods are nature's theme park. Mary Poppins has a summer house here.

When you enter the sticks, on the other hand, you are immediately, almost magically, covered in burrs—those things that stick on you like Velcro that you can't pull off your clothes. Ticks, which sit waiting patiently like people waiting on the five o'clock bus, find places on your body you've never seen. Chiggers, God's revenge on the sticks, begin their work. Chiggers have something in their jaws that can cause misery for weeks. Thorns the size of ten-penny nails reach out at you and draw first blood, or whatever's left after the ticks and chiggers have done their work. Poison ivy grows like kudzu, and kudzu grows like kudzu. It's a scientific fact that nearly all of Alabama is covered in kudzu. If you fly over Alabama, it looks like green shag carpeting was installed overnight.

It usually starts raining when you are in the sticks. Actually, it starts *pouring*—what they call a real "frog choker." I've been in the sticks and actually heard frogs choking. It's not pretty.

The usual trip in the sticks, for whatever purpose—hiking, hunting, or looking for Sasquatch—begins at the end of a country road. Off the country road is a gravel road. The gravel road leads to a dirt road. The dirt road leads to a path. The path then leads to the sticks. You hear a banjo strum. Another frog chokes. You are now 100 miles from the nearest Stuckey's. Your phone doesn't work. You hear Ned Beatty scream somewhere in the distance. There is nothing now...nothing but the fierce wilderness of the sticks surrounding you like Indians on Custer.

You wander aimlessly through blackberry brambles and poke sallet. Civilization is just a rumor. You crash and turn and search for even the most remote clearing. Stumbling forward into the green, itchy oblivion, you are now officially classified as a missing person. No one has ever been here. Not Lewis. Not Clark. Not even an Indian. This is untouched land. Then, as you feel the overwhelming remoteness rise up from the kudzu, you see it.

A stove. Probably something from Sears. Not an ancient, woodburning wonder, but a stove like you saw in your Aunt Velma's kitchen last Thanksgiving. Somebody carried a *stove* into the heart of darkness and dumped it there, along with some bald tires and a half-filled garbage bag of drywall.

No, you are not in the woods, you are in the sticks. As man asks, "Is there life on Mars?" and as we ponder the building of the pyramids and formations of crop circles, why has no one solved the mystery of the stove in the sticks? (Where is Stephen King when we need him?) The truth is that it's why country people go to the sticks. When you hear them announce they're going hunting, they are really not after squirrels or wild turkey; they are really hoping to find another Kenmore. And if they are lucky and go far enough, a fridge.

My agent, Frank, asked me, "What does this have to do with country music?" It has *everything* to do with country music, although you wouldn't know it if I didn't explain as follows:

All the artists in the Country & Western world fall into one of those two categories. Jason Aldean, Gretchen Wilson, and Brantley Gilbert are from the sticks. Keith Urban, Ronnie Dunn, and Carrie Underwood are from the woods. One is not any better than the other, just different.

Do not make the mistake of noticing "sticks" rhymes with "hicks." Just because somebody is really, really country doesn't mean they ain't smart. Conversely (I love saying that), the more sophisticated-looking, "woodsy" type could easily be a hidden dullard. The difference is that one of them might collect beaver pelts and the other has a house filled with Louis XIV antiques.

I made that mistake early on by insinuating to Conway Twitty that he probably didn't know what I was talking about. Conway, to be honest, probably wouldn't have done all that well on *Jeopardy*, but he knew what was going on. He shot back, "Son, you know we get CNN at our house just like you do." It was a little lesson. Just because someone is standing in front of you in tiny running shorts, a skin-tight T-shirt, and a polyester ball cap perched on his head doesn't mean he don't know *some* things. After all, Mr. Twitty had recorded some of the most "woods"-like songs in country history: "Love to Lay You Down," "That's My Job," and "You've Never Been This Far Before." I never mentioned to him that he also recorded "You're the Reason Our Kids Are Ugly" with Loretta Lynn. That song is from the sticks. I hope, Frank, you now understand.

Waylon Jennings

WAYLON JENNINGS WAS AN OUTLAW. I knew Waylon. He was Lonesome, On'ry & Mean, as one of his albums was titled. He took country to CBGB's in New York City and flattened them. He had quite a life story that's been told several times, but now I get to tell my Waylon story.

First of all, he was hilarious. He was kind and intelligent and very friendly, but most of all, to me, he was a total stitch. He didn't care one gnat's ass what anybody thought of what he said. You had to be prepared for an answer if you asked his opinion. He also held court on a variety of other subjects that floated through his mind, and it was always a hoot.

Ding! Ding! Ding! Learning moment alert!

It was Ol' Hoss (a name my father had also called me) who taught me to stop worrying about others' opinions of me and just have fun and live it up. He also had a way of saying things that summed up the situation like no one else could.

John Lennon liked Waylon, and I always pestered Waylon about their relationship because I am a Beatles fan. Waylon was in the

Crickets with Buddy Holly. John Lennon named his band the Beatles because he loved the Crickets so much—there's a lot of stuff going on there.

On the air, I once asked Waylon what in the world John Lennon saw in Yoko Ono. She's an intelligent, artistic person, but I never felt *Vogue* was gonna chase her down for a cover shoot. We were "live" and Waylon didn't quite know how to answer my question as truthfully as he usually did. What he said was, "Have you ever had a horse eat corn out of your hand?" I paused for a second to figure that one out. He just smiled at me and raised his eyebrows like, "Come on, dude, he's a guy. Do the math." I will let you figure it out, but I always thought that was the best answer you can say publically without actually spelling it out. If you can't figure it out, please call me.

I was also one of the three people to play golf with Waylon the single time he played golf in his life. He was living in Nashville, wasn't touring or appearing as much, and thought perhaps golf would be fun. I should have told him the truth up front. He'd had open-heart surgery and complained about it constantly and how he needed to "get out somewhere." It was me, Tony Joe White ("Polk Salad Annie" soul-singing Southern white boy), music publisher/all-around character Bob Beckham, and Waylon.

We got to the golf course and there, standing in the middle of the country club golf pro shop, was Waylon Damn Jennings in all his leathery glory—black T-shirt, leather vest, black jeans, and boots—not exactly up to the usual country club dress code.

In that familiar voice of his, he barked, "These sissies told me I can't play unless I have the right outfit. Who gives a cowfart about how you look playing golf?"

Beckham took him aside and said, "Calm down, I'll buy you some clothes." He then proceeded to pick out the single ugliest horizontal striped red-and-white polo shirt in the store.

Waylon pronounced, "The jeans stay, the boots stay, and I'll wear this shirt, and I'm gonna look like a damn barber pole."

It took a few minutes to calm everyone down. It was *Waylon Jennings*, for cryin' out loud, and the clothes police sort of looked the other way as we strode toward the first tee.

Once there, Tony Joe pulled out a box of pink balls and explained to Waylon, "These are the latest balls. All the pros use them, and I wanted you to look good."

Waylon eyed them suspiciously and said, "Son, I've got balls of my own, and if you are screwing with me I'll cut off your head and shit in your neck."

Tony Joe: "Trust me, Waylon. Would I do anything to embarrass you?"

Now understand Waylon had never picked up a club, putted a ball, or even been to a golf course before. This was like spotting Bigfoot at a Chamber of Commerce lunch. I could see many faces up against the window of the pro shop trying to figure out what was gonna happen.

After a thirty-second lesson, I handed him a rented driver, put a tee in the ground and one of his lovely pastel balls on top. It was then that Waylon learned all you need to know about golf and how a man enjoys this lovely, pastoral sport.

A mighty swing, a rush of air, and the ball shot sideways, hit a sign ten feet right and ricocheted into the bushes.

"Golf!" Waylon grunted. (He actually said, "Fuck!", but since both words are four letters and mean basically the same thing, I used "Golf!") He was now a part of the grand tradition.

"Try one more, Waylon." I teed up another. Tony Joe was suddenly very interested in something off in the distance. I could see his shoulders shaking from laughter. Beckham was rooting around in his golf bag for a spare bottle of vodka.

Whack! His drive dribbled forward about thirty yards. I beamed like a parent at his kid's T-ball game. "Now we're off. We're playin' golf."

And we did…for nine holes. Us playing and Waylon kicking the grass, shouting and cussing, and scraping the ball along the fairway—the way most people play every day. Some of his divots required a backhoe to fill in.

When we got to the turn, Waylon got out of the cart and said, "Boys, I've now played golf. It ain't for me. When I swing, I can feel the bones in my chest move around. That ain't good, and I ain't good. I'll see ya down the road."

And we stood and watched the Outlaw, Mr. "Ain't Livin' Long Like This," stroll toward his car in the parking lot. And yes, he looked like a barber pole.

I know I shouldn't tell this. I'm probably not the only one he told, but I've never seen it or heard it from anybody else. I hope his beautiful wife, Jessi Colter, won't mind.

It was a blazingly hot summer afternoon. I was at the old Music Row hangout called Maude's Courtyard. A whole book could be written about the people and the stories that came out of what was actually a nice restaurant that the songwriters and singers sort of adopted and actually took over during the afternoons. We played golf in there, liar's poker, smoked cigars, and generally did very little songwriting or singing. We did have a *lot* of cold ones.

Waylon sat down next to me at the end of the bar and said, "Hoss, you would not believe what happened to me yesterday."

This was coming from a guy who'd roomed with Johnny Cash, been the voice of the *Dukes of Hazzard*, performed in every honky-tonk in America, floated above the stars with Willie Nelson, and had almost single-handedly changed the sound and politics of Nashville.

"What happened to you, Waylon?"

"Now, don't go blabbing this story on the radio. As if you could, but somebody sent me one of them machines."

I was hooked. "What machines?"

"I don't know what it's called—'The Autoblow' or something— but you stick it on your wand, and it does the rest. It's battery-powered, or you can plug it into your cigarette lighter in the car."

"It feels like the real dealio?" I waded in a little deeper. I thought I had the picture.

"It's amazing. I know, I used it yesterday."

That was about all I wanted to know at this point, but he continued.

"I was in my car driving home."

You should know that Waylon had a white Cadillac convertible that looked like a land yacht. He was impossible to miss in this beauty.

"Hoss, I'd had a little nose candy, and I was kinda hopped up, and I saw that thing in the backseat and I thought, Well, I'll just stick it on while I enjoy the ride home." ("Stick it on" meant to insert your member into the suction tubing on the end. TMI.)

"I was doing fine 'til that thing started to do its job. The faster it went, the faster I went. I think I was doing eighty miles an hour going down Hillsboro Road. I was OK 'til I saw the blue lights come on. I thought, Oh, NO! So, I floored it. I just couldn't think straight. I didn't know which would be worse—to be caught by the cops wearing this thing on my pecker or doin' eighty down a country road with cocaine in the glove box. I couldn't decide what to throw out of the car."

I guessed. "The Autoblow?"

"Nope, the real blow. I three-wheeled it onto Old Hickory Boulevard toward my house. I decided I'd rather be caught with the sex thingy than drugs. I don't think they send you to jail for having an affair with a machine, but they frown on drugs."

Since Waylon was sitting here with me, I cleverly figured out he had not gone to prison.

"How'd you handle it?"

"Well, I figured if I could just get in my driveway I could come up with somethin'. So I drove *around* my gates and through the front yard and stopped sideways in front of my house. The cop took the same route up into my yard. I yanked that thing off and stuck it under the seat and hopped out of the car and yelled, 'Officer, thanks for the escort. I'm fine now. I guess I had something that didn't agree with me. If you don't mind, I've gotta dash for the crapper. If that's all right with you.' We both froze there in the driveway for a second while he absorbed what I'd said. I think my fly was still open, too.

'Mr. Jennings. You were going mighty fast, but I had that happen to me once, and I almost didn't make it myself. But, sir, you gotta slow it down.'"

I was howling by now, and Waylon put his hand on my arm and said, "Hoss, the best part of Outlaw is the Out part. *Out* of jail. Scared me to death. I'll leave the jail stuff to Merle Haggard. I got that machine out of my car and threw it in the garbage so I wouldn't be tempted no more."

Waylon Jennings settled back on his bar stool and sighed. "Now buy me a drink and I'll tell you why you never visit a truck stop in Texas with Willie Nelson at four in the morning when he's been smokin' on the bus."

I miss ol' Waylon a lot.

Hunting

I WAS FOURTEEN. I was armed. I don't know how old Dad was. Dads are always just older. When you look back, you realize how impossibly young our parents were to have such problems as wars and the Depression. These were tough people. Brave people. Country people. He was armed, too. We were mightily prepared to defend ourselves against rabbit attacks—killer rabbits, as Monty Python later warned us about. Run away! Run away!

In case you are not "huntin' learned," as they say in Kentucky, the prime objective is to never let the wild things know you are in their 'hood. "Son, they can hear you *thinking*. Those ears didn't get to be that size for no reason. You just gotta never let them know you're here." Wise words from a master huntsman.

Right, Dad. *How* could they possibly know we're here? Just because you're walkin' through the brush, hacking and coughing, lighting up a Winston, whistling and humming some country song, and you're slathered in Old Spice and taking the occasional potshot at a tree or squirrel's nest, how could anything that has ears possibly know we're coming? It was like sneaking up on somebody with a marching band.

I was cocked and loaded. Ready for the moment. Hunting. The warrior of the frozen land. Snow was melting on the ground, and I looked for any sign. Suddenly, it happened—so fast I almost missed it. Out of the bush darted a huge rabbit. You never called them bunnies. These were rabbits. Wild game. Hunted and served up for dinner. Dad let out a war whoop and fired first. I saw snow and dirt kick up some fifty yards from the rabbit who took this as a warning that one, these guys can't shoot, and two, I could get hurt accidentally.

He kicked into high gear. Then, with the precision of John Wayne and all the movie war heroes I'd watched, I raised my shotgun and slowly pulled the trigger. It sounded like a gun went off. Because a gun did go off . . . right next to my head. I saw the rabbit yip into the air, turn over, and land headfirst into a snowdrift.

"You got him, Son! Son, you got him!"

I got him, all right. Three or four pellets probably had clipped his shoulder and head. The little thing lay twitching in the snow, which was slowly turning crimson. Life was running into the frozen white.

I got him. I got him, and I didn't want him. I wanted him to jump up and shoot me the bunny bird and hippity-hop off down the trail. I looked at Dad and, and being twelve years old, tried not to cry. It didn't work. Dad looked at me, put his hand on my shoulder, and said, "I'm sorry there, Hoss. I reckon I'll finish him off." Dad raised his gun, aimed right at the rabbit, and then lowered it. I think I saw tears in his eyes. He said, "Let's move back a ways." We walked away twenty-five yards or so. While I stared off into the sky, I heard Dad's gun take the little guy out of his misery. We walked home in silence.

We took a lot of hikes in the woods after that day. We musta walked a thousand miles workin' stuff out, but I never fired a gun at anything alive again.

I don't judge people who hunt. I like steak and wear a leather belt. I get it. I just can't do it. My dad never raised a gun at an innocent target again either.

As we walked home in the snow, I seem to remember Dad singing an old hymn, "In The Sweet By and By." I probably imagined that, but it makes me feel better.

Dogs and Cats

I'M A DOG PERSON. I know there is the eternal debate between "us" and the "cat people," but I'm sorry, we're right. Dogs are better people. I can hear you now: "But you don't know how fabulous little Furgie can be. He snuggles and purrs and sits on the bookshelf and chases the laser beam!" I'm sorry—we're right. Cats don't care. Cats are standoffish and stubborn. Cats are dismissive and rude. Let's face it. Cats are French. Oh sure, Snuggles is thrilled to see you when you're opening a nine-dollar can of Fancy Feast, but just try to get his attention later.

How many times have I tried cats? Many. Too many. When I came home after a hard day of slaving over a hot microphone, I expected Calvin and Prissy to run to meet me like the conquering hero I was. Instead, all I got was a sneer from Calvin as he sauntered into the other room and Prissy arching her back and jumping on the couch. Now, I admit Prissy has reason to be upset. Prissy is a guy. You name a guy Prissy, you're gonna get some resentment. How can an animal be so difficult to sexually identify? After you remove the two obvious pieces of evidence, it's almost impossible. I am certain Prissy blames me for ruining his reputation in Catworld.

Dogs are good people. Dogs just know. Dogs are kind and gentle. Dogs protect you. Show me somebody with a guard cat, and I'll show you somebody missing some jewels. Prissy is missing some jewels, but that's not my fault.

Dogs understand and forgive. I think cats keep a detailed list of complaints in their secret hideouts. Cats hold a grudge and retaliate by peeing in your slippers if they can. Cats have meetings and take seminars called "How to Become More Aloof" and "Introduction to Furniture Scratching." Calvin, our giant Manx, would go *near* the cat box just to antagonize us. It was obvious that he knew why we had a giant box of litter. He understood the concept of proper bathroom habits. He just wasn't going to submit to our rules. "General vicinity" was good enough for Calvin to show his intelligence and independence. Calvin is gone now. I'm certain if there's a "Cat Heaven," Calvin is not there. He's somewhere right now taking a crap in Satan's shoes.

Brad Paisley is a cat. I tend to think of people as one or the other. Brad is friendly and smart and adorable, but he's a cat. I'm not saying he took a whiz in my closet, but I'm also not saying he didn't.

I met Brad Paisley at my golf tournament, which I held for years to support different charities. It was a glorious time. To be grudgingly honest, other people did most of the work. I showed up, swanned around as host, and played golf, and we raised some money for deserving people. If you don't play golf, you probably won't understand charity golf. Often, it's a long day with strangers on a sizzling patch of grass.

The Country King of Golf Tourneys is Vince Gill. Vince holds "The Vinny." See, his name is Vince and, therefore, his tournament is almost his name. It's a truly swanky and wonderful event. I played for as long as I could stand being a "celebrity" in "The

Vinny." The "celebrity" problem was that nobody knew I was the celebrity. Guys paid thousands of dollars and flew in from Seattle to play with famous people. The tournament was studded with big names: pro athletes, actors, singers…and me. I spent four hours carefully explaining who I was to the obviously disappointed three guys who got the worst celebrity draw in the tournament.

We gathered on the first tee and one always said, "I wonder who our celebrity is?" I have a radio show. I write TV shows. I have written some hits. It was all very cordial and painful at the same time. You should know that when people enter a tournament, they *all* expect to play golf with Vince Gill, Michael Jordan, and Justin Timberlake in the same foursome. I expect the same thing. Of course, you can't all tee it up with Charles Barkley, so there's your problem. Although I've seen Charles play, and I'm not sure that qualifies as golf in any way. I finally quit "The Vinny" (or they quit me, I can't remember). Thank God. It was too much pressure on me and Vince to keeping presenting *me* as a celebrity.

Vince has been a friend of mine for thirty years. We've played golf many, many times. I think his putter is still in a tree on No. 18 at Harpeth Hills. He misses a putt, and "It's Helicopter Time!" I throw clubs myself. It makes me feel better. If that's true, Vince should be the best-feeling human on the planet. I remember once during "The Vinny" that a man was seated on the bench by the No. 9 tee box. I spoke and he said, "Well, hello, Ger." He was just sitting there watching the players go by. He was old and gray and obviously weak, but he loved being there. It was Paul Davis. He wrote and sang several great pop hits: "Cool Night," "'65 Love Affair," "Come On Over," and "I Go Crazy." He was probably the biggest artist at the event, and no one even knew he was there. Paul had been shot years earlier on Music Row. It took his career and life away. He was such a gentle soul. I sat with him on that bench. I never saw Paul again.

Brad Paisley was escorted to my tournament to "meet and greet." He didn't know why he was there or what to do. I didn't either. I had him hand out prizes at the end as if both of us knew what he should do. He was funny and gracious, as always. He was a brand-new singer, and his record promo rep thought it would be a nice gesture for him to show up. It was, and he did. I thought at the time Brad was a cool cat. I was right. He was, and he is.

BP is among the cleverest people I've ever met. He can fire off a one-liner with the best of them. He is also significantly over-married. He is a world-class guitar player and a good singer. I've written songs with him several times. The last time, I had what I thought was a wonderful, romantic, and meaningful idea. He arrived, having just gotten married to Kim, and said he wanted to write a song he'd started at his wedding reception. You know how cats don't come to you, you go to them? I went to Brad. He wanted to write a song called "The Toilet Seat Song." Guess what we wrote. It's the pretty common story of a man who learns the lesson about living with a female. Leave the seat up at night and suffer the wrath of an angry and wet woman. Wonderful, romantic, and meaningful it was not, but that's fine. It was fun.

I have a theory that cats are always thinking about other stuff. Even when you are with them, cats have that far-off look in their eyes. They have other plans, and their minds are elsewhere. Brad Paisley is about half-Persian. He's looking at you, but thinking of catching a fish—just like cats do.

You know how cats suddenly have to be in the other room? They are quiet and peaceful, and then, BAM! They run like hell through the door as if somebody set their tail on fire? Brad also does that. One minute he's here. Suddenly, he has to be in the other room.

BP (yeah, still Brad Paisley) and I were sitting at my office trying to nurse a song to life one day. He said, "I've got a song on my album I love that I don't think is gonna see the light of day. It's a duet with Alison Krauss, 'Whiskey Lullaby.' Why don't you play it on the air once just to see what happens?"

I want to interject here that I think DJs get or take too much credit for "playing" a song. I know it's important and it helps, but the real heavy lifting happens from the songwriters, singers, producers, and record guys. Pushing a button that starts a record is really not all that.

I played "Whiskey Lullaby" on my show and changed the world as we know it. My old neighbor Bill Anderson and Jon Randall had written a masterpiece. I played it. Brad's recording with Alison was magic. Her vocals were perfect for such a heart-rending song. I was the one who played it. I've said that Alison Krauss often sings like she's trying not to disturb someone in the room with her. But the song I played that day—the duet by those two hillbillies (I forget their names)—was an award-winning record. I think Brad was pleased. He was probably distracted by a piece of string.

There is something magical about watching phone lines light up like Willie Nelson at a pot convention the first time you play a song. Certain songs strike a chord with people immediately.

The story here that I'm pretty sure Brad doesn't know is about the next song of his I helped break. It was called "The World." Here's how things actually work sometimes in the music business:

I was already in Brad's book as helping with singles because of "Whiskey Lullaby." I now had played "The World" several times. I'd come rockin' out of the news with this song at least once a day. Brad called me and said, "Hey, you think that's a hit? I think we're gonna go with that next." He was excited. I was excited. I'm certain there were powers-that-be at his label who were looking at the same decision. What I never told Brad the Cat or anybody is that I played "The World" by accident. I put his new CD into the player. I was gonna play his duet with Dolly, which was somewhere on the CD, but I always forgot to select that song. I was distracted or talking or reading the newspaper. So, I always played "The World," which just happened to be the first song on the album.

Now do you see why I think jocks get too much glory in playing a song? I accidentally played a certain tune, and Brad Paisley thinks

I think it's The One. *It was nothing more than my dumbass method of playing a CD. I stress again, I'm certain others picked it, loved it, wrote it, and fought for it. I just accidentally played it.*

After I played "The World," it changed the world again. I now had the golden touch so much that just playing a song by accident made a No. 1 record. The writers, producers, promotion people, Brad, his bus driver, his wife, and the president of the record company had nothing to do with it. Oh sure, the audience loved it and bought it and clamored for it, but I *played* the damn thing. Brad absolutely purred the next time he saw me. I was catnip, no doubt about it.

For years, I, along with half of Nashville, pitched Brad to host the *CMA Awards*. I blurted out as much as possible that *he* would be the perfect host. He's funny. He's a star. He wears a hat and Carrie Underwood doesn't. All the things you need in a host. Vince had done it so many times, he ran out of steam. Brooks and Dunn took a whack at it, but there were no raves, to be honest. It's a tough gig. One day, BP (Brad the Persian cat) called and said, "Guess what? Not for public knowledge, but I am gonna host the *CMA Awards* show. Can you help me write some of it?" I was thrilled he thought of me, and I agreed. I know he asked several other folks, which was smart, to think up stuff for him and Carrie to say.

I wrote 'til my eyes bugged out of my head. I did it twice, as a matter of fact—the first year they hosted and their second year. I didn't contribute all of the material, but I do remember sitting in a parking lot the day of the show on the phone with Brad for an hour. We discussed stuff down to the finest detail.

Writing jokes is a thankless job. A lot of folks assume it's easy. It's just like writing a song. Some days it just falls out of the sky. Other days you sit and think so hard your head hurts. Later that evening, he called and offered an excited post-show "thanks." I then saw him at Ronnie Dunn's after-party. Brad and I talked a little. He mentioned there was a chance that *somebody,* somewhere might do something, somehow for all my help. I joked and said, "Well, then, I guess you'll just have to write another song with me." I'm pretty sure he arched his back and hissed. Suddenly, he had to be in the other room. You know how cats are.

Broadway and Lower Broadway

THERE'S BROADWAY, and then there's Lower Broadway. Broadway is in New York City. Lower Broadway is in Nashville. Every so often, they intersect. I'm going to admit right here and right now that I love Broadway. I love show tunes and musicals and the whole thrilling thing.

I realize that, in many places, this will cause me to lose my "man card," but I don't care. At my age, my man card is not getting punched much anymore anyway. People ask me a lot, as if I'm some kind of Manhattan expert, "Where are the places to go, eat, and sleep in New York?" I actually know London better than I do the Big Apple. I always tell them to be sure and see some theater. It's exciting. We have a rule, by the way. If one of us—Allyson, Autumn, or I—don't like the show, we leave at "halftime." I usually know in the first five minutes if I want to sit through the rest of the show. I will have more on the problems of leaving early later, if "early later" is a phrase.

Lower Broadway is a touristy collection of honky-tonks, barbeque joints, and a few upscale restaurants. The music blares out the open front doors of the honky-tonks to entice people to come in, order a longneck, and listen to somebody sing old Garth Brooks songs. Nashville also has the fabulous Schermerhorn Symphony Center downtown. I always tell the conductor of the Nashville Symphony they ought to leave the front doors open so people walkin' by will drift in to catch him playing old Beethoven songs.

Tootsie's is the USDA-approved, Grade A honky-tonk. It's always been in that same place, just down the alley from the Ryman Auditorium. They've managed to maintain the historic "dive" appearance with just the right amount of neglect and poor lighting. I haven't been there in years but have been many times in the past. You really do feel like Kitty Wells or Willie Nelson might saunter through the back door at any minute. The lore is that *Opry* stars would sneak off between shows at the Ryman and have a half-dozen pops before going back for the late show.

Country stars usually don't think about the "other" Broadway. It's hard to maintain your redneck cred if you're on the Great White Way singing show tunes. However, every now and then one of the hillbillies busts through the gate and takes a shot at Broadway.

Gary Morris is one who did it. Gary has one of the finest, most powerful tenors in all of music. He's a powerhouse. I wrote one song with Gary that he recorded. Even I don't remember it. Gary had a series of hits including a fabulous version of "Wind Beneath My Wings," written by Larry Henley and Jeff Silbar.

I know both Larry and Jeff, and I wrote with Jeff in Los Angeles. Larry is hilarious, and of all the people in the world to write such a classic, moving song as "Wind Beneath My Wings," you would never think of old Larry. His earlier claim to fame was singing falsetto for the Newbeats on the '64 novelty pop hit, "Bread and Butter." Jeff moved to L.A. and wrote more pop stuff.

I have no idea if it's the whole story, but Larry told me he had most of "Wings" written when Jeff sorta popped into the room to see what was going on. Larry seemed to say that, one chord addition later, Jeff was a cowriter. That's always a tough one for songwriters.

Rodney Crowell, one of America's greatest composers, said to me, "Hey, if someone just adds one note and it's the right note you didn't have before, they are cowriters." I agree. There are dozens of Lennon-McCartney songs that were mostly written by one or the other. But that one idea always makes a song special. "Wings" has been recorded countless times and is the kind of classic every guitar slinger in Nashville aims for. It's the golden ticket to financial freedom.

Gary Morris is also one of the most confident men in the world. I don't mean that in a bad way. I almost said, "Bless his heart," which is the Southern equivalent of, "I'm saying something awful about somebody, but I don't want you to tell them." But he is. To me, he's not the most strikingly classically handsome man to ever stride onstage, but women just get weak-kneed when they are around him.

I especially remember the achingly young secretary at his office. She was barely qualified to answer the phone, but nobody cared because she was a total babe. Everybody I knew dropped in to "see Gary" and wound up talking to his receptionist for half an hour and forgetting about Gary. Her name was Faith Hill.

Gary decided one day to take his tenor to New York City. People talked about it like he'd decided to join a cult or something. Early on, people just didn't do that. His career was sort of in a glide path in country, and he's confident, as I said. I admired him for it. He did a little thing called *Les Miserables*. I think he actually played the part of *Les*. Or maybe it was Jean Valjean. I never did get to see him warble this pop opera.

Gary sort of drifted away from country and on to other things. He moved to Colorado. He started looking more like a mountain man. His great beard got whiter, and he did TV shows about shooting things. Inside him, however, there was always that voice. It must be like having a secret weapon. It makes you a confident guy. Gary Morris has every reason to be that. He conquered Lower Broadway *and* Broadway. I think that's as cool as it gets.

I've already mentioned a bit about Larry Gatlin, the Texas singer/ songwriter. He's also a serious part-time philosopher on anything people will listen to him talk about: politics, religion, and golf. Larry once hounded me to come see him in his play on Broadway. The irony of all ironies is that Larry Gatlin played the lead in *The Will Rogers Follies* on Broadway in New York City in that big theater next to the Sbarro and the SONY sign where the headlines go around a building in lights. *That* Broadway. Mickey Rooney, for God's sake, was in the play—Mickey "Andy Hardy" Rooney!

I always think anything with the word "Follies" in it is gonna be kind of lightweight. I was right. *The Will Rogers Follies* was written by theater heavyweights, but it was really an excuse to retell some of Will's great lines, with some songs in between. "I never met a man I didn't like." "A fool and his money are soon elected." "Be thankful we're not getting all the government we're paying for." Brilliant stuff.

The funny part to me was watching Larry Gatlin onstage, dressed as a dandy cowboy, spouting all these lines. I *never* saw Will Rogers; I only saw Larry Gatlin. To make sure *you* saw Larry Gatlin, Larry paused in the middle of the play to sing one or two of *his* songs. I can't imagine how the tourists put all that together. He's Will Rogers, he's funny, he's political, he sings these old-timey Broadway tunes, and BOING! He's singing "All the Gold in California." After the play, Larry kept me and Al waiting for an hour in the stairwell while Patrick Swayze and his wife, Lisa, chatted with Larry and Mickey. I just wanted to see Mickey.

For a brief moment, Tom Wopat had a country career. Yes, the Duke of Hazzard. Funny how that goofy show was connected to Nashville and me. Tom was Luke Duke and John Schneider (another country singer) was Bo Duke. Waylon Jennings was the narrator.

In college, I had played in Hazzard, Kentucky, as a rock 'n' roller. One night, I happened to be walking by a television set tuned to the *Dukes of Hazzard*. And, oh, my Lord! The Oak Ridge Boys were on the show, singing a song I had written—"Old Time Lovin'"—the first song I had ever recorded. I had written it by myself, and there were the "Oaks" belting it out to Bo and Luke and the Hazzard crew.

I never mentioned my "history" with the Dukes to Tom Wopat. He had moved to Nashville and was making country records. He visited my radio show, but mostly we played golf together. His country career didn't do much, but he was such a great singer and actor that he reinvented himself on Broadway. Broadway in *New York City!*

We flew in a big silver bird to the Big Apple on the invitation of my friend Tom Wopat. He was starring opposite Bernadette Peters in *Annie Get Your Gun*. So, picture this: we have Tom's seats for the show. They are the best—fourth row in the middle, just in front of the orchestra. You can actually see the facial expressions on the actors. Minutes before showtime, six or seven people were hurried into their seats. Right in front of us were Joe Namath and his wife and kids. I remember the noses. When they turned sideways it looked like a flock of macaws had landed in the audience.

Now, we're cookin': Broadway Joe on Broadway, my pal Tom onstage, and Bernadette almost close enough to touch. I got kind of bored with *Annie Get Your Gun* about halftime. We couldn't leave, of course. So, I did what everybody does when they are bored. You start looking at the program to see what's left for these people to sing. What I didn't realize is that the actors onstage could also see us. After the show, as we were gushing about how great everything was, Tom said, "I pointed you guys out to Bernadette during the show." I guess the actors talk a little if they ain't actin' all the time. He went on, "I had told her about you, your songwriting, and your love of Broadway. Bernadette hissed back to me onstage, 'HE'S COUNTING SONGS!'"

I was in the audience, minding my own bored business figuring out how much longer I had to sit there, while Bernadette Peters is onstage watching me calculate the misery. I vowed to never sit through *Annie Get Your Gun* again.

My apologies to Irving Berlin. There are fabulous songs and great parts in that musical, but for some reason, it didn't "speak" to me. I was done with *Annie Get Your Gun*.

Wrong. About a year and a half later, I'm on a private jet to Cancun, Mexico. Reba and Narvel Blackstock have a small, plain hacienda down south of the border. It's this little place with fabulous stonework, bedrooms that surround a massive courtyard, and a pool that fades into the ocean to infinity. If you get the chance, go with Reba and Narvel to their place.

On the flight down, Red casually mentioned she had some interest in appearing on Broadway. Allyson and I immediately knew she should do it, whatever it was. She'd knock them out, and we started the argument in favor of it.

She wanted no part of it. "I don't wanna live in New York City for six months."

"Are you crazy?"

"No way."

What play is it? Yep, you guessed it. Irving's masterpiece about Annie and a gun. By now, you probably know she decided she could live in "that crazy city." She actually loved it.

We went to see her and it was amazing. (I didn't count songs, either.) Reba turned into a whole new person on that stage. I think it was the best thing she could do. She became bigger in everyone's eyes. She conquered the Great White Way just like she'd conquered Lower Broadway years before. I was so proud of her. I don't think our jet conversation convinced her totally to do it, but it sure didn't hurt.

And now, my final Broadway memory: the thrill and the letdown. Al and I still laugh about it. After *Annie Get Your Gun* we went backstage with Narvel to see Red and the cast. We laughed and hugged and made plans to go to dinner at Josephine's in a few minutes. She said, "Y'all go on out the stage door, and we'll hook up at the car."

The stage doors opened directly onto the street. It's a little runway up toward the white lights. There was an enormous crowd waiting for the stars. We were the first people out. The crowd reaction was electric. It was like being shot full of adrenaline when that crowd roared for us—screams and clapping and smiles.

Then suddenly, en masse and also all at once, they realized it was nobody they knew. It was us. The collective joy went from jubilation and celebration to a death march in half a second. OOOoooooooh. It's who? Who are *those* people? It wasn't hateful, it was just reality. We weren't worth screaming over. Did I mention Al and I still laugh about it? I've done a lot of cool things in my life, but in that brief period between joy and reality, I felt what Reba must feel a thousand times a day.

QUIZZICLE #7

Which glamorous event did Kathy Mattea join me in attending?

A) Celebrity Leapfrog

B) Cow Chip Toss

C) Mooning for Mutts

Honey Pie

KATHY MATTEA IS SO ELEGANT and so poised, I am always amazed when she does something that seems out of character. She is one of those people you meet and think, *I better behave because she's classy.* Or at least that's always how I felt around her. She's not a stuffed shirt, by any means, as you'll find out, but there's always been an air of intelligence and no-nonsense about her that's slightly intimidating. That's why I was thrilled to see Kathy Mattea show up at the cow chip tossing contest.

Ms. Mattea has made some wonderful records. "Where've You Been," cowritten by her husband, is a piece of poetry and music about the tragedy of people getting old. She had a lot of hits and continues to record at her own pace on her own terms. I just love her.

For some reason unknown probably to everyone involved, there was a cow chip toss held on a farm in Mt. Juliet, Tennessee. It was really an excuse to get some friends together and drink beer and eat barbeque at Bob Beckham's place. Beckham has been a friend of mine for thirty years and is the chief excuse maker for anything involving hooch and people.

Two things happened that day that I will never forget. The first was watching the very refined Kathy Mattea "test" a cow chip for its tossability. Just in case you were born in a condo in downtown Chicago, a cow chip is the sunbaked version of a cow pie. Cows are not all that particular where they decide to "fertilize." It's usually a lift of the tail and "Look out, boys, she's gonna blow."

I have attended several wonderful Cow Bingo contests with this in mind. You put numbered pieces of plastic in a field and wait 'til a cow "marks" the number on your card. I once won a year's supply of dental floss playing Cow Bingo.

A cow chip throwing contest is a whole other sport. Sidearm is my method, but you have to select the proper chip. If you've ever skipped rocks across a creek (I was neighborhood champ for several years), you can toss a cow chip. Kathy knew, as all pros do, that to gain maximum distance, the chip has to be durable, thin, and Frisbee-like. This is when I knew Ms. Mattea was my kind of girl. Walking from pie to pie, testing for firmness and aerodynamics, was serious business. I am ashamed to admit I didn't apply myself as much as I should have. Although I can sling the B.S. with the best of them, Kathy Mattea won. The girl has got an arm like Roger Clemens. Distance, control, and direction are her talents. I know, in spite of all her gold records, winning that contest is her crowning achievement.

The other memory of that wondrous day in the sunshine involved a young man named Blake Chancey. Blake is Ron Chancey's son. Both are great producers. Ron made records with the Oak Ridge Boys, Garth Brooks, and Bob Seger. Blake went on to helm recording projects with Mary Chapin Carpenter and the Dixie Chicks. I guess the little nut didn't fall far from the big nut tree. I love both the dad and the son.

We were outside most of the cow chip tossing day. Every now and then, I'd hear Bob Beckham's dog howl. Farm dogs do that.

They warn people of some unseen trespasser or impending danger that nobody but the dog sees. I didn't pay much attention, and nobody else did, either.

When we went inside the house later that day, a young Blake Chancey was sprawled on the couch in front of the television. Blake was too young and too cool to be involved in anything as tasteless as a cow chip tossing contest. He preferred watching an old rerun of *Baywatch*. I don't blame him. Pamela Anderson is one of the most talented actresses to ever run in slow motion in a red bathing suit down the beach.

Bob and I entered the den. Blake looked up and said, "Bob, there's something wrong with your TV remote. I've been trying to switch around and it doesn't work. Maybe the batteries are dead."

Punch, punch, punch. He was right. The television didn't respond at all. Again, punch, punch, punch. Nothing. We heard some barking in the distance. Punch, punch, punch. No television reaction. Again, I heard a faint lonesome wail.

Bob grabbed the remote and said, "Son, stop hitting that. Oh, Jesus." He then dashed out the door. I watched out the window as he seemed to be running to where the barking came from. Blake and I decided to follow. Blake dropped what he thought was the remote. But it wasn't.

Shock collars have never been anything I want to use on one of my dogs. Owners and trainers swear by them. It actually teaches the dog lessons for life. I don't want to condemn anyone for trying to teach their "best friend" about safety and civility. The "shock" doesn't actually do any real damage to the dog, but let's face it, it comes as a shock. Certainly, if it gets several reminders a second for an entire episode of *Baywatch*. Bob felt terrible. I felt terrible. Blake was just mortified. The dog recovered just fine, but he always reminded me of Don Knotts after that.

QUIZZICLE #8

What did Terry Bradshaw ask me to do?

A) Think up a slogan for peanut butter

B) Wax his new Corvette

C) Trade pants with him

Don't Pass Me By

STEELERS FANS STILL SORT of quiver if you mention the name Terry Bradshaw. He's the Pro Football Hall of Fame quarterback with *four* Super Bowl rings. Rather than cow chips, he's still watching footballs being tossed, although now it's behind a desk on Fox *NFL Sunday*.

Most people don't remember that Terry was a country singer in Nashville, Tennessee. It happens a lot. Somebody has success in sports or modeling or business, and *here they come*: "I'm a-gonna be a Country & Western star!" There's always some producer or record exec who sees dollar signs attached and is ready to lead the way to a recording studio. Over the years, I think I've heard more bad music produced for the wrong reasons than anybody who's ever lived.

Every now and then, however, the "star" could actually sing. Nowadays, even *that* isn't a problem. Studio wizards can auto-tune a talent-free singer into success. If you hear a song with that otherworldly sound to it, that pitch-perfect vocal that doesn't seem human, chances are it isn't. It's an athlete or a rapper or a model being "fixed" by modern technology.

Terry Bradshaw could, and probably still can, actually sing. I'm not saying he made Ronnie Dunn want to quit showbiz, but he had a nice tenor voice. It's the voice you'd hear in the church on Sunday when somebody stepped out of the choir and sang a verse by his lonesome.

Jerry Crutchfield is a producer, musician, and business exec. We have done a *lot* of things together: commercial jingles, songs, and anything we stumbled across that might work. He's one of the few people who can pick out a hit song and turn a nobody into a somebody with one hit. He did it over and over. It's a talent few people have. "Crutch" taught me a lot.

Terry came to town, recorded some C & W songs, and embarked on his new singing career. I saw him a lot during those days. He and Crutch also decided he needed a side business to capitalize on his fame. That's where Terry Bradshaw's Peanut Butter came in. I wasn't part of the business plan, but I was part of the creative team. Bradshaw turned to me one day and asked, "Can you think of a slogan for peanut butter?" I've done a lot of goofy things in my life, but that day I started by staring out the window at home trying to dream up a slogan for crushed goobers in a jar.

I had several slogan ideas, most of which I knew Terry wouldn't like. Picture a big jar with Bradshaw's mug on the front. "It's nuttier than I am" was my favorite. I didn't even have the nerve to submit it. Second only to "Terry's Nuts!"—which was not a crowd favorite either. "Pass the peanut butter" had a nice football-y ring to it, but was shot down. "From Super Bowl to Super Jar!" Nope. "It takes a goober to know a goober." I thought Terry's picture on the front would make that work. No way. I even tried "PBJ. Peanuts, Bradshaw, and Jelly." Not even a glimmer.

"It's not peanut BUTTER, it's peanut BETTER!" Yes, I know. It doesn't have the joyous zing of "It's nuttier than I am," but that was the one they went with.

Somewhere in my attic I think I still have a jar of Terry's nuts.

QUIZZICLE #9

Who said, "Thanks for letting me gherm you"?

A) Al Sharpton

B) Neil Diamond

C) Pee Wee Herman

She Came in through the Bathroom Window

ONE OF THE WONDERFUL side benefits of living in Nashville is that you get to meet visiting superstars. I'm not talking about the "Gone Country" types Alan Jackson references—the ones who have fallen out of favor in another kind of music and now want to try "Country & Western." I mean the ones who genuinely have affection for the place and sometimes even move to Twang Town.

I once was hosting some charity event at the Tennessee Performing Arts Center. As usual, I was barely aware of who was on the bill or what was going on. A guy poked me in the back as I stood backstage and said, "Gerry, I'm Peter Frampton." I nearly fell over. Peter lived in town for a few years.

Jazz guitarist extraordinaire Larry Carlton lives just south of the city. I will miss seeing Donna Summer at dinner parties and on New Year's Eve. Felix Cavaliere of the Rascals and "Groovin'" fame appears every now and then. I've been to Steve Winwood's house a lot and ruined most of his wine collection. Stevie is in England most of the time now. You get the idea.

These people aren't "carpetbaggers," they just love living here. I always think, anyway, *So what? So what if they* do *come to town to try and make a record?* Rosanne Cash once said to me out of frustration, "It's not a *religion.*"

Rose took some heat from country purists for some reason I've now forgotten over one of her records. There are still a few of those types left around here. Some people are still upset they use drums on the *Opry*. But Rose is right. It's *not* a religion. It's just a town where music is made, and if somebody wants to live here, good for them.

I've been to dinner parties many times with Sheryl Crow. When I look at the list of songs she's written that I love, I'm amazed she even speaks to anybody. Sheryl and her babies called Nashville home. She's one of those people who make you feel good just knowing she's in the same room. After a "fun" dinner with wine, my favorite memory of Sheryl is seeing her playing an unplugged bass guitar while Reba McEntire banged on a cowbell and sang at the top of her lungs.

One of my many songwriting heroes is Michael McDonald. Mike has a house in Leiper's Fork. It's an old farmhouse, and he converted one of the little houses nearby into a studio. Yes, *that* Michael McDonald...Doobie Brothers/Steely Dan Michael McDonald. If somebody asks me to name my favorite pop song, I always say, "What a Fool Believes." Mike wrote that with Kenny Loggins. The performance, the story, the lyrics, and the music are all perfect.

He's written so many classics, it's kind of scary. And he did it all while singing in a language no human can understand! My favorite Michael McDonald album, *What The Hell Is He Saying?*, is played all the time. And, believe it or not, I actually wrote with Mike. He's hilarious, he's sweet, and he's an intimidating piano player. I plunk around on the 88s. I can write songs, but watching him do it is also, like I said, intimidating; there's no other word for it.

After forty years of mauling a Steinway, his hands look like meat hooks—big, gnarly, angry fingers sticking out of muscular canned hams. Kim Carnes (who also lives in Nashville) sang "Bette Davis Eyes." I got to see "Mike McDonald's Hands." Plus, when he's just sitting there writing and making up lyrics, he sings *just like* Michael McDonald! Even lyrics I just wrote I can't understand when he sings them—one of the great thrills of my career.

So, back to the "gherming." In case you're *not* from around here, a "gherm" is a slightly derogatory term for someone who gushes over a star. Getting ghermed is a common event for somebody who sings for a living. There is a fine line between gherming and stalking. Recording artists, for the most part, are wonderful. I'm not talking about me, but usually the actual star I'm with. People want to take a picture or say hello. I can't tell you how many times I've seen people come rushing up to Reba or Ronnie Dunn or whomever and say, "You're my biggest fan." It's always funny. They're excited, and, in the moment, it comes out wrong.

I can also say I've never seen one artist/famous/music performer be rude in any way to anybody. I've seen them hide before they get attacked. I've seen them move to a quieter or hidden table, but not one single incidence of the "Leave me alone, peasant" attitude. Never. And there are some fans who can be pretty forward. The ones with the "I bought your album, and I *made* you what you are today" body language drive me crazy.

Of course, I welcome anybody attacking me for an autograph or a pic, but, for some strange reason, folks give me my privacy. It's amazing how huge fans of mine act like they don't even know who I am in public. How they manage to contain their raw excitement and passion is astounding. They can sit two feet away and carry on like it's not the most heart-pounding moment of their entire life.

Speaking of taking pictures, Merle Kilgore was a real piece of work. He wrote two classic songs: "Wolverton Mountain" and "Ring of Fire." The latter he wrote with June Carter Cash, Johnny's wife. He also managed Hank Williams Jr., and that always sounds to me like saying you were in charge of a herd of buffalo. I think you just try to head things in a certain direction, but you don't really control anything.

I loved Merle because he was always cheerful and always paid for the martinis. I imagine the martinis made him so cheerful.

We were sitting in a restaurant somewhere when we noticed a quasi-famous singer stand up and have a picture made with an excited fan. Merle said, "Johnny was great about that usually most always." I asked, "What do you mean, 'most always'?" Merle leaned in and said, "Well, if John R. was in an obvious rush or in the middle of something else, he would ask me to take the picture." Sounded like a signal to me. It was. He explained, "John wouldn't be rude, even though the tourist obviously was taking advantage of him. The lingering, long fan story about their life and how they'd seen the star in some city twenty years before. I would grab the camera and say, 'I'll take this for ya, honey.'

"After much posing and trying to get the damn camera to work— usually the flash wouldn't go off or the batteries would be dead—we'd take a memory shot and they would walk away. Then Johnny Cash would say, 'Where'd you cut me off?' In taking the photo for the fan, I would only include Johnny's arm or leg or half his hair in the picture. We didn't do that all the time, but it did make us feel better knowing that, back in Arkansas, this nut would try to convince his family, 'THAT's Johnny Cash's left hand on my shoulder, I swear!'"

I've been so tongue-tied in front of some of my heroes, God knows what I actually said. One of those was Neil Diamond. Neil has been a huge star for almost as long as I can remember. "Cherry, Cherry" and "Solitary Man" and dozens of others take me all the way back to the gym at Simon Kenton High School. Hopping around in my socks like a mental patient to Neil Diamond records.

I wasn't at a dance or anything, I just enjoyed hopping around in my socks.

Neil came to Nashville to write songs and record an album. It had the faint hint of "Gone Country," but nobody cared. It was thrilling for all my friends who got to write with him and talk to him and listen to him. He gave big black guitars to a lot of the guys when they finished cowriting. I didn't get that lucky, but he did drop in one morning on my show. He'd been listening because he was living in town for several months. Just before we went on the air, I said, "I hope I don't gherm you." He looked at me as if I'd spoken in tongues.

"*What* me?" he asked. I explained the term and he threw his head back and laughed. "Wow, I love that. I know exactly what it means." I bet he did. When someone fills up the space that's exactly the height, depth, and width of Neil Diamond, people notice you. When you sound exactly like Neil Diamond when you speak, it's Gherm City.

I still have a framed piece of paper that reads, *"Gerry, thanks for letting me 'GHERM' you." —Neil Diamond.*

Available Names Left

I HAVE CHECKED with both the Country Music Association and the International Naming Rights Society for their lists of names not already taken for singers and bands. As you know, it's all in the name. Would Keith Urban or Tim McGraw be as big as they are without those cool names? Of course not. Even though several of these great names may have been claimed by the time you read this, here is the list of country names still available at press time:

Amish Gun
Hoots McGillicuddy
Lionel Twain
Billy Joe Bob Buddy Barnes
The Weasel Squeezers
Bart Grooks
The Concrete Plowboys
Ramblin' Roy Puckett
The Hickersons
Lupe Leibowitz

Whistlin' Bill Anderson
Skank Williams Jr.
Fussy and the Britches
Chocolate Tractor
Dinky Friedman
BeezelBubba
Cornelius P. VanderPlaatz
The Stump Squatters
Righty Frizzell
Jimmy Earl Dickerson

Whole Hawg
Patty and the Perverts
Trailer Swift
Nuns Without Habits
Flagpole Johnson
Grandma Jones
Zacchaeus Rodriguez
Beano and the SBDs
Angel Bambi
Pluckin' Pete Peterson
Doofus Rufus
The Downtown Rednecks
Cuss Cusstofferson
Willie Ectomy
Delores Funk
Mongo Lambert

Uncle Ned Peevis
Tick Melcher
Scootin' Bill Harbaugh
Barbara Mandrill
Dingus
Bumpkin Corleone
Fancy Shack
Merlene Fassbinder
Otis and the Jailers
Crotch Moxley
The Foggy Minded
   Mountain Boys
Sasquatch Morgan
Suzy Bogus
Kix Brooks

Buddy and Julie

HE EXTENDED HIS ARMS to push his shirt cuffs out a bit. Shooting your cuffs, it was called. It was a custom-made shirt, after all. The high collar and silk-print tie with the hand-made suit gave him a sort of Elvis/Riverboat Gambler/TV Preacher look. Expensive Italian shoes completed his getup.

He glanced in the rearview mirror to make sure his "piece" was on straight. It wasn't just any piece. It was a $3,000 natural-hair glory lid that was so magnificent and so meticulously crafted, *nobody* knew he was follicle-y challenged. The trick he'd discovered years ago, when he was young, was to go "toup" early. Just like Grandpa Jones went "old" early. If there's no one alive who has seen you without a full head of hair, then there's no one who can even wonder if your wig-hat isn't the real deal.

He'd fooled them all...all except for anybody who spent ten seconds looking at his pompadour. For every one of his years in the music business, from average songwriter to average producer to big-time music publisher, he'd walked the wig-hat walk. *And* he never appeared in public unless he was dressed in full-blown success regalia. He loved to flash that gleaming porcelain smile. Yes, it was just a tad *too* white. Urinal White was what he'd asked for, and that's what he got. It was blazing and blinding, just the way he liked it.

Buddy liked to wink a lot when he made conversation. It made people feel like he was really engaged and concerned. He was also a "point and clicker." He'd finish off a one-liner with his index fingers pointed like pistols after a thumb click. He piloted a Corvette convertible colored a tasteful and very royal blue. He'd considered canary yellow, but thought that might seem cheap or showy.

It was a stormy night, so he put the top up (mostly so he wouldn't lose his). This chick singer was going to be downright impressed.

She was a singer, but not *just* a singer, according to her Texas bio. She had a voice like an angel. Someone had once suggested an angel "like Tommy Lasorda?" She didn't get the joke. Her press shot was sexy and gauzy—a "come hither" half-smile peering out from underneath a cowboy hat. Her blouse was opened only enough so that her church wouldn't disown her, and she was squeezed into a pair of Wranglers. She had laughed after the press shoot and had told her girlfriend that when she took the jeans off it was like opening a can of biscuits.

Nashville had been forced to wait awhile for her arrival because of a couple of marriages and financial problems that were not her fault. Now, she was finally in town. She was ready for Music City. She was footloose, and also with a free-enough fancy. This little town was not gonna know what hit it. All the bad times were behind her now. She smiled, knowing she was about to hook up with one of the movers and shakers on Music Row to discuss her career. She was on her way. She hummed "Ain't No Stoppin' Us Now." She pranced out of the hotel door onto the sidewalk.

Oops, a little chunky, he thought. Not a problem, though. He could send her to his trainer. He was parked half a block away in the 'Vette.

Obvious dye job. That color blonde doesn't exist in nature. For a second, he drifted away and remembered being a teenager and Linda Gratowski. Ahh! Those were such wonderful, carefree days.

He'd been naturally drawn to Linda Gratowski because of her magnificent hair—a beehive that pointed toward God all the time. Her God Compass, she'd called it. Linda never mentioned his comb-over, and he adored her for that. That and Linda Grawtowski had gazongas for days. When you're seventeen, you notice things like that and think about them about every five seconds. He was hoping she'd let him play "motorboat" again after they made an appearance at the high school dance. He'd also brought a bottle of Maker's Mark, which he hoped to empty into her and speed the "motorboat" process along. As they prepared to go inside the school gym, Linda drained the pint of Loretto, Kentucky's finest bourbon. Her eyes rolled around and she belched, "I'm ready to party now."

Fire up the Evinrude, he thought. They had not been dancing for more than five minutes when Linda staggered like an old boxer and slurred, "I think you better take me home." He held her up and escorted/dragged her to his car. Great, he thought. Just my luck that she can't hold her liquor. As he navigated the winding back road to her house, she leaned her head out the window and unleashed the gates of hell. His friends always called it "selling Buicks in Europe." EEERRUROPE EEEEEUROPE BUUUUUUUICK. It was horrifying.

She was hurling all along the side of his recently waxed Corvair, and it distracted him. He jerked the wheel and veered off the road for a second. It was then that he heard her scream and saw her head fly off. Oh, NO! She's going to need her head. He must have swerved too near a mailbox or something. Oh my God!" he repeated over and over. He had to take Linda Gratowski home to her father, Big Mike Gratowski, without his daughter's head! This was not gonna be good. He was only seventeen, but he knew parents frowned on little things like that. No head. No Linda. No motorboating.

Then he saw what had really happened. Her head was still on. It was still there! Relief washed over him like warm water. But her magnificent God Compass had blown into the night. She had been wearing a wig!

In the dim moonlight, she turned and screamed again. Her hands went toward her obviously connected head—what looked like a pair of pantyhose stretched over tiny ringlets of mousy brown hair. He thought, She looks like a Brussels sprout.

"*Go back! Go back!*" *she pointed and pleaded. He slowed down.* "*It's back there in the ditch!*" *She wailed,* "*That hair was brand new!*" *Then she sold another Buick.*

They never found her beehive and never spoke to each other again.

Buddy got out of his car, leaned on the top of the door, and wolf-whistled.

Oops, a little old, she thought. Not a problem, though. She could send him to a doc she'd once dated. *Couple of nips and a tuck, and BAM! Instant youth. And get a load of that thing on his head. Oh, well.* She smiled and skipped toward him.

"You look FABulous!" they both said at the same time.

Buddy made the first move before they went "to the studio" (he owned a small studio where he took potential "clients"). "Why don't we stop up to my place and have a drink?"

Wow, he doesn't waste much time, does he? she thought with some resentment.

"Great! I'd love to see it," she purred with all the enthusiasm she could fake.

It was a small building on Music Row with eight apartments inside. It used to be a "boutique hotel." They had "boutiqued" themselves out of business, so they switched to condo/apartments. There was a small pool shaped like a banjo and a creaky elevator to take you to the second floor. His place was half of "the penthouse" (if the second floor of *anything* qualifies as a penthouse).

Buddy had worked hard on this love den. He'd designed it himself and had successfully demonstrated how the music business works to many talented singers from all over the world. He couldn't wait to show her his latest addition. It was his proudest creation.

They hurried from the car through the dark entryway. The skies were getting kinda scary-looking. There was a rumble in the distance. He unlocked the door, reached in, and turned a small white knob. The lights rose to a faint glow, and a disco ball began to turn on the ceiling. Tiny pieces of white began to twinkle around the room. He turned another knob, and his album of self-made Sinatra instrumentals began to play faintly in the background. She stepped into the splendor, and he headed to the bar.

"Name your poison," he shouted over his shoulder. "The bar is fully stocked, and the bartender is on duty." It was at this point she considered for roughly five seconds, *How bad do I want a record deal?*

"Vodka martini. Double, straight up," she answered him and herself at the same time.

"Comin' atcha, sweetheart."

Two of these and she'll be ready for my coup de grace. A little relaxin' juice, and then I show her the magic. They were now starting the continuous dance of the biz. Somebody in power takes somebody under his disco ball. Sometimes it's innocent. Every once in an azure moon, it actually works. Most of the time, it just keeps people busy.

People get off the bus in Nashville every day with dreams and some kind of talent. It's not the same town it was twenty years ago. There were vanity record labels in every other ramshackle old house along 16th and 17th Avenues. It was almost unspoken but understood that you *could* get a record deal. Sometimes you just had to pay for it.

It was sad how many people mortgaged the trailer or sold the farm to finance a dream. They'd sing in some shag-carpeted studio into an old microphone. The dreamers poured their hearts into the bad song while bored and jaded studio players plunked out the same notes they'd played the day before. It was ugly. It took advantage.

It has slowly faded out of sight, finally. Nowadays, the business is more sophisticated. Talent gurus "work" with people to make their dreams come to life. Most of the con artists have been forced out of town. The real people are the only ones left along Music Row.

"Tell me truly, Julie, do you love me?" Buddy warbled in his hoarse tenor. He still had it—the voice that made women weak. Julie, noticing it was the first time he'd said her name, giggled and clapped once.

"Wow, I've never heard that before," she lied. Of course, she'd heard it a million times. She'd even bought the old Bobby Sherman album it was on so she could hear how the damn song actually went.

Julie decided to do a little business. "How much does getting a record made cost? I'm not exactly floating in money these days."

Bud was in. "Oh, darlin', you don't have to give that a second thought. You have talent and you have beauty and you have me. You just think about what kind of sports car you're gonna buy and which designer dresses you like, and leave the business side to me. I've heard you sing, and this is gonna be easy."

Yeah, right, Julie thought. *If easy is what you want, easy is what you're going to get. I've done the mattress mambo with worse than you.*

She smiled and cooed at him, "Oh, Buddy, I just don't know what I could do to ever repay you for all you're gonna do for me."

Bud was def in. A flash of lightning outside almost blended in with the disco shards of white. Now it was time for him to unveil the magic. He said, "Can I show you something? It doesn't mean anything. I don't want you to take it the wrong way, but it's just so much fun to see." The sky rumbled quite a bit louder outside.

He didn't wait for her to protest. He walked to the middle of the room and clapped his hands as loudly as he could. She was slightly startled. Then she heard a slight movement in the wall. It was moving! Something was coming out of the wall! It started to protrude more and more... the wood end of something grew into the room. It was a bed. A bed just came out of the wall, just like that! To her, it was an odd combination of creepy and amazing.

Bud started to close the deal. "It's hooked up to a Clapper. You know, 'Clap on, clap off. The Clapper.'"

"Yes," she muttered. "I know the Clapper." She drained the second martini on the bar. She attempted a little joke. "Maybe at times like this, the word 'Clapper' isn't a good one to bring up to a lady."

Buddy laughed and bent over slightly. "I never heard that one. You're right. I'll come up with a better phrase. Now, if you'd like, I can clap again and send the bed away." He laughed at the word "clap" being used again.

Julie stood frozen for a second. *This is it*, her mind raced. *This is what it all comes down to—a guy in a wig and a bed that works with a Clapper. Is this how show business works?*

Buddy was pouring another martini when she made her decision. Julie walked toward him and grabbed his tie. She led him toward the bed like a pony.

"Maybe you can show me how some other things in this room work." She kicked off one of her high heels and kissed him on the mouth. His Aqua Velva made her slightly dizzy for a second.

They slid out of their clothes. They fell into the bed. "Strangers In The Night" played quietly. The dim lights played over their slightly chubby bodies. There was thunder and lightning both inside and outside "the penthouse." Bud was almost in. Suddenly, a flash outside was followed by an enormous clap of thunder. *Oh, no.* Not clap? Yes, clap. Julie noticed the movement first. Buddy leaned in and pressed to the sheets. He smothered her with a kiss. Before the lovers could untangle, the bed was almost into the wall. Julie laughed nervously and felt something above her head with her hand. It was more wood.

"Has this happened before?" she asked. She noticed how muffled the sound was. "It feels like we're in a coffin."

Buddy rolled off her and whispered, "It *is* a coffin." Then he let out his best Bela Lugosi scary laugh.

"Not funny, Buddy." It was black as midnight. She said, "Do you hear that?"

"I don't hear a thing. What?"

"Nothing. I don't hear a thing, either. No music, nothing. I think the power's off."

Bud cocked his ear in the dark and agreed. "I don't hear anything, either. And no, this has never happened before. I just had it installed a week ago. This is the first time I've done this."

Julie felt better and more pure than she had a right to. At least she wasn't 138th on the list of Clapper Flappers who'd been here before.

She spoke into the total blackness. "How do you open it from the inside?"

Buddy stared at the same darkness and didn't respond. He started to feel a little closed in.

All hints of romance went out of her voice. "Don't tell me you don't have an emergency switch or something. Who knows we're here?"

Buddy spoke carefully. "Nobody knows we're here. I had no idea we'd wind up in here. I'm as shocked as you are."

"Don't hand me that." She was getting panicky. "You hauled me up here to get a little action before we got down to business."

He put her straight. "Well, you sure got down to business easy enough."

"Who knows about this place?"

"My business manager, couple of songwriters, and you." Buddy sounded a tad nervous.

"We're stuck in a wall in an apartment in a building that nobody visits or checks or anything?"

"When the power comes back on, it'll surely pop us back out," he said with absolutely no conviction.

"Jesus, Buddy. What were you thinking? We could be stuck in here for days. What if nobody thinks to look in the *wall* for us? Oh, my *God!* I'm gonna die because of a Clapper. Get me the hell out of this box. I'm gonna FREAK OUT!"

Julie started to flail around in the crypt and cry a little. She began banging on the walls and shouting for help. Bud was now definitely in, but not the "in" he'd hoped for. They both flat-out freaked and started screaming and banging. The original banging was no longer an option. Julie started grabbing for a knob or a handle or anything she could pull. She was frightened out of her pants. She was also out of her pants.

Then it happened. As she fought with the darkness, her fingers became entangled in something. She clenched her fist and in one Velcro-sounding moment, Julie snatched Buddy bald. She screamed like she'd been attacked by a limp, hairy monster.

"Oh, Jesus. What *is* that?" She gave it a fling away from her toward the end of the crypt.

Buddy's scalp began to burn. She'd managed to undo a lot of glue, adhesive guards, and more. Bud had the Toupee 9000 that connected to his head with metal snaps. She'd yanked off his masterpiece with such gusto and fear, he literally felt light-headed. It was at their feet somewhere in the dark.

Suddenly, in the distance they could hear a faint strain of "My Way" being played on the Dobro. The power was back on. The bed didn't budge.

Buddy said, "I have a plan. You have to follow my plan precisely. You must do *exactly* as I say or we're both gonna die in here."

Julie listened carefully and noticed the music had come to the part where Frank sang, "And now the end is near."

Buddy continued, "The Clapper won't work because we're not in the room with it. I'm going to crawl down to the bottom of the bed. You brace yourself with your hands against the top. Put your feet on my shoulders and we'll push the bottom of the bed out through the wall."

"You mean break the wood? OK." She sounded skeptical, but it was at least a plan. She couldn't understand what all the fuss was about doing exactly what he said.

"When I'm in position, put your feet on my shoulders and, on three, we'll push. Then you must keep your eyes closed for another five minutes. Agreed?"

Julie repeated, "Feet on your shoulders. Push on three. Keep my eyes closed for five minutes. What is wrong with you?"

Buddy was grunting his way to the bottom of the bed. He put his feet against the bottom board and guided Julie's feet to his shoulders.

"Just do as I said, OK? Can you do that for me?"

"OK, but you keep your eyes closed then, too."

Buddy sighed and said, "Fine. I won't look at you in the disco light. You keep your eyes shut, and we'll be even. Ready? One...two...thuh-ree!"

It was a mighty heave. Julie drove her tootsies into Buddy's shoulders, and because of the sheer pain he shot his feet toward freedom. He heard a slight cracking noise and things began to give way. It was either the bed or Buddy.

"One more time," he said through clenched teeth.

Julie pushed with all her might and broke her promise at the same time. The bottom of the bed flew off and light rushed in and Buddy went flying out. She couldn't help it. She looked toward the light. She first noticed a glint of metal on top of his head dancing in the disco beams. He had four tiny, shiny horns. She noticed something furry was stuck between the bed and the wall. Buddy landed on the floor with a thud. She scrambled forward, eyes wide open.

He sat upright. He was naked and bruised, and he was bald. She was naked and bruised, and she started laughing. She couldn't help herself; it was an uncontrollable laugh—the laughter you couldn't stop. She laughed the "laugh of people when somebody farts in church" laugh. She laughed so hard, she fell out of bed beside Buddy. Buddy was so immobilized, he didn't even recoil when she touched one of the studs in his scalp. He was mortified. He was ruined. He was Linda Gratowski.

It took five singles before Julie had a moderate hit country record. Once she broke through that wall, she had another, bigger hit. Then her next went to No. 1 and stayed there for five weeks. She eventually had a *Greatest Hits* album released. Music Row was in love with her.

Everybody always remarked how much strength Buddy had shown. He had believed in her star dream when nobody else would. He was truly a genius. He had put so much of his own time and money into a project—much longer than anybody had before—and now it had paid off. That following year, Buddy was named producer and publisher of the year.

Julie started dating a senator and sang at the White House.

Shania and Kroger's

I HAVE A LONG HISTORY with grocery stores. Kroger's, in particular, goes way back to my childhood. For many summers, while I was battling my way through the teenage years, I worked at Kroger's. I realize it's actually Kroger Company, but everybody I knew growing up called it Kroger's. Can we just go with that? You realize Publix is not spelled correctly, either, and Piggly Wiggly isn't exactly inspiring. I was a produce clerk, cashier, and general flunky at several Kroger's for many a summer.

I was the genius at the Ludlow Kroger's in Kentucky who took it upon himself to put the truckload of bananas into the freezer for protection. I didn't realize bananas don't do all that well in subzero temps. We had a sale on black bananas for several weeks because of my industrious work habits. I also had the joy of crawling into the produce truck to check for tarantulas. I still have a massive case of arachnophobia because of it. I'm also scared, pant-peeing crazy scared, of spiders. If you've never opened the back of a truck and had a giant, furry, eight-legged monster come leaping out at you, you've never had any fun. Tarantulas are actually fairly tame, but I never wanted to get close enough to one to actually test that theory. The tarantulas didn't want to be in that truck full of bananas any more than I wanted to find them. We achieved détente early on.

I was the one who fell off a ladder into a table full of cantaloupes while changing a fluorescent lightbulb. Another summer sale. It was yours truly who put the wrong prices on cans of soup, which were snapped up immediately for one cent apiece. I stood in the meat department mesmerized by the meat cutters. I saw them get hypnotized by the monotonous motion of sawing up a chicken and buzz off a thumb every now and then. As an aspiring piano player, I quickly realized six fingers were not good if one day you wanted to become Liberace.

I especially enjoyed watching the thieves. Nobody was really dangerous, just sticky-fingered. We had one old guy who came in every day and walked laps around the store to get free samples of food on little toothpicks. Lunch every day included a couple of rounds through the store. One of my friends was a guy who worked for private security. We all knew most of the "pickers," as they were called. People who would eat, nosh, drink, and sample their way around a Kroger's. There would be a trail of half-eaten Twinkies and empty bottles of Coke on shelves every night. It was as if they said, "Hey! The stuff is just sitting there. Why not have some?" It never occurred to these folks that it was stealing.

Two or three times a week, I watched the security guy chase somebody into the parking lot with a canned ham in their shorts. My favorite was a woman who was waddling around the store. The private eye pointed her out to me. "Look at the way she walks. Somethin' ain't right." She'd disappear for awhile into the restroom and then come out and waddle the aisles some more. When she got busted, it turned out she was putting on pair after pair of pantyhose in the women's restroom. If she hadn't been so greedy that she had to walk like John Wayne, she'd have gotten away with her crime. The waddle did her in.

I also remember with some pain that the store manager loved Guy Lombardo. He chose *Guy's Greatest Hits* as the music of choice over the speaker system. Even today, if I hear Guy and those damn Royal Canadians honking though "Harbor Lights," I get hives. Over and over and over with that damn saxophone. It's the same effect I see guys who drive ice cream trucks have, with that tinkle-bell version of "The Entertainer." It's no wonder those guys are nuts.

I also flirted like crazy with every girl who came through my checkout lane. I actually requested to *not* work the "10 items or less" express lane. If I got a mom with her teenage, sullen, and bored daughter in tow, I didn't want them whisking through too quickly. It's not called the checkout lane for nothing. While they were checking things out, so was I. While Mom watched me like a hawk as I rang up her groceries, I casually asked the daughter, "Who's your favorite singer?" If she was particularly babe-a-licious, I even volunteered to push the grocery cart into the parking lot and help load up. I was just that wonderful of a young man; I only wanted to help all I could. Several times I offered to ride in their car to help unload at the daughter's house, but that was probably crossing the line.

Today, I rarely go into a Kroger's. When I do venture in, it's because I am in the area and can't wait for a pill or lunch—usually both. I generally wind up in the same checkout line because I don't like that self-serve deal. I'm against *all* self-serve deals because I always think the company is not paying somebody. I don't want to self-serve at the airlines' check-in. I like it when the agent does it. That way I feel like there's actually a seat and a plane waiting for me. Otherwise, I always think I'll get to the end of the boarding ramp and step off into empty space.

I'm not a self-serve guy. I don't like those Korean restaurants where they bring you raw chicken and some soy sauce at a table with a grill in the middle. I didn't go out to a restaurant to cook my own damn lunch. Hire a guy who cooks. I'm not a self-cooking guy.

At my usual checkout lane, a tiny, bent-over grandma works as the bag boy. I used to be a bag boy, and that job is called "bag boy" even if it's worked by a tiny, bent-over grandma. I spent years learning to put the loaves of bread in the bag first and then placing the soft drinks and cans of liquid concrete on top. I know how the system works.

And, of course, you also have the choice. Grandma always croaks out the question, "Paper or plastic?" Bag technology is a big deal. You either ask for the plastic, which means you end up with hundreds of environment-choking bags in the trunk with each single bag only holding a lightbulb or box of Cheerios... *or* you go with the paper bags, now with "handles," which come loose just as you're almost in the house. Hellman's mayo and Ding Dongs crash and disperse on the steps.

My wife says people who bring their *own* bags to the grocery store are just showing off. Flaunting their tree-hugging goodness for the rest of us Earth haters. How did we send people to the moon and not perfect the technology of paper bag handles?

Tiny, bent-over Grandma makes me feel guilty. She never knows where one load of groceries ends and another begins. She usually starts packing somebody else's Cool Ranch Doritos in with *my* celery. She should be home and not packing up groceries all day. I'm not being sexist, I just wish she didn't have to work at the wrong end of an endless line of groceries. She should be home doing grandma things: watching the grandbabies and knitting doilies and betting on the ponies on the internet.

How did she get to this place? What confluence of the stars got TBO Granny into such a situation? This (and you thought I'd never get here) is where Shania Twain comes in.

Talk about wanting to check out somebody's groceries. Shania was gorgeous. I first met her early on, when she was trying to have a hit with Norro Wilson as producer. Norro, by the way, is a perfect example of why you should never let a small child pick out their own name.

Ms. Twain didn't really hit the jackpot 'til she hooked up with Mutt Lange. Mutt is legendary for his songwriting and producing talents. I suspect he *also* picked out his own first name. Together, he and Shania made some explosive records: "Any Man of Mine." "You're Still the One." "Man! I Feel Like a Woman." Combine a signature sound with great vocals, and you get a lot of hits. She also was one of the first to be marketed by videos. The vids exploded, too. They went off like rockets because, on film, she's even more gorgeous.

Shania was constantly criticized for her records. I *never* understood why music people would say, "She's pretty, but she can't sing." I would nod and then go online and watch her singing somewhere live, and she sounded like she could sing to me. Oh sure, her lyrics and songs weren't going to make poets tremble, but so what? And if being able to sing perfectly was now a requirement, half the town would be looking for a new job. But she *could* sing.

I'm certain all that small-town, Music Row talk made her defensive. She always seemed like she was going to be attacked when I spoke with her. She was lovely but a little unsure of herself. Guess what? Your parents get killed, you raise your younger brothers practically by yourself, you get a little unsure. I always thought she should be hugged and applauded. The jealous reaction, however, was pretty intense. Some of that seeped into the public opinion but not enough to keep her from becoming a huge star.

About a hundred feet from my songwriting office was a vegetarian restaurant. I could never remember the actual name of it. We all called it "Weeds and Seeds." I went there twice a week and often saw Shania and Mutt enjoying a plate of something that looked like horse feed and grass trimmings. This was usually the daily special. I ate there because it made me feel healthy. I never actually enjoyed it, but they had wine, so it wasn't a total lost cause. I often saw Emmylou Harris chowing down on a big pile of leaves and tofu. When we all left, nobody smiled. You just knew your teeth looked like the hood of a tractor.

The joy was spotting Mutt in a natural setting. There are more pictures of the Abominable Snowman than there are of Mutt Lange. Supposedly, he bought *all* the available shots of him and hid them away. They looked happy when I saw the two of them sitting there. I always thought of them then as "Mutt 'n' Honey." They were on a break from making an album. The musicians who played on the sessions with Mutt at the helm said he was pretty demanding. He'd have them all play and play, and take a shot. Usually, from what I heard, he'd "fix" it himself later that night. Their relationship went south years later in a bad way. I know Shania is now married to the husband of her former best friend. *Former* being the key word.

Shania has a great phrase. I've seen her probably twenty times in my life to speak or do an interview. She's like me. She can't call up a name immediately like Garth does. Shania is so cool, however, she sees you coming and says, "Now, *there's* a face that looks familiar." I've stolen that. It tells the other person, "I know you, I want to talk, but give me a clue here, pal."

I know Shania struggles with dysphonia. Stress in life strikes at your vocal chords. It's an insidious problem that takes away the one thing singers have. Can you imagine? You're worried about your voice, the worry affects your voice, and the spiral continues 'til you can't sing. I am hopeful that, from what I hear, she's on the mend. I also hear rumors of a Vegas show like Celine Dion's. She deserves it. I want her to feel like a woman again.

Old Black and Whites

I WAS A "SURPRISE" to my parents. I have one sister, Carole Jean, who is thirteen years older than me. She got married at sixteen and moved out of our home, so I don't know her as well as some family members know each other. I was three and more concerned with making vowel sounds and discovering my feet. We still chat now and then, and recently she sent me a box of old black-and-white pictures my mother had kept in her attic.

My mom was hilarious. As I mentioned earlier, she was on my radio show for years. She was also *not* a hoarder. She threw out most of the things I left behind when I went to college. I could have killed her. My baseball cards—gone. My collection of old records—gone. My entire collection of Hardy Boys books—ditto. All are now probably worth upwards of $285—lost forever.

However, she did keep pictures, and I'm going through them trying to recall who is who. I have a single picture of my dad's mother, Grandmother House. She is right out of the Amish-Mama playbook. She wasn't Amish, but she's wearing that long, black dress. It's tightly buttoned up and very prim. She's got a gray bun and is built like grandmas are supposed to be built—round and firm.

My dad's pop was a character. Will and Emma House lived on a farm in Kentucky. Every single visit, my grandfather asked me to give him a hug because, "Your old grampa won't be here next Christmas." Those are always lovely words for a six-year-old to hear. "Death is imminent, so get ready for it, sonny boy." He gave me the same "final hug" speech for about twenty years. My only memory of Grandma is "Grandma is in the kitchen." I think she was born in there and slept in there. I loved to go to their farm because they had a root cellar. As rural as that sounds, it is. It was a huge mound dug behind their little farmhouse. It had a door on the backside, and you walked down steps to enter. It was beneath the earth. It felt like an adventure. I ran to the root cellar the moment I got there. One time, you were in the dark, cool root cellar and saw the few jars of beans being kept cool. Another time, you saw the hams hanging on a rope. And another time, you looked around at the dim stone walls. Then fun in the root cellar was over. Root cellars are good for storing stuff that spoils in the house and are a real blast for about two minutes. After that, it was time to visit Grandma in the kitchen or discuss the future with Grandpa Kervorkian.

The biggest memory of my life was at age ten. Mom and Dad packed up the car to drive south to the farm for Thanksgiving. Thanksgiving was a big deal back then. It was the only time other than a week's vacation that we went anywhere. My father's family visited and there were other kids. We went to the creek, played in the barn, or, if things got dull, locked one of the girls in the root cellar—all quality activities.

Thanksgiving dinner was the pièce de résistance for me. Grandma produced the greatest food in the world, and my dad reminisced. For weeks ahead of the special day, Dad described the golden brown turkey and the sweet potatoes and how fabulous the stuffing was. There wasn't a restaurant in Paris that could prepare apple pie like Grandma. I wasn't sure they had pie in France, but I went with it. Ten-year-old boys dream about food and bikes and root cellar adventures. Girls aren't in the picture yet.

I do remember some country music playing in the background of my memories of Grandma's house. There was no television to be watched, but a massive wooden radio stood guard in the parlor. The radio was so old that it only had one giant dial to find radio stations. The call letters of the big, 50,000-watt AM stations were printed right on the outside of the dial: WSM/Nashville, KDKA/Pittsburgh, WIL/St Louis, WLW/Cincinnati. I imagine that's where I first heard WSM and that "old-timey" country music. It all now feels like I was in a black-and-white Turner Classics movie.

But back to the turkey dinner. Thanksgiving morning in Kentucky is the same every year. It's gray and cold outside. The ground is partially frozen. When you walk in the woods, things crack beneath your steps, and crows are always bickering some-where in the distance. You pack some semblance of a suitcase and load up the car for the trip to Grandma's. Dad is already talking about how great dinner is going to be. One last Winston before Dad and Mom and I head down toward Falmouth, Kentucky. I fasted with only a bowl of Cheerios to make sure I had room for the feast. We were gonna arrive a little early, about two in the chilly afternoon, for a little visit, a few stories, and then down to serious drumstick business.

In that little farmhouse, the walls were so thin we could hear music in the driveway. The fireplace was smoking, and Grandma was in the kitchen. The stove turned Grandma's kitchen into a sauna. Yes, it was so hot in the kitchen that I couldn't stand the heat. So, like Truman, I stayed out.

The important thing was staking out an area at the big table. I'd been to many a family gathering and had been relegated to the card table—a flimsy foldout eating deal where the "kids" sat. This meant the drumsticks were long gone before the turkey was doled out to the card table ghetto. Not this year. I was already placing markers in front of the chair at the big table.

Time began to slow as I got hungrier. I politely spoke to my cousins. Girls who didn't know about anything that I wanted to discuss: baseball cards, crawdads, drumsticks. Grandpa did his Speech of Impending Doom for some of the newest little critters in the family. It *had* to be close to dinnertime. It was getting near three o'clock, and I'd heard stories of young boys dying of starvation in foreign countries because dinner was not served on time at Thanksgiving.

I finally decided to take matters into my own hands, hoping to get a sneak at ol' Tom in the furnace/kitchen. I braced for the heat and started the conversation. "Grandma? How's the turk-a-lurk [my mother's phrase] coming along? We about ready to sit down?"

Here is where I think I learned about life and expectations. It still scars me to this day to have been informed with the hideousness and unfeeling treatment of gray-haired relatives. I have never fully recovered from the disappointment we call the future. Grandma delivered the fatal blow. "Oh, hi, sweetie darlin'. The turkey? Oh, I don't think he's quite ready for the table yet."
I'm pretty sure she laughed a mocking laugh—the one people do in front of those who don't know what they know. Vicious, evil, bun-wearing mockers.

"Come here, honey. Look out Grandma's window. See? See? He's right there."

I stood on the kitchen chair she pulled up for me. I peered through the steamed-up window. There, doing quite a strut, was Tom T. Turkey. He was still *alive!* It was a world gone mad. How could a turkey, filled with stuffing and gravy and using the drumsticks I was assigned to share, be walking around in the yard? For the love of all that's holy, *how?*

I ran screaming from the room to warn everyone of the upcoming famine. People of Earth, the end is near! I ran straight into the parlor and saw my father. He had moved my chair to the card table, along with my "markers," and said, "Hey, Hoss. Come on over here and have a baloney sandwich. Your Grandma says this year we're eatin' at a decent hour like rich folks do. Supper ain't on 'til seven." He acted like he didn't understand the tragedy that was breaking out all around us. The poor man was oblivious to dying of starvation. Baloney would only prolong the inevitable. We were all going to die. Except for Tom, who let out a mocking gobble and flew on top of the root cellar.

Italians Do It Every Night

IF I CAN QUOTE Hank Snow again, "I've Been Everywhere." Of course, not *every*where, but pretty close. I think travel is the best education that you can have. That's why we've dragged our daughter, Autumn, around the world and back: England, Egypt, Japan, France, China, Italy, Morocco, and Cincinnati, Ohio, to name just a few stops. Seeing other cultures and learning to navigate a strange land makes you a better person. Autumn is a fabulously better person.

I also like to see places. I can spend up to fifteen minutes in a museum. I can sit in the front of a Parisian café for five hours. Museums need better wine and waiter service, I think. I could appreciate looking at old broken vases and Victorian chastity belts a lot longer if I had a glass of wine—and a little scooter wouldn't be a bad idea, either.

Al is a reader of little white signs—you know, the little white information cards next to the picture of a guy sitting on a horse with dwarves frolicking around. She wants to know who painted the picture and what the horse's name is. I'm generally through the museum by the time she's figured out how to operate that little tourist guide thingy they give you to explain it all—the thing you hold up to your ear and some guy tells you what century the thing you're looking at was discovered. I've spent most of my life waiting for her to come out of some museum or dungeon.

I thought I might give you some international travel tips. If you like country music, take your own along because it's not on the local FM stations in Italy or China. In China, by the way, they play Country & Eastern music. Although country does pop up in the weirdest places. We were in a taxi on our way out to the Great Pyramids in Egypt, and heard Merle Haggard singing "Mama Tried" on the radio.

I always think of Dolly whenever I visit the Great Pyramids. I don't know why, I just do. They're enormous. The pyramids, that is. Every single guy in Egypt has a cousin who rents camels, and they *all* insist you ride a damn camel for awhile. It's fun…once. After that, trying to do anything involves telling the taxi driver you *do not want to ride a camel* to go to your hotel.

Allyson and I still say one of the most exciting sights we've ever seen were the giant wooden doors as you walk out of the Cairo airport. We weren't ready for the culture shock. You stand behind the doors, and they open onto total chaos. Nobody pays any attention to traffic lights. People are praying on mats beside the road. Camels are available for hire to take you to your bus. You're surrounded by teeming masses of humanity. It's like stepping into a life-size beehive.

You should also be forewarned that the fabulous exotic Great Pyramids of Giza, the three famous monoliths in the desert, are not as exotic as you thought. You always see them photographed from the front. If you took a picture from the other side, you'd see the Holiday Inn and Taco Bell about a half-mile away. The actual pyramids are amazing. Being from Nashville and in the music business, I can only imagine how many roadies it took to set these things up. As you read this, Egypt is probably not safe enough to visit. I know I'm glad I went, but I was happy to leave. Walking around with two blondes and a big American face is like strolling around at Talladega in a tuxedo. You tend to stick out a bit.

If you do decide to risk it, take a side trip to Luxor, the Valley of the Kings. I know Steve Martin visited there, because King Tut is buried there. King Tut was the Toby Keith of his day. The temperature at Luxor is usually around 146 degrees. No rain, and the sun is brutal. It's like the old days at Fan Fair at the Nashville Fairgrounds. And just like Fan Fair, the only word you need to know is *baksheesh*. When somebody has his or her hand out for a tip, a favor, a drink, or a bribe, that's *baksheesh*. I'm used to it because I am in radio and the music business. I'm used to somebody needing something to get something done. It's an art form in Egypt. Did I mention that you can also take a camel ride on the way to the airport?

My wife is relentlessly cheerful, as I've said a hundred times. It's just so irritating to be with someone who is always happy and says things that make you bend over laughing. I deserve a medal, don't I? On vacays, it's my job to plan the hotels, the itinerary, and most important, where we eat. I *love* it. I can spend hours on the computer before any trip, reading reviews of restaurants and hotels that used to be nunneries. We were in Rome having a glorious time when I noticed a tragedy in my schedule. I confessed to Allyson, "I made a drastic error in restaurant schedules. Tonight's designated dinner stop will mark the third evening in a row that we have rezzies at an Italian restaurant." I don't know what I was thinking. It was a glaring misstep of epic proportions.

Her reply? "No problem, hon. The Italians do it every night."

Me: "Do what every night?"

Her: "Have Italian for dinner. I bet they go for months before they have anything but Italian, 'cause they're Italian. Imagine how many nights they have Japanese in Japan."

We had Italian that night, and it was fabulous. She was right.

Speaking of Japan, it was tough. Tokyo and the lights and the sights were amazing. The Ginza shopping district makes Times Square look like Dothan, Alabama. The Japanese really like their buildings covered in advertising. I warn you, however, these people are serious about their language. You can go for days and not find a person who speaks anything but Japanese. There are a few printed signs, but overall it's full-frontal Japan. If you're jet-lagged, as we were, and wake up at three thirty in the morning, go to Tsukiji. It's the fish market and the source of all the seafood eaten every day by the people of Tokyo. We got up, dressed, and caught a taxi that took us to the most amazing collection of things from the sea I'd even seen. It's enormous and it's squiggly. I once had sushi with Jeff Cook of Alabama, who explained all about raw fish to me. Jeff Cook is from Ft. Payne and not Shinjuku. He has not a clue what real sushi is. It's businessmen at a counter eating from a plate of live, squirming eels. It's things served as a delicacy that look like they fell off a garbage truck. Japanese cuisine is *seeeeaaaa*food. It's the Patsy Cline of raw fish. We once walked thirty blocks because we saw an arrow pointing to a McDonald's. I'm not sure what was in that Big Mac, but it was a welcome relief.

We also got treated like dirt in Japan. Because we bombed them, I realize they can be a little ticklish. But *they* started it. We finished it. Neither my father nor Allyson's dad had one little good thing to say about the Japanese. You get years ripped out of your life to float around on a ship (which they both did) because the "Japs attacked us," and you don't like certain folks. The Japanese didn't like us, either.

Sometimes, when I hear the word "discrimination" bandied about, I think back to a ritzy, steel-and-glass, upscale dining place in Ginza, the posh neighborhood of Tokyo. This was probably my only time of truly being treated differently because of what color my skin was and what nationality I looked like.

My family—Allyson, Autumn, and I—entered and took a seat at one of the lovely tables. We waited for service, which was a little slow. Waiters sauntered by and looked elsewhere. Probably the language barrier. After a long wait, I finally waved at one of the servers and mimed we wanted to order. He just stared and walked on. Suddenly, it began to occur to me we were being *ignored!* We weren't getting slow service, we were getting *no* service. Our reaction was a slow burn. This just doesn't happen to *us.* You have to wait on people, it's a *restaurant,* for cryin' out loud. It's quite an awakening to realize you are about as welcome as a banjo at the symphony.

We walked as slowly as we could out of there. We weren't offended (that's a lie; we were P.O.'d as hell), and nonchalantly moseyed our little old American butts out the door. Stupid restaurant. We didn't want to eat there anyway. It's the only time in my life this has ever happened to me. I can't imagine if that was the regular routine, if you had to wonder if somebody would let you eat at their counter. It would make you rage at the world. You'd be Toby Keith.

The massive area was lit by burning oil lanterns. As the sun was setting, the flames cast an eerie, spooky glow over the square. As your eyes adjusted, you noticed monkeys on leashes, bears asleep on rugs, tables filled with snails, and piles of goat brains. People were drinking and laughing and fighting. You noticed a man having a tooth pulled by someone with his leg on the patient's stomach. Strange music floated through the evening heat. Men looked at you with blank stares as if they wanted to either shake hands or pull a giant knife out of their sack. Bladders of wine were hoisted toward the sky and shared by the crowd. A woman gave a greasy character with no teeth a haircut. Steel griddles were covered in shrimp that danced as the oil heated beneath them. A shout in the distance, and somebody held up a steaming animal leg.

Yes, it looked exactly like the tailgate before an Eric Church concert. Exactly.

Or, it could be you've walked into the Djemaa El Fna. The open-air market/restaurant/mall/pub/farmer's market/dentist's office/barbershop/yard sale of Marrakech, Morocco. I've been back-stage at a lot of Eric Church concerts, so this place wasn't a total shock to me. It was still a bizarre bazaar anyway. During the day in Marrakech, you see women totally wrapped in rich, black cloth. Allyson says she still remembers locking eyes for a moment with a woman with only a slit in the traditional chador for her to see. It wasn't confrontational or angry, just one person sizing up another. Travel does that to you. You realize, underneath it all, humans are basically the same everywhere. People with families and jobs trying to make it to five o'clock and get home to feed the kids.

I always asked a driver or guide, when I heard some music, what the song was about. The melodies were intricate and nothing Dierks Bentley would record, but the subject was the same: a love gone wrong, a story about a hardworking man who didn't get what he deserved, or riding your camel into the desert for some privacy or a party. It might as well have been something by Jason Aldean—the Moroccan version of "Big Green Tractor."

I still get a chill thinking of nights in Morocco. The air is warm and filled with incense. Women and men, covered head to toe, move like ghosts as the wind whips at them and they disappear into invisible doors and twisting alleyways. And there ain't a Cracker Barrel for 10,000 miles.

The French and country stars of the '60s and '70s have a lot in common. They drink like fish. They smoke like chimneys. They do what they want and couldn't care less what people think of them. Ray Price could have been French.

It's not as bad in Paris today as it was the first time I went to the City of Lights. Back then, everybody smoked—the men, the women, the babies, and the dogs. You would see nannies puff-ing away, pushing a stroller with a pint-sized Parisian, lighting up a Gauloises. The French also don't care what they eat. If at one time it was part of an animal, then fire up the grill, Pierre, dinner's comin'!

I think it's hilarious that there is a "Country Music Association" in France. The thought of François in a cowboy hat singing "All My Exes Live in Toulouse" is just funny to me. I've discovered over the years in the music business that a lot of American artists claim to be "big" in Europe. They can't get arrested in the States, but somehow people in Provence love their music. It might be true, but I'm just sayin' I don't think Alan Jackson is planning a tour de France anytime soon.

The one thing I love about Paris is the showbiz look of that city. I once was seated beside a lovely man on a flight from Paris to London. I couldn't help but notice he was reading a lot of letters with the heading "Directeur de la Lumiere." In the worst French possible, I asked him what that was. It looked to me like "Director of Light." It *was* Director of Light. He explained to me in flawless, accented English that his job was to make sure everybody in Paris looked good at night. It ain't called the City of Light for nothing. His mission was to put a golden glow on couples walking along the Seine or sitting in a small café with a glass of Sauvignon blanc. Why, it's just like the *Grand Ole Opry* with berets. The *Opry* gives you a special spotlight, and so does France.

A few times I've been scared traveling. Once when the girls and I were lost behind the city wall in Luxor, the stares from guys sitting on their haunches were creepy. We were also stopped by a hotel manager from wandering too far down a road near our hotel in the Valley of the Kings. He just shook a finger at us and said, "No, no. You no go. Very dangerous that way." It looked almost exactly like a backcountry road in Tennessee or Kentucky...lush and green and almost romantic but probably precarious. We took his advice.

St. Petersburg, Russia, was the worst. It's a beautiful city with churches that take your breath away. The Hermitage is a stunning collection of artifacts and paintings in a building founded by

Catherine the Great in the 1700s. If you wanted to look at all 3 million exhibits, it would take untold years. Allyson would still be there today, on the second floor, reading about some lamp. When we were in Russia, it was more like the Wild West. It's been years, but I still get the willies thinking about that city. We walked past stores with such opulence and then passed a poor Russian squatting on the sidewalk, with a single head of lettuce for sale.

We had a young guide named Olga. I think there's a national law that young, blonde guides in Russia be named Olga. She was a terrific guide, but there was a sadness about her I never could get my head around. I always imagined she left us and returned to a gray apartment in the shakier part of town.

I asked Olga to take us to Nevsky Prospect. It's the Fifth Avenue of St. Petersburg. She acted like it wasn't all that great an idea but agreed to lead us into the crowds. What happened next is so typical and so scary at the same time. Young gangs of Russian boys gathered around Allyson and Autumn shoving sweatshirts for sale into their faces. They held items up high and babbled on about how we should buy them.

Al finally had enough and shouted, "No!" Just as suddenly as the throngs of young street vendors had appeared, they were gone. They just disappeared, like Dave and Sugar. Olga stood in front of us and was a little wobbly. Then we noticed what she knew had happened. They were pickpockets. Allyson had kept our passports in a little leather bag she wore on the front of her belt. It was unzipped and empty.

I tried to calm things and said, "It's not that bad. We can get new ones." Olga disagreed, much to my shock, and said, "No, this is bad, very bad. This is *very* bad."

Great, I thought. *I'm gonna wind up sitting on the sidewalk selling a head of lettuce.*

We did what everybody does when confronted with being stuck in a foreign country with no passports and no visas—we called our radio producer in America. I called Devon O'Day. In a heart-beat, Devon was on it. While we sat like potatoes in our room, she went to work. She called Vice President Al Gore's father's office in Carthage, Tennessee. She actually got the former senator on the phone. He said, "Let me see what I can do."

A short while later, Dev told me she answered the phone and heard, "This is the vice president's office." It always helps to have the vice president of the United States' dad start the ball rolling for you when you're stuck in Russia. We were told to go to the U.S. Embassy with new pictures of ourselves and await further instructions.

That Saturday, we walked up to the guard station of the American embassy. An officious young Marine said the embassy was closed. I said, "Did you get a call from the vice president's office?" He sort of snapped to, looked at a list, and said, "Oh, you must be the Houses. Yes, sir. Just a moment, sir."

He made a phone call, and we were in. The whole security affair is quite similar to going backstage before a Tim McGraw concert. If you can mention the right name, you are welcomed inside with open arms.

I fretted and worried the whole time. The day before, we'd spent hours slogging to one Russian government office after another, trying to get a visa to get out of Russia. It's no wonder Russia was in such trouble. Nobody cared, nobody worked, and nobody helped. It was a lot like Music Row the month before Christmas, except there were actually bottles of vodka sitting on desks. Empty vodka bottles. I guess it helps to have a little Stoli to get you through a busy workday in the Soviet Union. Come to think of it, that's also a lot like the Music Row offices.

Olga stayed with us as we went through security with our new visas and the passports that had been handmade by a slightly disheveled embassy employee. He'd come to the office on a Saturday to help out some fellow citizens get the hell out of St.

Petersburg. Allyson had said it best (as usual), "Everybody in that city was just deflated. They had no reason to want to do anything. They lived every day with no reason to smile."

We boarded the plane and landed a few hours later in Venice, Italy. As gray as St. Petersburg had been, Venice was as sunny and blue. I will never forget the exhilaration of riding in the back of a water taxi across the Laguna Veneta. It was a brilliant day and seventy-five degrees, and me and my girls were out of Russia and going to have Italian every night in a row. We laughed like schoolkids at how free we were. I don't think I ever felt more American, either.

American and free.

We stood—Al, Autumn, and I—on Wangfujing Street. That's the "main drag," as my mother used to say, in Beijing, China. The clouds were managing to squeeze out a little misty rain on the shoppers and the few tourists on this busy thoroughfare. We'd just been gawking at a Chinese pharmacy across Wangfujing. Shelves filled with tiger paws and dragon lips and God-knows-what-else in hundreds of rows of tiny jars. The Chinese still practice "natural" medicine, and from the looks of the people, it works. We were in a strange land—the only non-Chinese in either direction.

The rain began to pick up a bit. I noticed a small, elderly Chinese woman in traditional garb crossing the street. She was walking directly toward us. Uh-oh. Customs in other countries are strange, and I figured we'd probably done something to insult half the population. She approached, she bowed, and then she opened an umbrella and held it over our heads. Such a simple gesture, but it told me what people in China were like. They were like everybody else. Usually, folks are kind and helpful and ready to laugh. A smile is universal in its message. I've never smiled or received a friendly grin such that I didn't know things were going to be all right.

Sometimes I think Music Row has the Great Wall of China surrounding it. It's tough to penetrate and to go around. Strangers from another land, like Arkansas, have to learn where the gates are and how to go under or over or through the barriers to get inside the Forbidden City.

We were told by our Chinese guide to turn left when we got to the Great Wall. I had no idea how huge the Wall really is. It's like a double-lane road on top. It has gates and entrances every few miles to walk along the upper Wall. "Turn left" was good advice from our guy. As we walked with a few other Americans along an empty section of the Wall, I looked back at the other side, and it was packed with Chinese. I don't know if the custom is to go one way, but the populace obviously stayed the course. Our side was almost deserted.

Just like Nashville, they buried a lot of people in the Wall when they constructed it. People just got covered up in the course of living their lives. It happens in Twang Town the same way. Nashville has a lot of rules, too. You go a certain way. You do things in a particular manner. Outsiders can sometimes get lost in the shuffle or get buried in the wall.

Autumn loves to remind me that our guide for the whole Chinese trip was not named Dong. I, apparently by not listening, never learned his real name. I addressed the poor guy as Dong the entire trip. I yelled "Dong!" in crowds to get his attention. He spoke perfect English, and I spoke two words of Chinese. One of them was "Dong." Our last day, as a big treat for Dong, we invited him to breakfast. The Great Wall Sheraton had a buffet to make Waffle House pea-green with envy. Sausage and bacon and eggs and pancakes in metal warming trays. I half-expected the Chinese guy manhandling the little fry griddle to ask me if I wanted things "smothered and scattered." That's Waffle House-ese for, "How do you like your hash browns?" We slid in a booth and I said, "Dong, have a good old-fashioned American breakfast on us." I was certain he was about to have the meal of a lifetime.

He was horrified. He carefully poked at the bacon and examined the waffles like they were nuclear waste. Dong looked at our food just as we'd treated the traditional Chinese meal. We had been good at pointing at words or signs on a menu and hoping to win the Menu Lottery at most authentic Chinese eateries. We *never* won once. I once managed to order sea slug and lemons. Autumn cheerfully pointed at some squiggles and received four or five chicken feet standing ankle-deep in brown dishwater. The Chinese have Chinese *every day*. And they never get tired of it. Chicken feet get old to me after a few days.

Our last day in China, I tipped Dong fifty bucks. He told me he couldn't accept it. I was stunned. A fifty isn't all that much, especially for slogging around after Americans and having to look at pancakes. He carefully explained that would be his apartment rent for the next two years. It would throw things out of whack. He lived in government housing and would probably get noticed for having so much extra dough left over after his two dollar rent bill. I think China is a bit different now, but not much.

I do know that if you want to thrill and amaze Chinese people from the "outer provinces" like Mongolia, where everybody has the same serious "Moe"-do haircut, or if you want folks to stop and stare and ask to have a picture taken with you, take two fabulous blonde beauties with you. In fact, if you are planning a trip to Mongolia anytime soon, give Allyson and Autumn a call. They'd probably go.

Prior to visiting Spain, the two things that I'd had contact with that sounded Spanish were gazpacho and Freddy Fender. Freddy is, of course, neither Spanish nor gazpacho. Gazpacho is awful; Freddy is good.

My Rascal Flatts pal, Jay DeMarcus, told me that when they played the White House for George W. Bush, they served gazpacho. He said "When we hit the stage, I said how thrilled the Flatts were to be there, but, 'Mr. President, our soup was cold.' It got a big laugh."

I knew Freddy Fender only through my producer friend Ray Baker. Freddy recorded two monster hits: "Before the Next

Teardrop Falls" and "Wasted Days and Wasted Nights" (the Music Row theme song). Freddy had quite a career and looked a lot like porn star Ron Jeremy. I'm not sure if that hurt Freddy or helped.

Ray told me that one afternoon he and Freddy went into Baskin-Robbins. Freddy spied the chocolate and said, "I'd like two scoopses of brown." Maybe he was more Spanish than I thought.

The rumor was that the reason Freddy sang so high on "Teardrop" was because he was singing to a track made for Jeannie C. Riley. He hit the notes anyway, and it was a smash.

But getting back to Spain (which I'd like to do), we went there to see the World Expo in Seville. The world expos were events held around the planet in various cities. It's sort of like Epcot Center for real. They have pavilions built from all the countries. We visited the one in Hanover, Germany, and Lisbon, Portugal. The best, however, was in Seville.

We first flew to Madrid and spent a few nights having roast pig and sangria. We did the sights and then hopped on the bullet train to Seville. These people are serious about being Spaniards. They have Spanish food every night for weeks at a time.

They also have bullfights—one of the cruelest and also most exciting things I've ever attended. I bought seats right behind a matador, and it was amazing. The pageantry, the emotion, and the terror were all there in equal proportion. The crowd screaming, the music, and the bullfight itself were mesmerizing. I'm not sure I want to go to another, but I'm glad I went. I fully expected a great barbeque after the event, but that didn't happen. Just like you never see pet shops in North Korea, you see a lot of steak houses in Spain. I think there's a correlation there.

I love music, and in Spain, you see and hear it everywhere. It's like a Friday night in NashVegas. I still remember walking down a street and seeing six guys in black pants and white shirts sitting in hardback chairs at the end of a one-way alley. Surrounded by the old stone buildings and the cobblestone streets, these guys knew it was a natural amphitheater. They clapped and stomped, and two guitars flamenco'd into the night. In my town, they have The Bluebird Café. I don't know the name of a club in Seville, but a nice alleyway was just as good.

Autumn was twenty when we went to the World Expo in Seville. She was totally babe-i-fied. They had massive parties and dance clubs—discos, if you will—every night. We saw shows where Fred Astaire and Ginger Rogers were projected on giant water sprays and danced on the lakes. We saw fireworks. We heard bands and sampled food from all over the world. It was really as alive as you can get. We heard that chest-thumping bass from a mile away as we approached a massive covered dance arena. There, thousands of folks were ordering tequila and jumping into the lights and onto the throbbing floor. A gorgeous young Spaniard walked by and smiled at Autumn. She was gonna dance the night away. I told her that we were going back to the hotel but wanted her to get home pretty soon. She was a woman but still my little girl. I watched her jump into the flailing arms and happy dancing crowd and said, "Pedro." His name, he had told us, was Pedro.

Hours later, I was staring in the dark at the ceiling. It seemed like hours, anyway. I finally said out loud, "Are you awake?"

"Yes," Allyson answered. "She's not back."

Frankly, I'm not sure it had been that long. We were a little disoriented and jet-lagged, as always. Then again in the darkness, Allyson asked, "Are you worried?"

"Me? No, not at all. Let her have some fun. Why should we worry? We know she's somewhere in Spain with a guy named Pedro." That's like being in Moultrie, Georgia, and asking strangers, "Have you seen my daughter? She's with a guy named Bubba." We now were immediately panic-stricken.

I suddenly felt like I was the worst father who had ever lived. But then a key rattled in the lock, and Autumn sneaked into the room, where we had all bunked together. I didn't say anything. Al said, "Hi, honey, we're glad you're home." Autumn told me years later that they'd just danced and had struggled to talk because of the language barrier. I have the feeling he was a good kisser. She just said, "He was *so* sweet." I still don't trust anyone named Pedro.

My favorite city in the world to visit is London. They speak English there. Not the kind of English they speak in Kentucky, but close. All Londoners think country music is cowboys and people shooting guns and sayin', "Howdy, ma'am." Of course, a lot of Hollywood types think the same thing. In reality, only about 50 percent of the Nashville population shoots guns and says, "Howdy, ma'am."

I also think the Brits are hilarious. My grandmother was born and raised in England during the early part of her life. She called me "Li'l Bit. Grandma and her second hubby owned a strawberry farm in Ohio. Carl had one arm. He'd blown the other one off in a hunting accident and had walked for miles with his arm inside his overalls. He made it; the arm didn't. I remember him rolling a cigarette with a paper and tobacco pouch with one hand. I haven't seen anyone else "roll" a cig except for some friends of mine from England. However, most of them have two hands.

I still have friends "across the pond" and get pictures of their kids now. We've probably stayed in London as much as we've been anyplace except for our house. I was on the BBC for years with my friend Nick Barraclough. He's a Beeb Two radio star, and I'd go to Reba's studio once a week to talk to him about Nashville over a satellite connection. He even came to the States to broadcast the *CMA Awards* for Radio 2, and I cohosted with him. He loves country music and did everything he could to get the Brits to like it, too. The songs strike a chord deep inside him, as they do with people all over the world. I'd always say to him about a particularly great song, "Why didn't I *think* of that?" Nick always replies, "Of course, you knew all those words. Just not in that order."

Please go to London. It will do you good. Take the morning Virgin flight, as we always do. You leave New York City at 8 A.M.

and arrive in London at 8 P.M. You then got to bed and wake up without the jet lag. I've done the overnight flights to Europe and have spent most of the trip trying not to fall asleep in my mashed potatoes.

For fifteen years, we stayed at a small hotel, the Capital, in Knightsbridge. It's down the street from Harrods, and Graham is the concierge there. The last time I saw Graham, he said, "Welcome back, Mr. House. We just had your friend, Mr. Willie Nelson with us last week."

I inquired how Willie had handled himself during his London stay. Graham smiled that proper Brit smile and said, "Oh, he was quite lovely. I don't know what he was smoking up there on the top floor, but the maids who went up to clean have yet to come down."

QUIZZICLE #10

Who said, "And some days we'll dress like pirates"?

A) K.T. Oslin

B) Pete Rose

C) Keith Richards

The Pirate Song

YOU GUESSED IT: K.T. Oslin. If ever there was a show-biz chick, it's Kay Toinette. Toinette is certainly the result of somebody losing a bet. If you've been within a few miles of Nashville, I'm certain you've heard K.T. laugh. I know you've heard her hit songs. She recorded in town for years and had big smashes like, "80s Ladies" and "I'll Always Come Back." *Nobody* sounded like K.T. and that's because she is a total original. I just can't tell you how much I love her. She's one of the few people who say things that amaze me and catch me off guard. And she is always hilarious.

K.T. was actually in the original Broadway production of *Promises, Promises*. I know she will be delighted when I mention it because the original production of that musical was in 1892. She was a chorus girl and, from what I understand, spent the rest of her time working as a secretary for Thomas Edison.

Decades later, she moved to Nashville and wrote songs. She worked her way up the ranks and became such a wondrous star. Her career lasted quite awhile, and we had lunch together whenever things slowed down a bit.

For some reason, I've been to 297 meetings at one time or another about starting a television show. I always go because you never know when the *next* meeting will pan out. *This* could be the one where we create the next TV sensation. But we never did or do.

Because K.T. and I hit it off so well, both on and off the air, her manager decided we should do a television show together. We met with some boob tube production people and tossed around ideas. I thought we might do a talk show and maybe even show the audience the upcoming topics on-screen. Maybe have a clock and when time was up, we'd move on to the next topic. (Much like the now-successful "Pardon the Interruption" on ESPN.) Nobody stole my idea or anything; I just came out of radio, where everything is presold and kept short. "The show must be fun and loose," one of the producers said. "It ought to be you and K.T. just winging it and having fun," another chimed in. I knew we were cooked right then because "winging" it hardly ever works. You can ad-lib, for sure, but "winging" isn't good television. It just doesn't happen.

If you watch when Letterman or Jon Stewart get up to receive their Emmys, they don't get up alone. Forty-five writers also get up onstage with them. All that "winging" came from hours of people thinking up the ad-libs and the instant humor for the shows.

Jim Stafford recorded "Spiders & Snakes" and "Swamp Witch." He is a first-class comedy writer and comedian. Years ago, he told me (off the air) that he'd sit around practicing "panel" for the Tonight Show *with fellow writers. Before Jim went on the* Tonight Show *with Johnny Carson, he practically sketched out the whole couch conversation. They rehearsed it. They tweaked it. He'd go on, and it would be as smooth as silk. Johnny asked the questions, and Jim related the stories as if they had just come off the top of his head—the true mark of a real comedy guy. Rehearsed spontaneity. I think that's pretty common knowledge now, but back then I was stunned to hear Johnny and his guests weren't "winging" it. Ah, showbiz.*

Jim also hosted a show called Those Amazing Animals. *When it got canceled, he said I missed a helluva barbeque.*

As we were about to wrap up the TV production meeting, somebody else said, "K.T., what do you want the show to be?" She looked right at him and said, "Some days we'll dress like pirates for no reason whatsoever." Everybody laughed, and we all made plans to meet again soon to get the ball rolling. As we walked to our cars, K.T. looked at me and smiled that knowing smile of hers. "Another meeting, more big plans, and you know what will happen? We'll make plans for another meeting 'til everybody sort of wears themselves out planning."

She was right, as she usually was. We never dressed as pirates.

The Elegant Warriors

OUR VET IS DR. LADD. We've sent all manner of dogs and cats to him to get poked, prodded, and cured. Dr. Ladd is also a good-looking dude. I almost had a man crush on him. Allyson gets all dreamy-eyed whenever one of our mutts needs its teeth cleaned. Her friend Bonnie says he's so cute that several of her friends are taking road kill in just so they can stare at Dr. Ladd.

The Doc is a total pro and is always gentle when one of our "babies" is there for the final "visit." Is there anything sadder than taking that ride with a little furry thing that's been with you for fifteen or sixteen years? I've done it several times. Dr. Ladd pets his head and says, "He's a good little boy, isn't he? You want them to live a good life, and when that time is over, it's time to say good-bye." I hate to cry in front of a good-looking man, but I've done it.

Over the years I've met a lot of elegant warriors. People who are so iconic and so famous you wonder if they ever "lived a good life"... or at least a normal life.

Spotting the warriors is amazing. It's watching Art Linkletter, in his mid-nineties (!), sweeping in to discuss his new book. This was a guy who hosted a milestone TV show, *Kids Say the Darndest Things*, and he was still working the room. It's Larry King asking me, "How long have you been local?" (I wasn't, by the way; at the time, I was national on XM Radio.)

It's flying next to Tony Bennett with Naomi Judd and laughing together about his days with Sinatra. I did one of the last interviews with Fay Wray. Fay is the girl who got famous being squeezed by King Kong. Yes, *that* King Kong. Empire State Building gorilla-meets-blonde. I asked Fay if she still monkeyed around, and she almost hung up on me.

Pat Boone is the whitest singer in the history of music. Pat was born in Nashville and became a singing sensation in the '50s and '60s. Pat rerecorded R&B songs in his "smoother and more acceptable to most of America" style and hit it big. He's a great guy—a milk-drinkin' family man. His kids were *not* milk duds. Daughter Debbie had "You Light Up My Life" and drove us all crazy with that classic. Pat was almost eligible for Social Security when he showed up shirtless in a leather vest one day. He had recorded an album of heavy metal songs in "Boone style." As I recall, the album sank like a stone, but it was fun. I still get a thrill when I hear one of his earlier hits, "Moody River."

It's seeing Jed Clampett standing in front of you. The patriarch of *The Beverly Hillbillies* came to see me. It was just surreal. He was so old that he was that sort of translucent-skinned, fragile thing we all become when we're ancient. Inside this frail frame, however, was the guy who danced with Shirley Temple and was supposed to be the Tin Man in *The Wizard of Oz*. ("The Tin Man" is also one of my favorite Kenny Chesney songs.) Buddy was allergic to aluminum dust (aren't we all?) and lost the part in that wondrous film. I was so dumbstruck by his appearance before me I never asked *one* question about *The Beverly Hillbillies*, which I know disappointed him to no end. He'd probably never been asked a question about Jethro or the cement pond before.

I noted earlier that when I was a pup living in Jacksonville, Florida, I performed in a play with George Hamilton. (Back then, I thought I could act and spent a lot of the audience's time proving I was barely acceptable.) George is a true Hollywood story. He told me he didn't have two nickels to rub together when he moved to Tinseltown, but he rented a Rolls-Royce and rode around as if he were richer than a king. Everybody bought his act because he was talented, tall, and tan. He made a gazillion dollars from producing a movie about Evil Knievel. The thought of George playing Hank Williams, however, is still hilarious to me. He is so far from Country & Western, he's in another dimension. Yet, you still see him sometimes on an old movie channel, all duded up in a Nudie suit and a big hat. It's like Donald Trump playing Fred Sanford.

My best brush with bumping into greatness was literally that. When I lived in L.A. in the '80s, I went to a lot of showbiz parties. I knew some folks who knew some folks. I remember standing with a glass of Champagne, and some elderly gentlemen backed into me, and I spilled my bubbly all over the floor. He sort of stammered and apologized, all at the same time. We've all heard that, "Well, uh...oh my...uh...excuse me there, pal...I...uh...did I do that? Oh...well...well...Jeez...I am so sorry. Let me get you a napkin...uh...you all right?" I laughed and said I was fine. Who could get upset at Jimmy Stewart?

Speaking of L.A., I was on the radio playing country music one early morning when the phone rang. I talked awhile with this guy, who wasn't really an old warrior then. In fact, he was on the most popular TV series in the world. Then, as if he was embarrassed that he hadn't introduced himself, he said he was Bobby Ewing from *Dallas*. Patrick Duffy loved country music, and he'd drop in from time to time before he went to straighten out J.R. at Southfork Ranch. He was just a ray of light to be around, and it's no wonder he became such a star.

Bob Hope is probably the most famous person I've ever met. We all know his story, and it's an amazing one: vaudeville, radio, movies, television shows, and all those USO tours. Has anybody not seen Bob standing on a warship or a rice paddy telling jokes to men who are fighting a war? Barbara Mandrell always calls him Mister Hope when she talks about him because she revered him so much. There is just something elegant and professional about people like Bob Hope that gives you faith in humanity and show-biz. He was a huge, worldwide star for sixty years. Leslie Townes Hope came to Nashville, and I introduced him.

The Tennessee State Fair is a quirky event, at best. When I got to Nashville, it was a lot less "quirky" than it is today. Ours is more like a carnival and farmer's market combo than, say, the Ohio State Fair. The midway is not exactly jaw-droppingly amazing. They have a guess-your-sex booth. The freak show has a bearded man. It's more low-budget, if you get my drift. Some of the prize pigs only have three legs. This is *not* a Hollywood production, our State Fair. One of the rides is a tractor with a flat. During the golden years of the State Fair of Tennessee, when I was a pipsqueak of a radio geek, they had some pretty serious acts appear on their stage. They hired the usual gamut of old musical acts such as Paul Revere & the Raiders or the Temptations. And in and among the goat-roping competitions and the ham demonstrations, they brought in a big name like Mr. Hope. (I was actually asked to appear at one of the ham demonstrations, for obvious reasons.) I was asked to warm up the crowd and then introduce Bob, as if the biggest star in show bidness needed to be introduced. Like most fairgrounds, the stage is atop a concrete bunker and next to a racetrack. The seats are bleacher-like affairs with a capacity crowd of about 12,000. So, the stage is set. It's late in the afternoon, and the radio guy, me, is ready to do five minutes and bring on the *real* comedy. I am so excited when I see a long, black limo snaking its way through the maze of buildings behind the fairgrounds.

When I talk about elegant warriors, I mean showbiz vets who are always prepared and have only the best people to handle stuff for them. My proof is that, when the limo rolled to a stop, and I stood by to welcome the star, Bob Hope had been prepped. Door opens, out steps Old Ski Nose, and he says, "Hello, Gerry." I nearly fell over. The pros know how to do it right. They get names of local towns and local hot spots and local personalities and sprinkle them throughout their act, and everybody leaves thinking they are the greatest people who ever lived.

Here's when I proved I am *not* a pro, that I am really more quali-fied to run the Tilt-A-Whirl than I am to emcee a packed show at the State Fair. I went onstage a little shaky, did a few jokes, and actually got some laughs. I was as thrilled as the crowd to see Mr. USO standing in the wings. "And now, ladies and gentle-men, please, a big Tennessee welcome to America's favorite star, Mr. Baaaaaahhhhhb Hope!"

When an emcee typically finishes his clichéd intro to insert-famous-name-here, he usually walks off the stage and normally watches from behind a pile of public-address equipment. Me? Do I shake hands with Bob Hope and graciously cede the stage to him? *No.* I am so enthralled with the star and the stage and the night and the fair that I walk about five feet and then just *stand there*. I'm still on the stage! Hope looks at me and smiles and shrugs and goes into his act. I'm still there like a giant doofus for all the world to see. More Bob...more geeky/gawky boy not moving an inch. Bob, being the pro that he is (after all, he has done shows where people are shooting at him), is hardly fazed by his new co-performer. He plows on, and the King of Awkward continues to grin like a moron from stage left. After about fif-teen minutes, I feel a tug on my elbow and then the words I will never forget: "Son, come on over here now. Only Mr. Hope belongs onstage." It was the show producer, and he was kinder than I probably would have been. Bob Hope *killed* that afternoon.

He sang and he did patter and he reminisced and made every-body love him more. I stood behind that pile of PA equipment 'til "Thanks For The Memories" rang out and his show was over. The movie star of the *Road To...* comedies made his way toward the car. As he passed, he stuck out his hand and said in that famous nasally tone, "Thanks, pally. If it hadn't been for you, I would've bombed out there. And believe me, I've bombed and been bombed onstage, and it ain't pretty." With that, he was gone. The elegant warrior.

HE LOOKED LIKE SOMETHING OUT of a hairdresser's western. It was an over-the-top outfit at six in the morning. Who goes out dressed in full frontal horse opera regalia? Marty Robbins, that's who. "Out in the West Texas town of El Paso" rang in my ears every time I saw Marty. At the time, he had a Frito Bandito mustache and a leather jacket and pants to match. Along his arms, he had fringe. On his pants, he had fringe. He had... (drumroll) "Fringe in Low Places." (Insert bucket-o-fish, the inside studio musician joke for a rim shot.)

He was glorious and western, and he was a gentleman and a star. Marty Robbins was part of my childhood soundtrack. "Devil Woman" still kills me. "Don't Worry" was the first time a fuzz-tone was used on a record because somebody played through a broken mixer.

Marty wrote most of his hits and had what I call an emotional tenor. Like Roy Orbison and others, Marty delivered what Bruce Springsteen so brilliantly called "three-minute operas." I think that's what is missing from today's country music. I don't think it has to be that old-timey mountain music, but it would be nice to hear somebody deliver a great song once in awhile. How many times can somebody be happy in the mud in the sticks in a truck with some chicks?

Marty's son, Ronnie, had the family office across the street from my office. Ronnie did a really great stage impression of his dad. I imagine that's what Ronnie actually sang like, but it always looked like he was "doing" Dad. Nobody can re-create Dad. Frank Jr. couldn't do it. Paul McCartney's son suffers because of it. Does anybody remember Doug Hitler? Of course not. Originals put such a stamp on their image that trying to follow it is impossible—what a burden to bear. Look at what Chaz Bono went through, or, as I call him, Partly Sonny.

Marty was so graceful. He laughed his way with such ease through a crowd. He stopped to hear for the thousandth time how much somebody loved "El Paso." He wrote songs and sang and drove race cars 'til the end.

Brentwood is just a hop and a skip from Murfreesboro Road, where my radio station was located. Marty often did a television interview downstairs and then just popped in on me. I was always glad to see him. The last time I spoke to him, he was wearing his cowboy getup. I saw a lot of costumes in those days. Marty had a closet full of ivory-white suits with red flowers and yellow cacti and embroidery for days. When he arrived in his "outfit," I prodded him with, "You look like Gene Autry's limo driver." He thought that was hilarious and, after shooting me the bird (it was radio, after all), pronounced, "And just for that, I'm singing one of the boss's songs." He had a little gut-string guitar with him and proceeded with "Yesterday's Roses," written by Gene himself. He sang it like he was in front of a million people. Not long after that, his heart let him down. My heart was broken, too. He was an elegant warrior.

I actually met Gene Autry at some radio dealio many years ago. Gene was ancient at that time, but his speech to the convention was amazing. He told the story of how he came to write "Here Comes Santa Claus." He was in the Rose Bowl Parade, next-to-last in the line of participants. Ol' Kris Kringle was right behind Gene, who was

astride his horse, Champion. *The kids along the way would have normally been thrilled to see "The Singing Cowboy," but instead they
shouted, "Here comes Santa Claus!" and ignored him. Gene had the
good sense to write what he heard.*

*I still remember the opening of his speech to a packed crowd of
radio men and women. "It's so nice to be here in Nashville, especially
to see the ladies here today. Why, it's just like looking out on a beautiful
garden of flowers. A beautiful garden of beautiful flowers." He took a
professional pause and then delivered, "Of course, I do see an occasional weed here and there." It got one of the biggest laughs I've ever
heard. He was ninety and still rockin' the house.*

*I also met Roy Rogers, but he was more interested in his steak. Get
along, little dogie.*

It's not often I have a guest call me an ape and am happy about
it, but it did happen once. He filled the room not only with his
physical presence but also that attendant outsize star power that
few people possess. He was older and had battled cancer and
people who wanted to take a gun from his cold, dead fingers. He
wore a long overcoat instead of his usual sandals and leather gladi-
ator outfit. I remember he was there plugging something. It's what
old showbiz gladiators do—they have a new project and fight to
make sure it's successful.

Charlton Heston had recorded the Bible. Who better to read the
"Word" than the guy who made *The Ten Commandments*? It was
just kind of scary to have Ben-Hur stride confidently in and shake
your hand. My first question was, "What have you got to say for
yourself?" He shot back his iconic line from *Planet of the Apes*,
"Take your stinking paws off me, you damned dirty ape." That
voice! Now, I've had the same exact thing said to me by Martina
McBride and Jennifer Nettles, but it's funnier coming from a guy.
This obviously was not Charlton's first trip to the Colosseum.

I poked and prodded him about the Bible and asked him repeatedly if he'd found any loopholes while reading it. He was generous

to laugh, but quite serious about his new work, and we wound our way to the end of an hour. The most memorable part of the day was the shocked reaction of my station manager, John King, after the show.

"Did I just see *Moses* walking down the hall?"

QUIZZICLE #11

What can you say that makes your friends suspicious it's an April Fools' joke?

A) "Mark on your schedule a reminder for the first of April. We're going catfish noodling with Reba."

B) "Drop whatever you're doing. We're playing golf with Engelbert Humperdinck."

C) "Hey, next Thursday is the first annual Banjo Burn on Music Row. Bring your banjo by and throw it on the bonfire."

Fool on the Hill

ACTUALLY, ANY ONE OF THOSE answers could probably be true. Reba is up for anything, especially if it involves wading in a muddy creek and sticking your bare hands into a hole. Noodling is fun and healthy except for the snapping turtles and the tapeworms. I'm not sure what on earth possesses a ten-fingered hillbilly to try such a sport, but it's done around these parts. It's one of many odd things I've suggested to Reba that we do over the years.

Burning banjos has for years been a dream of many people. During my career, I've tried to start many "events" on Music Row. Way back when, I was part of the group that dreamed up the Swine Ball. Some advertising and political friends of mine, over drinks, thought it would be fun to spoof the Swan Ball—the swanky dinner dance in the ritzy part of town that neither I nor anybody I know have been invited to attend. It's actually a lovely evening, but the crowd I run with ain't gonna pass the admissions test for the Swan Ball. So, we did what outsiders do—we started the Swine Ball.

It was originally intended to be a "tacky" event. Everybody would wear polyester jumpsuits and plastic shoes. It has morphed over the years, no longer requiring our guidance, into more of a pig-based celebration.

I also tried desperately to get the city fathers to approve having all the fire hydrants on Music Row decorated to look like Little Jimmy Dickens. What fun for the tourists visiting the heart of country music to see tiny hats and big guitars in a custom suit on all the hydrants of Music City. That idea not only didn't go down with the City Council, but Jimmy himself was kind of irritated by it.

I suggested several times we have a late-night banjo burnin' by our station. It also went nowhere. I guess too many folks saw *Deliverance* and felt a kinship with those who pluck for pleasure. Another fabulous plan that didn't work out as I'd hoped and dreamed.

I *did*, however, once call my two Hall of Fame songwriting pals, Bob DiPiero and Tom Shapiro, and say, "Drop what you're doing tomorrow, we're playing golf with Engelbert Humperdinck." "Engie," the massive star of pop's early days, actually had some reason to visit Nashville and pick songs, as he was in town recording an album. Two of his biggest hits, "Release Me (And Let Me Love Again)" and "There Goes My Everything," were from the pens of Twang Town songwriters. He did my show and then said that he wanted to hit the links. I called and left messages for my two guys to complete the foursome.

Hours later, I got a call from DiPiero. For some reason, he's always suspicious of my plans and ideas. Bob is one of the greatest people I know and the authentic godfather of my daughter, Autumn. He said, "House, I just realized tomorrow is April Fools' Day, and you invited us to play golf with Engelbert Humperdinck. If this is one of your pranks, I'm going to kill you because I canceled a bunch of stuff." See how some people are? You can't even invite them to play golf without arousing suspicion. I called and swore on his goddaughter's eyes that it was true.

Engelbert is cool and suave and a Vegas showman. He was managed by a guy named Gordon Mills, his old roommate. Gordon had previously hit it big managing another singer named Tom Jones. Tom also was in town for awhile when he recorded "country." "Green, Green Grass of Home" was a huge hit for Tom Jones, and he loved that kind of music. I will say the most ridiculous sight I've ever seen was Mr. "What's New Pussycat?" in a cowboy hat. Puhleeze, Dr. Sex Bomb, lose the lariat lid.

When you play golf with people, you start discussing all sorts of things. As usual, with three songwriters and a singer, you start discussing showbiz and how awful it can be. Bob, Tom, and I all lamented how the business was difficult at times. Blah, blah, blah. I am still frozen by the memory of Engelbert looking up just before teeing off and saying, "Wait 'til your manager loses everything." What? Yes, Engelbert and Tom's manager cost them *millions*. They are back in the black now, but Gordon Mills had siphoned off around $320 million to pay off gambling debts to the Mob. (I half-expected DiPiero to say, "Thanks.") Tom Jones and Engelbert were victims of the cliché of all showbiz clichés—they'd trusted somebody else with their money. I almost felt guilty taking the four dollars Mr. Humperdinck lost in the golf game. But, hey, you have to pay off your bets, right?

White Is 1,000 Colors

I HAVE LEARNED DURING the 150-odd years of my marriage not to examine things too closely in our house. Here's what happens if I do:

I once picked up a lamp and looked at it for a second. You know how, one day out of the blue, you just wake up and want to examine your lamps. Allyson saw me on my illumination examination and said, "I don't like that lamp, either." I actually didn't have anything particular against it, but casually said, "Maybe it's time we got a new one." Then it started. Once she'd bought a new lamp, she noticed that the cabinet she put the new lamp on didn't seem "quite right" now. We went cabinet shopping. Then, because it was a different cabinet, we had to get a new picture to hang over it. The walls were now clashing with the painting and, frankly, ruining the lives of nearly everyone within a square mile.

After we had the kitchen walls painted, the room next to it had a sort of "mismatched" feel to it. The simple act of examining a lamp had cascaded into a landslide: a new cabinet, a new painting, new wall colors, and, suddenly, we now need a new kitchen.

This brings us to the "while we're at it" syndrome. You know the drill. You're tearing up the carpet to put down hardwood floors and, "while we're at it," why don't we put a new roof on the house? You pick out a new stove and, "while we're at it," what about planting some cedars in the backyard and look at another house in Florida we can redecorate? It's a slippery slope, looking at lamps.

I have a point here, so stay with me. Anytime we have a decorating discussion, we look at paint samples. Allyson loves white. I love white. It goes with anything. Just in case you are not aware of this, there are now 1.52 million different variations of white available for your choosing. *And* you have to look at every one of them. Inspect each tiny cardboard "sample" and bring them home and hold them up against the door and ask, "What do you think of *this* white?" Men, be warned, you can't just glance up and say, "I like it. Let's go with that one." *Oh, nooooo.* Because if the attention sensor goes off in the co-decorator's head that you didn't sweat and struggle with the choice, then the choice is tossed out like yesterday's cat litter.

What about country music? Did author boy forget about some tie-in to country music? That's not far away, I promise.

My wife has confessed to me a secret my own mother had told her. Mom passed along what is apparently a secret evil method to get things changed around the house. Women are devious people. Mom instructed my Mrs. as follows: "I'd ask Homer [my father] the first time if he'd like to change the wallpaper in the living room. He'd always say, 'Aw, it's fine with me.' I'd wait a few days and then ask, 'What about a different style of wallpaper in the living room?' Basically, I'd get the same response. But the third time was the charm. When I'd say, 'Hey, I'm thinking some flowery wallpaper in the living room would perk things up around here.' He'd reply with, 'Fine with me. Whatever you want, honey. I think that's what we need.'"

The poor guy never had a chance, worn down by the time-honored method of repeat asking. Allyson knows that with 1.52

million choices of the color white, I will eventually break and beg for something called "pale eggshell latte."

Here it comes. Most country singers are a variation of white. I don't mean skin color; I mean they are just ever so slightly different. Some are off-white, some baby-white, some ivory, and a few antique whites. Although, it's also true most country singers are white. I've spent decades trying to decide what it is that separates people who make music in this town. What is it that attracts fans to jump aboard the fan wagon of a certain particular brand of white country singer? Is it a particular song? Sometimes. Is the artist very attractive? That helps. Do they have so much charisma they just can't be denied? That's also good, but no guarantee. The plain fact is *nobody knows*. You can, of course, ask nearly anyone, and they'll act like they know, but they don't. You can have a pretty good guess, but I've seen the experts pick somebody who never sees the light of day. Some artists who are often called the "whole package" strike gold, while others strike mud.

As long as we're talking about shades of white, two colors are "radio" acts and "seat-selling" acts. Often they are one and the same. I've been friends for years with two great singers—Richie McDonald of Lonestar and Marty Roe of Diamond Rio. Both of those bands had enormous hit records. Lonestar's "Amazed" was a smash all over the world. Diamond Rio knocked it out of the park with "One More Day." Their bands are filled with good-looking, intelligent, funny guys. They had hit after hit on the radio, and yet they never got to the stratosphere. I loved to see these bands coming through the door. They do have people who will drive across the country to watch them in concert. But they never got close to the supernova that Alabama was. Four dudes from Ft. Payne—Randy Owen, his cousin Teddy Gentry, Jeff Cook, and hired drummer Mark Herndon—rocked Nashville like an earthquake. Randy was charismatic, but his voice wasn't America's greatest. Teddy was gentle and a good bass player. Jeff played guitar and sang harmonies OK. But, somehow, some way, those songs and those boys made musical history.

Brad Paisley even had a hit just referencing "Old Alabama." Brad, whose career has been over for years, knew that perhaps he could hang on just a little longer if he sang about a group people liked. Brad is a good judge. Why? It always struck me as odd that Alabama's signature song, "Mountain Music," wasn't mountain music at all. It had a rockin' track and searing guitars. They sang about that good, old-timey music that took you to the mountains. I never heard Bill Monroe or anybody from the mountains who sounded like that.

Earl Thomas Conley was a slightly blue shade of white. He had soul. ETC wrote smash songs and sang with such heart and conviction, it was painful. Earl even had four No. 1 songs from one album. He played the game, recording and writing and touring and singing until it just wore him out. The white-hot spotlight was just beyond his reach. It never quite shone on him. I haven't seen Earl Thomas Conley in years, but I hope he's relaxing on a porch somewhere with a cigar and a glass of red wine. All those hits, and yet not enough folks picked his shade as their favorite white. It sure was mine.

If you'll excuse me for a moment, I have to go downstairs and move a lamp.

Marriage

I ALWAYS LIKE TO INTRODUCE Allyson as my first wife. She happens to also be the only wife I've ever had, but it keeps her on her toes. We recently celebrated our 127th wedding anniversary.

You know you've been married awhile when you both agree *not* to buy each other anything for that special day and instead spend the dough on new wallpaper for the guest bathroom—you know, the bathroom nobody ever uses. The one with the "good" towels with the gold embroidery that say, "Welcome." I once wandered in there accidentally and got in trouble for ruining the area for visitors. I have thought many times about putting some yellow police tape across the door in case a nonvisitor should try to desecrate the sanctity of the holy lavatory.

The only reason I've stayed married for so long is my cheery and forgiving attitude. My gift is having such a sunny personality. I never get upset with a brooding, sullen, moody, tortured soul living in the same house with me. Somehow I've managed to never fret over wasted days and wasted nights, not to mention wasted cash chasing some cockamamie dream. My future sainthood is guaranteed because of my unerring belief in life's blessings and celebrating the moment… living in the now. Never criticizing or doubting my partner, but always uplifting and reaching out when things get rough. Every sunrise is a precious prize and should be celebrated.

What? Why are you reading this and acting like something doesn't sound right? I'm serious. The only way this marriage has lasted is because of what I've just told you. You can believe what you want. I'm sticking to my story that only one person has held this thing together for our 127 years of wedded bliss. Don't you start trying to pick things apart this late in the game!

When I look back at how innocent we were when we got hitched, I get almost scared. I got a job in Ithaca, New York. I was working at a tiny, tiny station in my college town and got offered a job in New York. We had been living in luxury—a trailer built on a gravel lot in Richmond, Kentucky, that actually got whacked by one of the semis that used our front gravel yard to turn around. We returned from a short trip to find the front of the trailer cracked open. You could look inside and see all our stuff. It's a bad sign when thieves can actually reach into your house and take whatever they want… but they don't. It still depresses me that our belongings were so awful they weren't worth stealing.

We packed all our worldly possessions in a 4 × 6 U-Haul trailer and took off with about $200 in cash for New York. Allyson was pregnant, and I didn't even have enough of a clue about the dangers out there to be concerned about moving so far from anyone we knew. I do remember my daughter being born a Yankee. It was the happiest day ever. I just stared at this little bundle for hours.

I also remember having to finance the hospital bill for her special delivery. During the paperwork, I asked the administrator, "If we miss a payment, do you come and repossess our kid?" The taskmaster took her work seriously, and I didn't get the response I wanted.

Some people are lucky and find a partner early in life. I think most love stories are luck and geography. Everybody has a match somewhere out there, but finding it is a matter of timing and location. I just happened to grow up three or four miles from my long-time female companion. From elementary school to middle school and then high school and even college, she's always been there. Allyson always remarks, "When you've been together all that time, it takes away the ability to lie about the past. How can you make good stuff up when the other person was there, too?"

John and Martina McBride have a great relationship—a sound engineer and a singer with a voice as big as the world. They got started early, just as we did. They are great friends to us, and we've spent a lot of time together. They move like fish together through the troubled waters of showbiz. You know the drill: finishing each other's sentences and laughing at each other's habits. Being married to your best friend is good. John always has her back. When Martina is onstage wailing her heart out, John is on the other end of the microphone making sure everybody can hear how great she is. A team.

Now, I don't want to start the "How Small Martina Is" jokes here. Yes, she's the last one to know it's raining. It's true, her picture on the cover of her CD is life-size. What other star shops for clothes at Gymboree? Who else calls Paul Williams "Stretch"? I'm not going to get into those jokes because I know she's sick to death of them. SICK TO DEATH, I said. But how on earth such a little person can have tequila and not get affected is beyond me. I always think it's a trick. Every rare occasion, we've had a tiny bit of Patrón. Not all the time, but every now and then, you have something to celebrate—like finding a new piece of Beatles memorabilia.

John McBride is the proud owner of the Beatle Bunker. He has more Beatles artifacts, albums, tapes, and pictures than Ringo. It's one of his passions. He has the original tape of the first Beatles recording with the original notes. He's that kind of Beatlemaniac. Because I'm one,

too, I think it's amazing. When I wanted to give a friend a copy of the
Beatles' Butcher Cover *album as a gift, I called John. For a pittance,*
he offered to sell me a real copy of that rarified album with the Fab
Four and meat and baby dolls on the front. What they were thinking
when they did that picture is beyond me. It was snatched from public
view pretty quickly and thus became a real collection piece. I told John
I felt bad taking from his personal stash such a rare and precious item.
He shot back, "Oh, don't worry about it. I've probably got a hundred of
them." You see what I mean about being The Collector.

I am almost certain the tequila thing is a trick. I slam one back.
Martina pours hers in a potted plant when I'm not looking. I have
two, and I get wobbly. Any more than that and I start seeing visions
of José Cuervo or the Alamo. Martina doesn't change even a little
bit.

Speaking of little bit, I'm not going to mention the fact that
it's hard to drink someone under the table who's already at table
height. She is SICK TO DEATH of any "little" humor. Martina is
actually just two lungs and a larynx.

Look, all I want to say is how happy I am for my friends, who
still hold hands and have three beautiful daughters. Some of my
favorite moments ever have been sitting around Martina's kitchen
as she flutters about in a little sundress, cooking for us. She loves
it, and I'm always willing to accommodate. I'm just that kind of
friend. She is a fabulous chef, which is no small thing.

I also remember the last time Martina and I had lunch. We went
to Noshville, a Nashville deli. Martina was dressed all in black and
wearing a shiny red leather beret. She was just standing there by
the counter when a fat lady sat on her head.

QUIZZICLE #12

Who had the most amazing baby ever?

A) Chris Cagle

B) Inez Godzilla

C) Nicole Kidman

Here Comes the Sun

SOME PEOPLE GET INTO the music business by sheer force of will. It's not as if they are incredibly beautiful or sing like an angel. They aren't the songwriter of the century, nor are they so clever they defy logic. These folks just *will* themselves into some form of stardom. It's really kind of admirable how drive, desire, and a driven need get them a record deal. They just won't go away. Chris Cagle is like that to me.

I first saw Chris Cagle perform at a New Faces Show at the Country Radio Seminar, an annual industry conference in Nashville. He had a sort of Tim McGraw–lite act and moved like he was the biggest star in the world. Sometimes it's fun to see a singer take the stage and perform as if he's opening the Olympics. Chris had all the confidence in the world. *Good for him*, I thought, as he blasted his way through "Play It Loud" and "I Breathe In, I Breathe Out." I had seen hundreds of people stand on the tiny stage in front of radio program directors and DJs, and usually they soon dropped out of sight. Chris didn't do that. He kept on making records and forcing people to get in line. I watched with fascination how some pretty good songs—and Chris singing them—kept getting in front of the radio public.

I got a glimpse of what Chris thought of himself during a conversation early on in his career. He kept referring to these "Cagle Heads" out there who "keep demanding more of my music and me." Now, Jimmy Buffet has "Parrot Heads" because he is a national treasure and has a forty-year history of hit making and worshipful concerts. I wasn't sure this early in the game there were that many "Cagle Heads" storming the gates.

My second indication that things were a little inflated was when I dashed into the men's room outside my studio. Radio people always make a dash for the john during a record. My club soda habit usually caught up with me about 8 A.M. There, standing and taking care of business, was Chris Cagle. Then I noticed he was singing and singing a song I sort of knew. It was "What a Beautiful Day." Cagle was by himself, taking a leak, and singing his own song at the top of his lungs. I guess we all hum our own song once in awhile, but that's in the shower or the car, maybe? I don't know of another person who takes a whiz and sings one of their hits at the same time, especially alone.

The crowning glory of Chris' view of life was during an interview. I know he won't like this, but I am pretty sure this is how it happened. Chris' girlfriend was expecting a baby. He announced on the air, "My kid is gonna be the most amazing and brilliant kid ever." Fair enough. Every father thinks his spawn is better than anybody else's. I know *I* thought that. However, Chris went further than any proud papa had ever gone before. He said that during their sonogram he could see his son's image. We're talking in the womb now. Chris announced to the radio public, "When I say smile, he smiles."

I smiled, too, and said, "Maybe he recognizes Daddy's voice."

Chris pressed ahead. "No, he hears the word and knows what it means. I say smile and he does."

I asked as gently as I could, "So, your baby speaks English in the womb?"

Dad swelled up and said, "Yes, isn't that amazing?" The conversation continued on from there, but I was kind of reeling at the incredible news of the fetus that was already communicating with the outside world.

When I was driving home, my cell phone rang, and it was Jamie O'Neal of "There Is No Arizona" and "When I Think about Angels" hit records. We're great friends, and I love her. She is also one of the most amazing singers on the planet. She did several demos of my songs and lifted them to a better place. It's scary how good she is.

Jamie paused and said, "Did I just hear Chris Cagle say his kid can understand English and he's not even born yet?" I confirmed what she'd heard. "Wow," Jamie almost sang (which is just how her voice is). "That is about the most unbelievable thing I've ever heard."

I told her, "Yeah, but he's a proud father-to-be and maybe a little excited."

Jamie replied, "Excited is one thing, but that is pretty out there. An unborn talking baby! I just wanted to make sure I heard what I heard this morning." We made plans to catch up soon and said good-bye.

You know what? Sometimes the excitement of fatherhood causes you to have an unborn English-speaking baby. (Or to think you have one.) It's a miracle, as I know from having Autumn, the most amazing daughter anyone ever had. I haven't seen Chris in quite awhile, but I hope he's somewhere singing "What a Beautiful Day."

The Flatts

AS I WALKED PAST the bedroom, I heard a frustrated search going on. Drawers were being opened and closed, and my wife was talking out loud to herself. She was obviously hunting for something she needed that very moment. I half-shouted, "What did you lose, honey bun?" She gave that vague "to herself and not to me" answer, "I can *not* find my under-why-er." That's how she said it. Under-WHY-er. Look, the girl grew up in Kentucky and had lived in Tennessee for most of her life, but I didn't remember her accent being so strong.

This was rural, in-the-sticks stuff. It sounded like people who pronounce words like "cold" as "code." Or if they are enjoying the fried catfish, it's DEE-lish-ious. It's country-speak, where one-syllable words suddenly have three, and cities like "Shelbyville" turn into one syllable—"Shelbv'l."

I wandered in to examine her newfound speech patterns in person and to also watch her search. She usually loses something, especially on trips. Often I wake up hearing the sounds of a thousand zippers in rapid-fire succession. Vroop-vroop-vroop, as she

zips and unzips the hundreds of pockets and travel bags and lug-
gage compartments looking for something of exalted value.

"Did you just say you can't find your under-WHY-er?" I half
mocked. At the moment, she was bent over with her head almost
in a bottom drawer of the Chester Drawers (which is how everybody in Kentucky refers to that large cabinet in the bedroom). She
looked up and announced in a slightly frustrated voice, "Yes, it's
a special bra I just bought. It's called the Underwire." Ohhhhh,
so it's *not* her accent changing, it's her clothes! Of course, I then
celebrated the fact she needed such support. She usually gives me
a disgusted look whenever I appreciate her talents. The woman
is impossible to please. Suddenly it was an Aha! moment. There,
among scores of frilly lavender unmentionables (that I just mentioned), she snatched out a silky piece of dangling garment and
pronounced it as her Under-why-er.

All this is to bring me to my story of the Flatts. Rascal Flatts—
Gary LaVox, Joe Don Rooney, and Jay DeMarcus—known mostly
on the "Row" and in radio as the Flatts.

If you combined the Everly Brothers and the Gibb Brothers and
the Marx Brothers, you'd get Rascal Flatts. They are that wonderful
gumbo of great musicianship, songwriting, and general wackiness.
Because one of my closest friends, Trey Turner, was their manager
through much of their successful career, I was connected to them
a bit.

Gary LaVox is, to me, the iPhone 5 of singers. You just wonder
how it works. I've been in studios and watched it. I've written
songs with him and watched it. It just comes so effortlessly, it kind
of makes you angry. Nobody should be able to sing like that with
one tonsil tied behind his back. He is LaVox, i.e., "The Voice." If
you listen closely to Gary sing, you'll notice he also uses *all* the
notes. If the melody is near several other notes, by God, he'll sing
those, too, just in case you want to hear every note close to the real
note. If notes were people, he'd be China.

The funny thing to me is that, instead of wowing a crowd of 20,000 rabid fans, Gary is just as happy sitting in a duck blind at five in the morning in thirty-degree rain. You haven't lived 'til you've waited for Gary to show up on his motorcycle with a German pot on his head. I've argued with him for years that the sport of hunting ain't all that sportin'. He couldn't care less and lives to look down the barrel of a weapon at the unluckiest deer in the world. He's as quick as anybody I know with a quip and is generous with his time. And I've never seen his wife naked.

Joe Don Rooney is the quiet sex symbol. I have played golf with Joe Don and his dad several times, and I know the little acorn is near the oak. His father is a gentle soul. Joe Don listens and cares. He also has a freaky Barry Gibb falsetto that you probably don't know you've heard singing up above Gary. Joe Don is also married to Tiffany Fallon. Tiff is a Playboy Playmate of the Year. She had apparently visited the radio station where I worked one afternoon. In my studio on my soundboard, she left a *Playboy* folded out and had signed it in a low and lusty place. I have never seen Gary LaVox's wife naked.

The final member of the group is the one I'm probably closest to, Jay DeMarcus. He's also married to an Allison. She's a babe, too. These guys *all* hit the Lovely Lottery. Jay's a bass player, a singer, a songwriter, and a producer. Check out his work on the last Chicago album. He also has a golf swing that isn't supposed to exist in nature. Defying all natural laws of physics and luck, he can swat the white pill forward in jaw-dropping swoops and curves. Joe Don can whack it, too, but Jay is his own special category.

As Trey (then the Flatts' manager) and I stood on a tee somewhere, he mentioned a Flatts song, "I'm Movin' On." My producer, Devon, had already discovered this tune on her own and had played it for me with that "Listen to *this*" look that people get. She was right. The story I got later was that "I'm Movin' On" was rejected by some people at the record company to even be recorded. Then it was rejected as an album cut. It was certainly never going to be a single release. Guess who played it. Guess who deserves zero credit for anything other than listening to people who knew an amazing song when they heard it. It was one of those wonderful warm exciting moments when you see a song being born. Trey drove their label's record execs around Nashville to record stores. (Remember when they actually had stores full of records for sale?) The Rascal Flatts bin was empty. People, ultimately the smartest or worst judges of hit songs, had heard it a few times and immediately said the magic words, "Where can I buy that?" I can't tell you the number of times people have called me to inquire where they might purchase a song I was playing. I always told them area muffler shops or flea markets in Uruguay. They accepted my answer and, I assume, headed to Midas.

I've also been told by the Flatts themselves that "I'm Movin' On" changed their careers. Suddenly, they were on another level. Their audience was bigger than ever, and it ignited a rocket under them. They are gracious to say I played the thing, but the truth is they *made* the thing. They wanted that song. They sang that song. The Flatts are stars because of their own talents.

As far as I can determine, Gary LaVox has never seen my wife naked. Or even in her under-why-er.

Taylor Swift

I HAD NO IDEA she was only fifteen when I met her in Nashville at BMI during a performing rights soiree, where the organization's songwriters and publishers, as well as numerous artists, gather annually to honor the music. She was being escorted by one of the nicest guys in the business, Scott Borchetta, who runs Big Machine Records.

Scott and I have a long history and friendship. It was Scott who worked one of my songs that had been recorded by George Strait called "The Big One," and made it the No. 1 song in the nation. I also knew his father from his record promotion business.

Scott's blonde, elegant, and amazingly mature "date" at BMI that evening was Taylor Swift, who was the first artist he had signed to his then fledging label. I didn't know who she was back some eight or nine years ago, but I did know I was truly impressed with her. As we chatted for some time before the ceremony began, we discussed her writing and her singing and her dreams. I remember watching her walk away, thinking she was probably going to get everything she wanted.

Scott did his job. A lot of people take credit for Taylor Swift. Certainly her parents, who moved to nearby Hendersonville to let their daughter take a shot at the big spotlight, deserve the "belief" award. But it's Mr. Borchetta, in all his Italian designer clothes glory, who deserves the "genius" award. He put it all on the line and started a company, raised the money, hired the right people, and set forth on a run of success rarely seen in any business. It's always easy to look back and say, as I do, that this person or that person has "got it." It's a lot tougher to actually do the work, take the risk, and make the decisions based solely on a gut instinct that somebody can break through.

For an artist to succeed, it's actually pretty rare—a combination of luck and sweat and songs and looks—and an angel or two. Taylor Swift had all those things and more. She had beauty, brains, and a laser vision of where she was going that I've never seen in anyone so young. And, "bonus time," she's funny, with comedic timing and a sense of improv that is a natural gift. Throw in "hit songwriter" in the star-making machine and what you get is the Taylor of today.

Taylor happened to be a guest on my radio show the same day that a large group from Leadership Music was visiting me at the station. Leadership Music is a great program where a select group of executives representing different sides of the business converge for a full day once a month to learn from each other. Taylor waltzed into the studio in a gossamer summer dress, carrying a big guitar and an even bigger smile. I interviewed her not really knowing much about her, except that Scott believed in all her tomorrows. She sang, she was funny, she laughed. She threw her head back and just let loose. Everyone in the room loved her, most of all me.

Thus began a radio romance. I played each new song with an honest enthusiasm about how great it was. Meanwhile, her father wrote me notes about his kids listening to me around the breakfast table before high school classes and said how great it was to be listening and laughing together. I got a call from her every now and then. She tweeted with great humor something I said about her, such as when I said her dad was walking around Hendersonville in a white robe and an aluminum hat. Like all teenagers, Taylor seemed to enjoy poking fun at her parental unit.

The hits started, and so did the press. The Big Machine was cranking up and starting to fire on all cylinders. TS was no BS and on her way. I even suggested she was about to get so successful she would soon make a gospel album called *Lord and Taylor*.

One day, we were preparing some commercials to hype the station, and the star who was originally going to do the promotional "spots" with me had to cancel. Yours truly suggested that we ask the new young blonde singer to do the commercials with us. Let me be clear: we were very much the recipients of goodwill when Taylor agreed to do them for the little exposure she received in return. The spots were funny and goofy and promoted her. The ads also promoted us as connected to this social whirlwind; it was a win-win for all.

Even then, three short years into the process, Taylor was fast becoming a star. Once, as she left the studio after a short visit, I said, "You're getting so big, in six months we'll never hear from you again." She apparently put a note into her phone, and six months later, to the day, she called just to prove us wrong. It was delightful. It sounds calculated, but even more, it was smart, professional, and just plain good.

Taylor started to orbit further out from us after that. I couldn't have been happier for anybody. I used to worry a little that she'd become the "dog that caught the pickup." I've seen that happen: somebody wants it so badly, and then suddenly they get it, and it all breaks down. Stardom is power. At a fragile age, it can often just ruin a person. We all know the drill. But I had no fear for Taylor. If ever there was somebody with her feet so firmly planted in reality, it was her. I never even heard a typical Music Row rumor about her. The Golden Girl was truly gold.

One morning I arrived at the studio to find a package lightly wrapped, addressed to me. It was a painting—a heart with wings, flying into a blue, starry sky. Written across the top were the words, "Because you believed in me." It was hand-painted and signed by Taylor. It meant so much. A gesture like that, so personal and carefully done...it was amazing. I put it on the wall and looked at it almost every day. The truth was, I really hadn't done anything other than talk to her, interview her, and enjoy her from afar. But she appreciated it and sent me a little reminder of that. Taylor Swift is that rare person who rode the rocket to stardom at such a young age and never lost her balance. Wow.

I WILL TELL THIS STORY from my side. It's all I got.

It's another BMI songwriters' awards banquet. The same Music Row event where I'd first met a young, blonde teenage wannabe eight years before. At the bar I bumped into a guy who said, "My daughter loves you." Of course, I immediately wanted to hear more from this intelligent speaker of wonderfulness. It was Taylor's dad. He regaled me with the old "family/aluminum hat" stories again. The conversation ended with, "She wants to see you. Come over to our table and say hi."

Now let me describe the BMI Awards. It's not the Kennedy Center Honors. It's a big deal, but it's the music business. People are roaming all over the room during the ceremonies. Jody Williams, the head of BMI's Nashville operations, happily calls out a song title, and the writers leap onstage for a picture. Fellow writers applaud and jeer and hoot. Half the crowd is standing at the bar as if it's a honky-tonk. Major country stars mingle around and look for their table numbers, just as everyone else does. It's kind of like the Golden Globe Awards with hats. A good-time free-for-all of glitz and camaraderie and too much wine. My idea of a perfect evening.

Halfway through the night, I slipped out of my chair and plopped down between Ms. Swift and her pa. Now, I might have walked into something. I know she had just gotten an award. It could have been bad timing. There was a lot going on. Oh God, little fifteen-year-old Geraldine is about to surface. But I did not get the reception I thought I would. It was not a massive, warm-loving hug that was my usual greeting. Not even a quick hug. Not a gentle welcome touch on the arm. Dad stared straight ahead and Ms. TS gave a short sideways glance and a noncommittal, "Hey."

I looked around for the cameras. I was thinking, *This is pretty good. I've been set up. Dad asks me over, and they are going to act like they don't know me.* But there were no cameras, there was no setup. They just acted like they didn't know me. After a long and embarrassing few minutes, I slowly did the walk of shame back to my seat. I remember legendary songwriter Don Schlitz yelling at me, "Hey, you working the room?" Apparently not, Donnie Boy.

I had noticed a sadness once before in Taylor during an interview. It was one of the times she was on the show and had broken up with "insert-name-here." I didn't know it at the time, but it was her birthday, and her heart was a little broken. I felt sorry for her. But she was a pro and said all the right things. She was a little cryptic, but she hung in there.

On this evening, however, Taylor was the *last* person I ever expected to be brushed off by. Again, to be fair, I might have wandered in at the wrong time. My choice of timing could have ruined a good moment. Usually, though, making the effort to tell someone to "hold on 'til this is over" is a fairly easy thing to do. If you're in the middle of something else and an old pal drops by, at least acknowledge their existence with a "Love ya, but gotta do this now" moment.

I'll survive somehow. I was a little bummed, as my wife will attest, but I've managed to overcome a small incident in a star's life. I really can't think of another instance like this one. It was surprising and unsettling, to say the least.

I know that even in my small walk of fame people have told me I didn't speak to them at the grocery store. I usually ask, "Did you say 'Hi' and I ignored you?" "No, you just walked on by on your way to the cereal aisle." Of course, this is from someone I do not know at all. They knew me and were offended I didn't use my psychic powers to recognize them and say, "Hey." So, little fifteen-year-old Gerry Girl needs to learn to understand people are busy. I'll also say Gerry Girl has never made a career out of songwriting and acceptance speeches that enigmatically target one heartbreaker after another. There's that.

Life goes on. I still watch Taylor with curiosity and wonder. What will she do for her next act? I hope it's all good. She's a big star who once painted a picture of a heart.

I gave the painting away.

The CMA

ONE OF THE GREAT ADVANTAGES country music has over other kinds of music, such as jazz, Gagaku (Japanese classical music), and Klezmer (Jewish dance music circa 1900) is that country has the Country Music Association. Search high and low, and you'll find no Gagaku Music Association. The Gagaku people just don't care. You could start with saying Gagaku or Klezmer causes brain damage and you would go unchallenged. Try it next time you're among friends. Denounce atonal punk rock as dangerous to your mental abilities, and everyone will just go along. They'll let you trash atonal punk rock (which is, frankly, not a bad thing to do).

I am perhaps the lone voice in the wilderness, which includes both the sticks and the woods, pointing out the dangers of country. I have been stalked, harassed, threatened, and, yes, even looked at funny by members of the CMA because of my stance. They also don't like the mention of brain damage and country in the same sentence, either.

They are a wonderful bunch of folks who work so hard to defend and browbeat or, should I say, gently persuade the world that country is good. This was the organization that, you may remember, created that wonderfully powerful slogan, "Country: Admit it. You love it." Sure, that has a hint of reluctance. Yes, it does bring in the argument that there is a considerable group of humans who can't stand it. It's a bit defensive, to be honest. It always reminded me of when your mother wanted you to go out with a girl who had a face that would frighten a warthog. Mom thought she was cute, the girl's mother was her friend at church, and Mom would say, "Come on. Admit it. Olga. You like her." Everybody, except your mother, knew that wasn't true, but you would smile and tell myopic Mom that you'd think about it. The CMA slogan had that kind of "feel" to it.

The truth is, country is wildly popular all over the United States, in parts of Canada, and in small pockets around the world. I've received checks for country songs I've written that were played in Sweden, Ireland, and Denmark. I cashed those checks and went immediately to buy myself one Chili-Cheese Pup at Krystal.

The CMA has managed to squash the brain damage thing for a long, long time now. I'm proud of them. Considering the success of the singers I know who play to 75,000 screaming cowboys and cowboy-ettes some nights, they must be doing something right.

I have written hundreds of letters to the Country Music Association detailing my ideas and theories for improving the profile, acceptance, and promotion of this twangy genre:

- If they could just work out a deal to get Ford to give everyone a truck. Imagine the excitement of a new F-150 owner being able to turn on a country station and immediately hear a song about the very vehicle he was driving.
- I think if more country & Western lyrics were readily available to tattoo parlors, country would have more skin in the game. If people in New York City were on the subway, riding behind a woman with every word to "She Thinks My

Tractor's Sexy" tattooed on her back, they would be hooked for life.

- Why hasn't the CMA done more to convince the Baptists to replace hymns with hits? There are a lot of Brad Paisley songs you can sing during Bible school. Why don't these people think? It's right there—free country promotion.

- What if McDonald's replaced Happy Meals with Hick-y Meals? You see how easy it can be? Simple move, and the CMA comes out looking like a hero.

- If you took any person who expressed a dislike for the music and simply let them ride on Willie's bus for an hour, they'd emerge as fans of country. They would also emerge much more cheerful and probably asking for a bag of Dorito's.

Advertising on Kenny Chesney's head, more alarm clocks that play banjo music, get the First Lady in some Daisy Dukes, a few mud bogs in the middle of the Indianapolis Speedway, Beyoncé and Jay-Z hosting the *CMA Awards*—these are all fabulous ideas I've suggested. They've all fallen on deaf ears. Sad, isn't it? A well-heeled, well-supported professional organization dedicated to promoting country music, and all I get are crickets.

The only thing that saves them from my wrath is that perhaps they have all been brain-damaged so much, they can't remember to call me.

Does anybody know if there's a Hard-core Elevator Music Society?

The Mother of All Headaches

IT BEGAN JUST LIKE every other day, with a gentle knock on the bedroom door. I stirred slightly and noticed golden shards of sunlight cracking through the brocade curtains. It was going to be a glorious one. Leopold came backing through the door, holding aloft the hammered pewter tray with my breakfast. He had been with us for years as chef, housekeeper, and general assistant. It was clear that he'd also had quite a snootful last night. I knew I would ask if he'd been drinking, and he'd say perhaps one glass of sherry. It was how he got the nickname "Leo the Lyin'" from my wife.

The Mrs. was a vision of elegance, out like a light with her Bose noise-canceling earbuds and silk sleep mask. I noticed the "chaw" of Red Man had fallen from her mouth and would probably leave a nasty stain on that pink Halston peignoir. I slipped out of bed just as she began to snore like Larry the Cable Guy.

Breakfast was the same: evenly toasted eleven-grain bread with two local (no more than five miles away) eggs, poached. This came with a glass of freshly squeezed pomegranate juice and one hand-chosen macadamia nut in a tiny silver serving cup. The coffee had to be made from civet beans and served steaming. Civet beans are coffee beans eaten, digested, and excreted by small Indonesian mammals and collected to make the best brew in the world. Leopold pulled out my chair and, with a flair, flipped the white cotton napkin into the air. There was just a whiff of Mennen aftershave coming from Leopold as I started to lift the Waterford cup to my lips.

The room started to move a bit. A large bird flew by my head and out an open window. Leo turned slightly, and his profile distorted into a variant of Nosferatu. I could vaguely hear the tinkling melody of "Here Comes the Sun" somewhere in the background.

I WOKE UP AND HIT the alarm clock: 3:40 A.M. The Beatles song stopped. I knew I had to bounce out of bed quickly or struggle with it later. It was pitch-black outside, and I walked like a newborn fawn toward the bathroom. I had a radio show to do and a studio waiting for me in an hour. I got ready and watched CNN by myself in a darkened kitchen with my usual bowl of Raisin Bran and a muffin smeared with Skippy. God, it was early. It was always early.

It was August 15th, the day I became the luckiest man in the world. It was also the anniversary of my wedding day. I knew I would spend most of today's show on one of my favorite topics: worst wedding songs you've actually witnessed. I had laughed loud and long at what some brides in virginal white had chosen to play as they walked down the aisle. "Wild Thing" by the Troggs was a perennial favorite, along with "She's a Brick House" and "Who Let the Dogs Out?" Some people's ideas of romance were hilariously different from mine.

People always called with a song so off-the-wall that I knew they weren't making it up. These were the days when I enjoyed doing radio immensely—me with the folks telling stories about their friends. It was always a joyful and funny time.

The show went exactly as planned. I almost always left right after 10 A.M. to head home and begin writing the next day's four-hour show. For me, it's nerve-racking enough to be live on the air, but it's paralyzing to show up unprepared. I always tried to write twenty-five jokes or bits every day to bring with me as a cushion. I was all pumped up from just finishing one show and used that "rush" to create some more stuff. This meant I could wrap up my workday about noon, have lunch, and then hit the golf course or meet a friend for a songwriting session.

Golf was the chosen activity of the day. Drift up to the course, run into somebody, and take off on a leisurely ruined walk through the woods. It was around 2 P.M. or so, and my pal Tom Shapiro was walking off the practice tee. We were, as usual, discussing what was wrong with the music business when I suddenly felt very, very odd. I excused myself from the conversation with the caveat we'd connect the following week.

It's called the "mother of all headaches" for good reason. It is. When your brain starts leaking, which is what happened to me, you truly feel like your melon is about to explode. What happened to me next is scary, amazing, and lucky.

Somehow I found my way to my house. It was one of those "no memory of driving" moments—you know, where you find yourself somewhere and don't remember getting there. As I was lying on the floor, I called my wife. Allyson always has her cell phone on her. But she *never* answers it; the ringy-thingy doesn't work or she doesn't hear it. (I've set her phone on stun, and I get bupkis.) The amazing part of the story is *she actually answered her phone!* Wonder of wonders. Here is the lucky part. The actual conversation went like this (read it and then tell me my wife and I haven't been together forever):

HER: "Hello?"
ME: "Where are you?"
HER: "Call 911."

I had only said, "Where are you?" and I guess from the pained tone in my voice that she immediately knew something was wrong. Either that or it was just the shock of answering her cell phone for the first time in modern history.

I honestly don't remember a lot of what happened that day. Allyson tells me it took *forever* for the 911 crew to arrive. Turns out they got lost on the way to our house, and the maps they had weren't all that accurate. Good system, huh?

When it was all over, I contacted the 911 Commission. The head guy told me that none of the emergency vehicles had GPS. I found that to be amazing information. I told the guy that even the Papa John's deliveryman has GPS. It's fifty bucks! Next time I need emergency service, I'm ordering a pizza. They're quicker. Mr. Commissioner didn't find any of this funny.

Allyson also says I said stuff to the EMTs that probably threw them off a bit. I was joking around and having a brain attack at the same time. They asked me (again, I don't remember any of this) if I had trouble breathing, trouble walking, or difficulty with drinking. She says I told them, "I fell asleep in a Dumpster last night. Does that sound like a drinking problem?"

I vaguely remember checking into the hospital, lots of commotion, and then my friend Dr. Bob Singer appeared in front of me. It helps to have one of the most talented neurosurgeons in America as your pal. One Friday we're at Bob's for barbeque, the next Friday he's leaning over you preparing to remove the side of your skull.

From what I understand, I had a leaky artery. Bob says he "coiled" it, which involved cauterizing it and sealing it off, I think. The brain, especially one exposed to so much country music, is a little touchy. If your brain gets blood on it, or senses something is wrong, it does what we all do. It puffs up to protect itself. That's a little simplistic, but generally it's what happens. This is why an aneurysm is so dangerous. Your computer decides to get bigger inside a box (skull) that doesn't stretch much.

I had three craniotomies. Bob told me later he opened a place in the skin over my stomach and slid part of my skull into it. It sort of looked like a cell phone pocket on my right side. Unfortunately, it healed up or I would never have to worry about losing my iPhone. Docs do this to keep the brain alive and warm. I spent several days teetering on the edge of darkness. I also had one of the worst haircuts in history. Long and sleek on one side, totally shaved to the skin on the other. I looked like the lead singer of some punk rock band or Gary Oldman in *The Fifth Element*. I also had about thirty-five staples in my scalp. I kind of felt dangerous.

I'll leave out the real gory stuff and just say I am lucky to be missing putts today. Bobby Earl (my nickname for him) says I recovered better than anybody could hope for. He had a lot to do with that and hates it when I tell him that. He's something, believe you me. Thirty days later, I returned to radio with a bald head and a new vision of what life was all about.

All my country music friends showed up to welcome me back. Vince Gill told me I was one of the few people who looked vastly improved after life-threatening surgery. Apparently, I need a long sleep in the hospital hooked up to a morphine drip to look rested. After a trip in the Morphinemobile, I also have a newfound understanding of Keith Richards.

I enjoyed every day and stayed on the air for years after my "adventure." I had a lot of panicky bouts with headaches. A lot of "OH, NO! It's happening again!" stuff because of a minor head tremor. It just takes time. Everybody goes through it, and it's tough.

One of the true delights of my career has been writing songs with Hal David. Hal, who passed away in August 2012, was a wonder. Hal was a force of music that is almost impossible to describe. Hal David wrote dozens of songs that form the musical fabric of American pop, even today. His words were just as important as cowriter Burt Bacharach's melodies to make hits like "Raindrops Keep Fallin' on My Head" and "What the World Needs Now" and literally a hundred other songs you know and love. I sent him melodies, and (as Allyson says) we watched like little kids as the fax machine slowly revealed Hal David's words.

Probably one of Hal's most obscure songs was from the hit musical *Promises, Promises*. It's called "Knowing When to Leave." I've read the lyrics over and over. It's actually about a relationship in the show, but it's also a great message for everyday living.

Knowing when to leave is one of the hardest things you'll ever have to learn, like when we lost our friend Sue, when the radio landscape began to change under my feet, and when I realized I had time left, but other things began to call to me more than blathering in front of a microphone. When I realized it would be OK, when I thought about sleeping 'til five forty-five in the morning more than getting up at 3:40 A.M., and when I asked myself the question, "Who wouldn't want to spend more time with Allyson House?" I knew the answer.

I leave you with the wise words of Zen Master Twang Dung:

Give up your dreams and go home.
It will be quiet there.
You are loved there.
Your dreams weren't all that hot anyway.

Acknowledgments

LEONA HELMSLEY was the Queen of Mean. I always thought she was a dead ringer for the Evil Queen in the Disney flick *Snow White and the Seven Dwarfs*. In fact, when she'd been quoted by a witness at her trial for tax evasion as saying "Only the little people pay taxes," I thought that proved it. Bashful, Doc, and Dopey paid taxes, but Leona didn't. Leona went to the big hotel in the sky several years ago, but she was vindictive, to say the least. You don't get to be the Queen of Mean unless you go out of your way to get even.

I don't want to get even like that. I only want to get even with people who are better than me. I want to get even by moving myself forward to their better place. I have met a lot of people I'll never get even with. They are so much more than the average human that they pull us all along. Some people just make us all try harder. I'm just trying to catch up.

Chet Atkins, Minnie Pearl, and Barbara Mandrell set the bar pretty high for a young guy learning about people and the music business. They were big, big stars and big personalities who took time with every single person they met along the way. I will never get even with them.

Jim Ridings was an assistant professor at my university. He had actually worked at a radio station. His wasn't the usual B.S. professorial "theory." He was patient with an idiot who wanted to talk on the radio. Allyson and I spent our honeymoon at his house in

Savannah. Two young birds trying to fly, and he let us nest there 'cause we were so broke.

A guy named Randy Bongarten was the head of the radio company I worked for a long time ago. He took the time to fly me to meet him in Phoenix. He counseled me on the bad move I would make if I left Nashville for some job paying a thousand dollars more in some other city. Because the first time I ever held a golf club was with Randy, I blame him for all the pain that game has caused me over the years. I'll never get even with him.

I'll never get even with Steve Hicks, the brilliant Texas businessman who ignored all the advice *not* to bring me back from California to work for his station in Nashville. Steve changed my life. Right now, I'm certain he's rubbing his forehead and thinking up some new plan to change the world.

I will never get even with Sue and John Cullen. We traveled the world together, Allyson and I, with these two angels. Sue worked with a company called What Color Is Your Parachute. She just glowed. My wife and John's wife were like sisters—great friends and so much alike. Sue thought everyone's dream would come true, and told them so. When we lost Sue, I changed. That's how much she meant to me. I carried her casket to a field in Texas, and I thought if anyone had so much to give to life, it was her. John remains a confidant and a friend you run across the room to hug.

There are hundreds of people I will never get even with. They made me laugh and prodded me along with humor. They were kind enough to point out I was screwing up. They believed in me. I should probably make paintings that say that and hand them out.

Big thanks to Bob Sellers, who introduced me to the speaker's guru, Duane Ward. Thanks to Duane for getting the fabulous agent Frank Breeden to work with me. Much big thanks to Tyler "Elvis" Ward. Couldn't have done this without you. How can I possibly thank Jeffrey Green and Lauren (Three Degrees) Virshup enough for their amazing editing job? Tom Schurr, who endured my "headache" and was so kind to me. Clay Hunnicutt, who makes radio a good thing. Also, I love Beth Stein and Beverly Keel, who both encouraged/harangued me into embarking on this adventure. I'll never be able to thank Glenn and the fabulous team at BenBella Books for all their help and belief.

A very special love-filled shout-out to my radio compadres Mike Bohan, Al Voecks, and Duncan Stewart for all the years of laughter. Nobody better at six every morning.

Props to Shane Tallant for joining our family and taking care of my girl. I give my heart to the most beautiful babies in the world in all of history, Holland and Willa. My apologies to all my golf pals who had to listen to me as I was writing this thing. But, most of all, for my darling Allyson.

About the Author

WHEN YOU WRITE A BOOK called *Country Music Broke My Brain*, you have to be qualified. There's no one who exemplifies that attribute more than Gerry House.

Gerry worked in the music industry's famed Music Row district in Nashville for thirty years, the last twenty-two of which found him behind the microphone every weekday morning hosting "Gerry House & The House Foundation," the top-rated morning radio show on WSIX-FM for over twenty years.

As Nashville is the songwriting and country music capital of the world, one can appreciate just how tough it is to entertain the entertainers in an entertainment hub (similar to getting invited to perform card tricks at the annual International Convention of Magicians). You better be good...really good!

In characteristic fashion, the title of Gerry's book draws a tongue-in-cheek correlation between his long career in the country music business and the brain aneurism he suffered in 2003 and the three craniotomies from which he fully recovered...or so he claims.

ALTHOUGH GERRY would gladly discuss his awards with you in person, it should be noted that he has won virtually every broadcast award possible. The Country Music Association awarded him Personality of the Year four times. The Academy of Country Music handed him seven awards. *Billboard* magazine, *Radio & Records*, and Leadership Nashville also gave him their highest honors.

The National Association of Broadcasters gave Gerry its presti-
gious Marconi Award for radio excellence and recently inducted
him into the Radio Hall of Fame alongside Bob Hope, Larry King,
and Ronald Reagan. Gerry reflects, "How this happened remains a
mystery. There is a forty-minute PowerPoint presentation available
if you would like to see it." He is the only country music DJ to be
inducted into the NAB Hall of Fame.

Gerry House, like the true multiple personality that he is, also
lives in the music world as a songwriter. Performing-rights orga-
nization BMI has honored him with awards for No. 1 hit songs.
He's had more than forty songs recorded by artists including Brad
Paisley, LeAnn Rimes, George Strait, Reba McEntire, Randy Travis,
Clint Black, Trace Adkins, and many others. His hits, such as "Little
Rock," "On The Side of Angels," "The Big One," and "The River and
the Highway," have sold millions of records.

Gerry is first and foremost a writer. It wasn't enough that he wrote
his own daily radio material for over twenty years. He also loves putting words into other people's mouths. He's written stand-up jokes
and TV scripts for years. The *ACM Awards*, the *CMA Awards*, the
CMT Awards, and now *American Idol* have all had big stars delivering Gerry's lines.

Along with his wife, Allyson, Gerry has spent most of his career
in Nashville. However, he's been heard all over the world. Four years
on XM Radio and contributing to the BBC mean he's been "on the
air" everywhere. In fact, Gerry notes that "I've been heard more on
radio in America than on any other household appliance."

Gerry is a piano player, a guitar player, and a golfer. You
are not in danger of being hit when he's at the piano or holding a guitar. He's a world traveler and writes either a joke or a
song every day. Gerry and Allyson live in Nashville near their
daughter, Autumn, son-in-law Shane, and twin granddaugh-
ters Holland and Willa. You can also find them at their other
home in north Florida.

Index